Experiential Learning in Philosophy

In this volume, Julinna Oxley and Ramona Ilea bring together essays that examine and defend the use of *experiential learning* activities to teach philosophical terms, concepts, arguments, and practices. Experiential learning emphasizes the importance of student engagement outside the traditional classroom structure. Service learning, studying abroad, engaging in large-scale collaborative projects such as creating blogs, websites, and videos, and practically applying knowledge in a reflective, creative, and rigorous way are all forms of experiential learning. Taken together, the contributions to *Experiential Learning in Philosophy* argue that *teaching* philosophy is about *doing* philosophy with others. The book is divided into two sections: essays that engage in the philosophical debate about defining and implementing experiential learning, and essays that describe how to integrate experiential learning into the teaching of philosophy. *Experiential Learning in Philosophy* provides a timely reflection on best practices for teaching philosophical ideals and theories, an examination of the evolution of the discipline of philosophy and its adoption (or reclamation) of active modes of learning, and an anticipation of the ways in which pedagogical practices will continue to evolve in the 21st century.

Julinna Oxley is Associate Professor of Philosophy and Director of the Women's and Gender Studies Program at Coastal Carolina University. She authored *The Moral Dimensions of Empathy: Limits and Applications in Ethical Theory and Practice* (2012) and has also published on topics in ethics and feminist philosophy.

Ramona Ilea is an Associate Professor and Chair of the Philosophy Department at Pacific University. She co-edited *Consequentialism and Environmental Ethics* and published articles in the *Journal of Agricultural and Environmental Ethics*, *Teaching Philosophy*, and the *Journal of Social Philosophy*.

Routledge Studies in Contemporary Philosophy

42 **Pittsburgh School of Philosophy**
Sellars, McDowell, Brandom
Chauncey Maher

43 **Reference and Structure in the Philosophy of Language**
A Defense of the Russellian Orthodoxy
Arthur Sullivan

44 **Civic Virtue and the Sovereignty of Evil**
Derek Edyvane

45 **Philosophy of Language and Webs of Information**
Heimir Geirsson

46 **Disagreement and Skepticism**
Edited by Diego E. Machuca

47 **Philosophy in Schools**
An Introduction for Philosophers and Teachers
Edited by Sara Goering, Nicholas J. Shudak, and Thomas E. Wartenberg

48 **A Philosophy of Material Culture**
Action, Function, and Mind
Beth Preston

49 **A Philosophy of the Screenplay**
Ted Nannicelli

50 **Race, Philosophy, and Film**
Edited by Mary K. Bloodsworth-Lugo and Dan Flory

51 **Knowledge, Virtue, and Action**
Essays on Putting Epistemic Virtues to Work
Edited by Tim Henning and David P. Schweikard

52 **The Ontology of Psychology**
Questioning Foundations in the Philosophy of Mind
Linda A.W. Brakel

53 **Pragmatism, Law, and Language**
Edited by Graham Hubbs and Douglas Lind

54 **Contemporary Dualism**
A Defense
Edited by Andrea Lavazza and Howard M. Robinson

55 **Reframing the Intercultural Dialogue on Human Rights**
A Philosophical Approach
Jeffrey Flynn

56 **How History Matters to Philosophy**
Reconsidering Philosophy's Past After Positivism
Robert C. Scharff

57 **The Affordable Care Act Decision**
Philosophical and Legal Implications
Edited by Fritz Allhoff and Mark Hall

58 **Realism, Science, and Pragmatism**
Edited by Kenneth R. Westphal

59 **Evidentialism and Epistemic Justification**
Kevin McCain

60 **Democracy in Contemporary Confucian Philosophy**
David Elstein

61 **Deleuze and Pragmatism**
Edited by Sean Bowden, Simone Bignall, and Paul Patton

62 **Mind, Language and Subjectivity**
Minimal Content and the Theory of Thought
Nicholas Georgalis

63 **Believing Against the Evidence**
Agency and the Ethics of Belief
Miriam Schleifer McCormick

64 **The Essence of the Self**
In Defense of the Simple View of Personal Identity
Geoffrey Madell

65 **Personal Autonomy and Social Oppression**
Philosophical Perspectives
Edited by Marina A.L. Oshana

66 **Domination and Global Political Justice**
Conceptual, Historical, and Institutional Perspectives
Edited by Barbara Buckinx, Jonathan Trejo-Mathys, and Timothy Waligore

67 **Hate Speech Law**
A Philosophical Examination
Alexander Brown

68 **Music and Aesthetic Reality**
Formalism and the Limits of Description
By Nick Zangwill

69 **Beyond the Analytic-Continental Divide**
Pluralist Philosophy in the Twenty-First Century
Edited by Jeffrey A. Bell, Andrew Cutrofello, and Paul M. Livingston

70 **Science and the Self**
Animals, Evolution, and Ethics: Essays in Honour of Mary Midgley
Edited by Ian James Kidd and Liz McKinnell

71 **Resisting Biopolitics**
Philosophical, Political, and Performative Strategies
Edited by S.E. Wilmer and Audronė Žukauskaitė

72 **Experiential Learning in Philosophy**
Edited by Julinna Oxley and Ramona Ilea

Experiential Learning in Philosophy

Edited by Julinna Oxley and Ramona Ilea

NEW YORK AND LONDON

First published 2016
by Routledge
711 Third Avenue, New York, NY 10017

and by Routledge
2 Park Square, Milton Park, Abingdon, Oxon OX14 4RN

Routledge is an imprint of the Taylor & Francis Group, an informa business

Library of Congress Cataloging-in-Publication Data
Experiential learning in philosophy / edited by Julinna Oxley and Ramona Ilea. — 1 [edition].
pages cm. — (Routledge studies in contemporary philosophy ; 72)
Includes bibliographical references and index.
1. Philosophy—Study and teaching. 2. Experiential learning. I. Oxley, Julinna C., editor.
B52.E96 2015
107.1—dc23
2015016899

ISBN: 978-1-138-92739-1 (hbk)
ISBN: 978-1-315-68230-3 (ebk)

Typeset in Sabon
by Apex CoVantage, LLC

To all the philosophers interested in experiential learning

Contents

Foreword by Peter Singer xiii

Acknowledgements xv

1 Experiential Learning in Philosophy: Theory and Practice 1
JULINNA OXLEY AND RAMONA ILEA

PART I
Philosophical Reflections on Experiential Learning

2 Practicing Philosophy: Philosophy with Children and Experiential Learning 21
MICHAEL D. BURROUGHS

3 A Short History of Experiential Learning and Its Application to Business Ethics 37
KAREN HORNSBY AND WADE MAKI

4 Performing Care Ethics: Empathy, Acting, and Embodied Learning 52
MAURICE HAMINGTON

5 Dewey and Collaborative Experiential Learning Indoors 65
MINERVA AHUMADA

6 Philosophy, Critical Pedagogy, and Experiential Learning 77
J. JEREMY WISNEWSKI

7 Implicit Bias, Race, and Gender: Experiential Learning and Dual-Process Cognition 89
DAN YIM

8 Cultivating Citizenship: Assessing Student-Designed Civic Engagement Projects in Philosophy Classes 101
SUSAN C. C. HAWTHORNE, MONICA JANZEN, RAMONA ILEA, CHAD WIENER

PART II
Examples: Experiential Learning Courses

A. Social Change through Philosophy

9 Emergent Learning in Independent Studies: The Story of the Accessible Icon Project 119
BRIAN GLENNEY

10 Taking Animals Seriously: Ethics in Action 131
KATHIE JENNI

11 Experiential Learning in a Social Justice Course: Philosophy as Transformative Experience 140
MEGAN HALTEMAN ZWART

12 Feminist Philosophy and Civic Engagement: The Educational Fair 149
SHARON M. MEAGHER

B. Service-Learning and Community Engagement through Philosophy

13 Engaging with Global Justice through Internships 161
ERICKA TUCKER

14 Cultivating Responsible Global Citizenship: Philosophical Exploration & Service Learning in Guyana 169
KATHERINE E. KIRBY

15 Studying War and Contributing to the Community 179
JOE COLE

16 Minding Philosophy: Service Learning and Intellectual Disability 189
DONNA S. TURNEY

C. New Directions in Experiential Learning in Philosophy

17 Collaborative Research Groups in the Experimental Philosophy Seminar 201
ALEXANDRA BRADNER

18 Philosophy as Practice: Zen and Archery 212
GREGORY A. CLARK

19 Teaching Philosophy by Designing a Wikipedia Page 222
GRAHAM HUBBS

20 Museums as the Philosophy Lab: Technology and Cognition Beyond the Brain 228
ROBIN L. ZEBROWSKI

Contributors 237
Name Index 243
Subject Index 247

Foreword

Philosophy professors are sometimes caricatured as absent-minded people, remote from real life, their heads in the clouds. That image of the discipline and those who work in it clings to an unrepresentative and increasingly outdated view of its subject. What I like most about *Experiential Learning in Philosophy* is that it celebrates the diverse ways in which philosophy connects with real life. Emphasizing that connection when teaching philosophy enhances the learning experience of students, and at the same time enables philosophy to have a positive impact on the world.

There is a long tradition of experiential learning in philosophy. In ancient Athens, Socrates asked his fellow citizens difficult questions about the way they were living their lives. In China, the sages were seen as sources of advice on how to live their lives. Presumably this was a two-way process—at least some of those who pondered Socrates' questions, or received advice from Mencius, tested out the precepts they had imbibed and provided feedback from which, one hopes, the philosophers were able to refine and improve their teaching. These conceptions of the nature of philosophy continued throughout most of the history of the discipline, both in Europe and in Asia.

If philosophy became, for a time, a more abstract scholarly study, removed from everyday life, that was an aberration that has now passed. To say this is not to deny that abstract reasoning is an indispensable element of philosophy, nor that there are philosophical questions that are remote from everyday life, but rather to say that there are many points at which abstract philosophical reasoning does have implications that make an important difference to how we live our lives.

Philosophy involves reflecting, thinking, and arguing. In my experience, students find this activity most engaging when it is about aspects of their own lives. It is easy to imagine that a woman who has unreflectively accepted the view that abortion is wrong would be led to think more deeply about that question if she finds herself pregnant at a time when she is unprepared to become a mother, or does not want to become the mother of this man's child. That experience is, fortunately, not one that everyone is going to have, but other moral questions are inescapable. We all eat, but we don't all appreciate that the choice of *what* to eat raises important questions about the moral status of animals, about our responsibility for climate change, and about global poverty.

For most of us living in affluent nations, the question of global poverty is raised more directly by our everyday decisions to spend money on things that we don't need, whether it is a soda, a new item of clothing, the latest digital device, or a vacation. Are such purchases justifiable, given that children are dying from diseases like malaria, measles, and diarrhea, and aid agencies that are highly effective in reducing this toll could save more lives if they received more donations?

My own preferred engagement with experiential learning—if that is not too grand a name for it—involves challenging students to think about these everyday moral questions, and more broadly, about the way they are living their lives. One way in which I have done this is by means of a Giving Game. I have asked students to decide which of several charities should receive $1000. The money is real (donated by me) and the charities are selected to raise ethical and empirical questions about the best cause to which one should give. Students are given information about the charities, drawn from the web pages of organizations like The Life You Can Save and GiveWell. Students then vote for their favorite charity and the money is disbursed in proportion to the votes each charity receives. It is not difficult to lead on from such questions to deeper issues about the nature of ethics and the role of reason in practical decisions.

It is surprising how profoundly a philosophy class taught in this manner can change the course of a person's life. Some students turn vegetarian or vegan. Others start giving to aid organizations. In at least one case, a former student of mine decided to pursue a high-income career so that he could donate half of his income—a six-figure sum—to effective charities. I know of at least two philosophy students who have donated one of their kidneys to a stranger. A discipline that can have that kind of impact cannot be brushed aside as irrelevant to real life.

As this book shows, experiential learning is not limited to applied ethics or political philosophy. It can be practiced in a wide range of philosophical subjects and learning contexts, using a variety of different techniques. The reader interested in helping students to see both the importance of philosophy by linking it to their experiences will find plenty of suggestions in the essays that follow.

Peter Singer
University Center for Human Values, Princeton University & School of Historical and Philosophical Studies, University of Melbourne

Acknowledgements

We would like to thank the contributors to this book for their excellent work and their prompt communication, and Sierra Barnes for her help in creating the index. We are also indebted to everyone at Routledge who made this book possible, especially Katie Laurentiev and Margo Irvin.

Julinna Oxley: My most heartfelt thanks go to Ramona Ilea for agreeing to co-edit this book with me. I invited her to help with the project after it had been conceived, and she brought more creativity, enthusiasm, organization, and discipline than I could have imagined. Her passion for experiential learning is unmatched, and I have learned so much from her about how to be a good philosopher, colleague, and friend. We made a great team and it is her dedication that has brought this project to fruition.

My teacher Alice Terry first introduced me to experiential learning in the 6th grade. I was one of five students in the gifted and talented program who went on an "awareness walk" in our town, where we came to the realization that it was dying. We decided then to revitalize it—we called the SBA, wrote to the Mayor, looked up building owners, drew up architectural plans, and sponsored a downtown clean-up day. Over the course of a year, we accomplished a lot: land was sold, a new park was put in place by the old railroad station, and buildings were restored. Amazingly, we never doubted ourselves. Alice's optimism and confidence convinced us that we could do it, that we could make a difference. She worked tirelessly alongside us, directing our efforts and explaining things to us that we didn't understand. Two years later, we received—and were the first "kids" to receive—the National Public Service Award for our efforts. I now realize how formative this experience was in shaping my ideas about education and community activism. My deepest thanks go to Alice. Her vision and creativity are unmatched. She inspired me to believe that anyone can make a difference, and I hope to do the same with my students.

I am also grateful to Coastal Carolina University for adopting and promoting Experiential Learning beginning in 2011. Donna Qualters (Northeastern University) helped framed my understanding of EL and convinced me that philosophers should, just as much as professors in other disciplines, try Experiential Learning. Coastal Carolina University also provided me with a research leave to work on this book, and provided funding for my EL courses over the last several years, for which I am grateful.

The idea for this book was conceived in 2013 at the Pacific APA, when I participated in an APA Committee on the Teaching of Philosophy panel on service learning. I found that other philosophers were doing amazing projects with their students, and realized that many were interested in experiential learning, but didn't know where to start. I am especially grateful to Matthew Altman, Sally Haslanger, Dan Hicks, Jana Hodges-Kluck, and Rasmus Grønfeldt Winther for instructive conversations at this conference that convinced me that this would be a worthwhile project to pursue. I also am also grateful to the anonymous reviewers at Routledge, Jerry Gaus, Justin Weinberg, Philip Whalen, and Rasmus Grønfeldt Winther, for providing feedback and offering extremely valuable ideas and suggestions along the way. The numerous submissions I received for this book were equally inspiring and useful in helping me to lay out the theoretical landscape of experiential learning in the discipline of philosophy. And finally, special thanks to Philip, my daughters Marigny and Parisa, and my parents Paul and Beverly, for their encouragement and support throughout the project.

Ramona Ilea: I want to begin by thanking my co-editor, Julinna Oxley, for inviting me to co-edit this book. She is organized, philosophically rigorous, attentive to detail, and cheerful—an awesome combination for a co-editor!

I am also thankful to the American Philosophical Association for an American Philosophical Association Grant Fund. This grant enabled Monica Janzen, Susan Hawthorne, Chad Wiener, and me to conduct the assessment studies we talk about in Chapter 8 of this book, and to set up Engaged Philosophy http://www.engagedphilosophy.com/, a web site that gives faculty and students tools to implement activist or service projects in philosophy classes—assignment guidelines, sample projects, and testimonials and data supporting civic engagement results. I am also grateful to Pacific University Oregon for a Faculty Development Grant and to the Center for Civic Engagement for a Civic Engagement Mini-Grant. These grants, along with a few other sources of funding, helped me to travel to over ten conferences to present my work on civic engagement, which in turn allowed me to hear some excellent talks, get feedback on my work, and meet a lot of wonderful people.

I also want to thank Stephanie Stockamer, Dave Boersema, and David DeMoss for giving me the needed encouragement and support to incorporate civic engagement projects in two of my classes at Pacific University Oregon. My interest in civic engagement started in graduate school, when I had the backing of my co-advisers, Naomi Scheman and Helen Longino; I am also very grateful to them.

A special thanks goes to my family and to my life partner, Gregory Oschwald. They are always extremely supportive, perceptive, and encouraging. I could not do everything I do without them.

1 Experiential Learning in Philosophy

Theory and Practice

Julinna Oxley and Ramona Ilea

I. EXPERIENTIAL LEARNING AND PHILOSOPHY EDUCATION

Philosophers, like other professors in the humanities, have long used the "sage on the stage" model of higher education: lecturing to students, giving quizzes and tests, and assigning papers. This style of teaching encourages a learning style called "knowledge acquisition," or didactic learning that involves the ability to practically apply theoretical knowledge to a specific question or situation. In addition, many philosophers use a kind of neo-Socratic method of classroom discussion, which involves engaging students in philosophical discussion of an issue or argument, and asking a wide range of questions as a way of getting them to think about the matter more carefully. Some philosophy teachers also use thought experiments to test intuitions and to get students invested and interested in understanding the relevance of philosophical questions and concerns to their lives and the world around them.[1] Students deliberate individually or in groups to consider and respond to a thought experiment, with the goal of developing critical thinking skills, as a form of active learning.

But in recent years, philosophers have begun exploring new and creative ways to teach abstract philosophical theories by seeking to incorporate *experiential learning* (EL) activities. EL is a pedagogy that encourages the instructor to direct and facilitate learning via practical activities, so the students apply what they are learning in the course to real-world problems or situations.[2] The goal of EL is to engage students in constructing new knowledge that impacts their lives and worldviews by creating opportunities for them to participate in events where they have a significant life experience. These experiences are generally sought out in activities that involve engaging in the world *outside* the classroom structure, such as service learning or travel abroad; practically applying knowledge in a reflective, creative, and rigorous way; or engaging in large-scale collaborative projects like organizing a fair or creating a website. EL is not merely about developing the skill of argumentation via active learning exercises or thought experiments; it involves carrying out complex, coordinated activities that require managing students and other stakeholders in an unpredictable environment.

Kolb's (1984) cycle of learning nicely captures the distinguishing characteristics of the EL process: begin with knowledge, such as the concepts, facts, and information acquired through formal learning and past experience; engage in an activity by applying the knowledge to a "real world" setting; and then reflect on this application, such that the analysis and synthesis of knowledge and activity create *new* knowledge for the student. Reflection is a key feature of EL, because, by reflecting, the student forms beliefs about her own process of learning that provides a deeper level of personal meaningfulness. Reflection is not just journaling or describing what happened; rather, it is guided by deep and engaging questions so that reflection is an essential component of high-quality learning. It is important to understand, then, that EL is not meant to *replace* the activities of reading, writing, listening, thinking, and discussing as the basic foundation of a philosophical education. Rather, by *supplementing* these activities with tangible and practical activities, a student's understanding of and commitment to the subject matter is augmented.

This approach to classroom learning has several advantages, which we will outline briefly here and examine in greater detail in the following sections. First, EL is one of the few instructional strategies that are considered "high impact educational practices," along with first-year seminars, learning communities, and undergraduate research.[3] Research on student learning reveals that students learn the most—in the sense that they achieve deep long-term learning, personal knowledge, and practical understanding—when they engage in EL activities that show the practical relevance of what they are learning in the classroom. Second, EL offers the opportunity for students to interact with their peers, which creates confidence and gets them used to speaking in front of others. They can develop relationships with students from different backgrounds and interact with professionals in the community. This enables students to navigate class and social norms as a way of developing practical social skills.

Finally, EL activities help to show that philosophy is not limited to analysis and abstraction.[4] Incorporating EL into the philosophy classroom provides the opportunity to facilitate understanding of the context of one's own life and the lives of others, and to think about action as grounded in theory.[5] When students participate in projects with the wider campus community through civic engagement or service learning, engagement outside class offers students the impetus and the raw material to achieve this goal by providing "opportunities to engage in problem-solving by requiring participants to gain knowledge of the specific context of their [project] and community challenges, rather than only to draw upon generalized or abstract knowledge such as might come from a textbook" (Learn and Serve 2015). In this regard, EL provides an opportunity to show the relevance of philosophical reflection to some of the most important topics in the world today, such as global justice, the treatment of animals, gender equality, and our technological future.

II. THE THEORY AND PRACTICE OF EXPERIENTIAL LEARNING IN PHILOSOPHY

The field of EL has a rich philosophical history that is rooted in John Dewey's educational theory, though some suggest that philosophers such as Aristotle and Rousseau are intellectual predecessors. Since several chapters in this book (e.g., Chapters 1, 3, and 5) provide comprehensive discussions of Dewey's educational theory, we will not examine it in detail here. Briefly, Dewey's contribution to experiential educational theory is to provide the intellectual framework for EL, by arguing that while traditional schooling involves "experiences," those experiences are often the wrong kind: they are mis-educative, in the sense that they inhibit growth of further experience on the part of the student (*Experience and Education*, Chapter 2). Dewey instead recommends that experiences be "directed" to a particular goal that is thoughtfully set by an instructor or educational mission. This directed learning should include student interaction with the external environment (broadly conceived) to provide a context for the learning and to promote a greater understanding of the world outside of the classroom. Providing a specific context or framework from which to understand one's purposes for learning will help to guarantee that the educational experience is genuinely educational (rather than mis-educative).

Dewey's ideas spawned a new movement in education, and a number of variations on his ideas have emerged, including the newer experiential learning models discussed in Chapter 3 of this book. Dewey's central views have remained intact, though, and EL has evolved into a pedagogy that can be taken in a number of directions, so that there is not just *one* way of doing EL. Rather, EL asks that instructors approach their courses backward and think about what the instructor would like for students to remember about the class a year or even five years from taking it. EL provides a novel approach to answering this question, by suggesting that, whatever the answer to this question is, engaging in an experiential learning activity will enable the student to do this more effectively—for example, to develop the skills and dispositions associated with that knowledge base.[6] For students to experience transformative learning, instructors need to do more than give riveting lectures and rigorous tests. The students will need to engage in a practical activity that impacts them on a deeper, more personal level than a traditional philosophy class.

In this introduction, we identify six types of EL that are relevant to philosophy: service learning, teaching pre-college philosophy, social activism and civic engagement, collaborative group projects, study abroad programs, and the broad catch-all category of *philosophical* EL. For EL to be successful, (a) the instructor ensures that the EL experience is relevant to the class being taught, (b) the instructor explains why the students are engaging in EL, and (c) the EL experience connects to the course materials directly and in a way that allows for reflection. Each of the authors in this book does this by having a structure in place to facilitate the experience for students and to provide multiple points of accountability for the students during the semester to discourage procrastination and to help them achieve their goals. In what follows, we outline the different types of EL and state briefly which chapters discuss this type of experiential learning.

Service learning is one of the most popular types of EL, and this is true in philosophy classes as well. Service learning can help students develop "the disposition to reflect well on the relationship between a well-lived life and a good community" (Valentine 2000) or the kinds of concern, care, and sense of urgency that are vital to recognizing and responding to one's duties as an ethical agent (Kirby 2009).[7] When successful, service learning is, then, a powerful antidote to an undesirable consequence of typical teaching—the concern that students end up becoming unreflective moral skeptics:

> [students] become overwhelmed when they have to face several seemingly plausible but incompatible approaches to moral issues. These students may conclude that we can never know the correct answer to a moral question or simply that there is no correct answer. Focusing exclusively on moral reasoning, then, runs the risk of creating clever moral casuists, jaded moralists, moral cowards, moral skeptics, or moral cynics. (Fitzgerald 254)

Cathy Ludlum Foos emphasizes that while service learning in public schools must follow liberal principles (thereby not endorsing a particular model of the good), it can still positively affect character by encouraging the traits of character associated with liberalism, increasing students' sense of responsibility and emphasizing that they are community members (Foos 2000).

Pedagogical research suggests that traditional service learning assignments get the results they target. Fitzgerald cites numerous studies showing that traditional service learning:

> improves academic learning. . .[and] social, psychological, and moral development: open-mindedness, personal responsibility, social responsibility, positive attitude toward others, a greater sense of efficacy, higher self-esteem, lower levels of alienation, moral development, and more controversially civic responsibility (251).

Similarly, H. M. Giebel references "a large study by Janet Eyler and Dwight Giles, using both surveys and interviews, which indicated that service learning had positive results for students in the areas of critical thinking, understanding and applying concepts, engagement and curiosity, personal development, and citizenship" (94). Haste and Hogan point to "abundant evidence that young people's participation in community organizations predicts longer term involvement in civic life as well as leading more immediately to greater self-confidence and team-working skills" (479). Chapters in the book that address service learning are: Chapter 3, "Experiential Learning in Business Ethics" by Karen Hornsby and Wade Maki; Chapter 9, "Taking Animals Seriously: Ethics in Action" by Kathie Jenni; Chapter 12, "Internships: Experiential Learning in Global Justice," by Ericka Tucker; and Chapter 15, "Minding Philosophy: Service Learning and Intellectual Disability" by Donna Turney.

Teaching pre-college philosophy is a type of experiential learning that is unique to the field of philosophy; it is when philosophy professors (or students) teach philosophy to people in elementary school through high school. Many graduate programs have philosophy outreach groups, and many universities, both large and small, do philosophy outreach in local schools, using the undergraduates or graduate students as the facilitators of the workshops with the target group. Doing philosophy with these populations is EL for the undergraduates and graduate students who participate; they learn to teach using basic examples and hone their knowledge of philosophy and their critical thinking skills in so doing. Chapter 2, "Experiential Learning and the Practice of Pre-College Philosophy" by Michael Burroughs, describes the connection between doing philosophy with young people and EL and articulates the benefit of these programs not just to the target group but to the college students who participate in the outreach programs.

Civic engagement and social activism are terms used to describe the individual students' outreach projects related to moral, social, and political issues. The goal of civic engagement is to deepen student learning in the college setting, contribute respectfully to communities in which they become involved, and produce lifelong civic leaders. Social activism is one type of civic engagement, in that it involves campaigning for a particular social, moral, or legal outcome. There are several chapters in the book that provide examples of how to do activism and civic engagement with students: Chapter 8, "Assessing Student-Initiated Civic Engagement Projects in Philosophy Classes" by Susan Hawthorne, Monica Janzen, Ramona Ilea, and Chad Wiener; Chapter 11, "Experiential Learning in a Social Justice Course: Philosophy as Transformative Experience," by Megan Halteman Zwart; and Chapter 12, "Feminist Philosophy and Civic Engagement: The Educational Fair" by Sharon Meagher.

Study abroad programs are also very popular EL courses because they involve traveling with students to sites associated with the course content (such as visiting museums, landmarks, battlefields, or religious sites). Study abroad has the dual function of providing students with cross-cultural experiences (where the majority of their education will take place, according to some), and providing them with educational content associated with the travel (Nguyen 2012). Students who participate in study abroad programs are highly satisfied with their experiences because they provide a way of culturally and socially situating the course materials. The chapters that explain how philosophers can organize study abroad classes are: Chapter 6 "Philosophy, Critical Pedagogy, and Experiential Learning" by Jeremy Wisnewski and Chapter 14, "Cultivating Responsible Global Citizenship: Philosophical Exploration & Service-Learning in Guyana" by Katherine Kirby.

Collaborative group projects involve learning by working together on a guided project. They are one way that doesn't necessarily require interaction with the world outside the classroom. In these projects, EL methods are adapted to suit the classroom environment by enabling students to work together in groups and take on projects that have a goal but not a determinate outcome. In other words, risk is involved in these types of group projects. They require a substantial time investment and include guided reflections of the collaborative experience; in this regard, they are not just any kind of group work. Chapters in the book that articulate how to do collaborative group projects in the philosophy classroom include: Chapter 5, "Dewey and Collaborative Learning Indoors," by Minerva Ahumada; Chapter 9, "Emergent Learning in Independent Studies: The Story of the Accessible Icon Project" by Brian Glenney; Chapter 15, "Studying War and Contributing to the Community" by Joe Cole; Chapter 17, "Collaborative Research Groups in the Experimental Philosophy Seminar" by Alexandra Bradner; and Chapter 19, "Teaching Philosophy by Designing a Wikipedia Page" by Graham Hubbs.

Philosophical experiential learning is the term we coined to refer to the practice of using distinctive activities to teach associated philosophical content. These activities are unique and suited to the instructor's interests and expertise and the goals of the course. For example, Maurice Hamington describes a course that includes acting exercises in order to learn about care ethics in Chapter 4, "Performing Care Ethics: Empathy, Acting, and Embodied Learning." Dan Yim teaches about implicit bias and seeks to overcome it by exposing privileged college students to underprivileged students and schools in an urban area in Chapter 7, "Implicit Bias, Race, and Gender: Experiential Learning and Dual-Process Cognition." Gregory Clark takes students to an archery range to teach them about the concept of practice, described in Chapter 18, "Philosophy as Practice: Zen and Archery." And Joe Cole's students do unique peace-related activities in a just war course, which he describes in Chapter 15, "Studying War and Contributing to the Community."

III. OBJECTIONS TO EXPERIENTIAL LEARNING AND RESPONSES

Despite the successes of EL, some philosophers think EL does not belong in a philosophy class. They might claim that EL is not suited to help students achieve the aims of philosophical education. Philosophy is about encouraging students to become good abstract reasoners, not about inspiring personal growth or developing social skills or civic interest. The main focus in teaching philosophy should be conceptual analysis, logical reasoning, and adept handling of words/concepts by way of argument, discussion, symbolization, and writing. Philosophy teachers should focus on these goals exclusively. Moreover, some might argue that EL even detracts from the ability of students to achieve the aims of a philosophical education. They might object that connecting philosophical theory to real-world experience corrupts philosophical theorizing, insofar as philosophical theory is rich enough by itself to be interesting without practical application. Seen from this perspective, student engagement in projects that do not have this aim is at best irrelevant; it might even detract from learning by emphasizing emotion-laden experiences at the expense of rational thought.[8]

Our response to the first objection is that it is based on a false dichotomy, by creating an opposition between philosophical reasoning and engagement with the "real world." It suggests that EL cannot help achieve the goals of a philosophy education, when in fact there is evidence that EL actually contributes to these aims. Our response to the second objection that practice corrupts theory is that is based on a narrow view of what philosophy is that developed in the twentieth century. In contrast, the view that philosophy ought *not* to be exclusively abstract and otherworldly has a rich and varied history. As many of the papers in the first part of our volume emphasize, Socrates in the agora, Dewey and Addams in the educational and social trenches, political philosophers, and feminist philosophers wrestling with the problems of their times all suggest that philosophy can be both engaged *and* true to itself in stimulating careful and critical reflection. It may, in fact, be truer to itself when the real world is used to construct theories, even abstract ones like social ontology. The simplifications and oversimplifications that are possible in many types of abstract philosophy, while helpful in clearing debris, need the complications and testing of the world to show whether they stand up to scrutiny.

The contributors to this book support this view of philosophy, offering convincing testimonies that students' understanding of course materials, for example, are deeper and more sophisticated when they engage in any of the forms of EL that we highlighted in Section I: service learning, civic engagement, teaching pre-college philosophy, collaborative group projects, study abroad, and philosophical EL. Empirical studies support our contributors' findings that EL has been shown to improve the development of the kinds of skills valued by philosophers. Surveys of faculty who use experiential service learning show that they value it because it improves analytical skills and problem-solving skills (Hammond 1994), skills that are often emphasized in philosophy classes. In fact, the top three factors that most strongly motivated faculty to use service learning were "increased understanding of course material," "increased student personal development," and "increased student understanding of social problems as systematic" (Abes, Jackson, and Jones 9). Collaborative experiences are also shown to increase students' cognitive thinking skills and to decrease their intolerance for ethnic, religious, racial, and gender diversity (Bosley 1992). "In addition, students who have collaborative experiences are better able to develop their critical thinking skills by learning how to engage in dialogic conflict with other group members" (Bosley abstract). Moreover, Kuh (2008), for example, demonstrates that high-impact practices such as service learning, collaborative assignments, diversity and global learning, learning communities, and internships, increase engagement and success in college students. Impact studies show that study abroad enhances both creativity and critical deliberation (Nguyen 2012). And although service learning projects are criticized for being too engaged in community involvement at the expense of academics, multiple studies show that service learning projects increase academic performance (Ash, Clayton and Atkinson 2005; Celio, Durlak and Dymnicki 2011, Vogelgesang and Astin 2000).

However, some philosophers claim that these projects do not belong in a philosophy class. On one hand, philosophers make arguments on controversial topics, especially in ethics or political philosophy, and yet they have not arrived at a consensus on many of these topics. EL projects in philosophy courses often require students to take a clear stance on an ethical or political issue, which, one might argue, is disingenuous and encourages the formation of opinion rather than argument, given that there is no consensus among philosophers. On the other hand, philosophers sometimes frame courses in a way that the instructor's personal opinion and philosophical commitments are more obvious, which, arguably, can be an inappropriate influence on students. In fact, the experiential learning projects in these cases presuppose some conception of the good, which, again, may be biased on the part of the instructor or overly political.

Some chapters in our book do describe projects that can be seen as political or as furthering a particular philosophical stance or concern. Kathie Jenni's or Ericka Tucker's chapters, for example, describe courses that require involvement with community organizations that have what some might take to be overtly ethical or political missions. However, this is not any more biased than teaching certain course materials (e.g., Peter Singer's *Animal Liberation*, or arguments about neo-colonialism) or assigning certain paper topics that require students to take a stance on issues covered in the class (or in this case, the treatment of animals and global justice). One might respond that allowing students to experience the issues firsthand gives them greater autonomy in forming their own opinions on the matter.

Furthermore, while it is true that philosophers have not arrived at a consensus on many issues, it is also true that there is more agreement among philosophers than some suspect. Most if not all philosophers are highly critical of racism, modern-day slavery, or factory farming, for example. Moreover, EL projects that require involvement in the community offer students choices of a variety of community groups that they can work with, so that they are not required to be involved with a group whose views they oppose.

Some philosophers will not be convinced by these responses and will continue to think that community-based projects are overly biased or political.

Nevertheless, these philosophers should not write off EL altogether. Not all forms of EL involve working with community groups or doing activist projects. These philosophers might be perfectly satisfied by other forms of EL represented in this volume: teaching pre-college philosophy, collaborative group projects, study abroad, and philosophical experiential learning activities (such as museum visits, website construction, or archery instruction). The focus of these activities is not so much on serving the community but on developing student understanding by applying the material learned in class to a practical situation so that they have educative as opposed to mis-educative experiences, those that provide a long-lasting understanding of course materials. While some forms of EL are indeed better suited to some philosophical topics than others, the goal is to give students an experience that allows them to feel the full force of the theory and not just examine hypothetical cases as the primary method of learning about philosophy.

A related objection raises the problem of forced voluntariness: students only volunteer with community organizations because they are forced to do so. This seems to defeat the point of volunteering.[9] Others fear that students will have to choose projects that do not interest them. Those concerned about these issues would probably stay away from a traditional service learning model (such as Kirby's in chapter 14) and opt for a civic engagement/activism model instead, giving students the freedom to pick the project that *they* believe in. When doing civic engagement projects, such as those assigned by Hawthorne, Janzen, Ilea, and Wiener (chapter 8), students choose projects *they* are passionate about, addressing a local or global issue, and they develop an aspect of citizenship of their own choosing—direct political interest, pressure politics, activism, volunteering in the community, charity work, or educating others.[10] However, even those doing traditional service learning or internships usually offer students many options. Tucker, Hornsby and Maki, and Cole, for example, give students a list of organizations that they can choose from. While students are still forced, in a way, to volunteer, having the freedom to select projects that interest them helps a great deal. Another option for avoiding the problem of forced volunteerism is to have students work in collaborative group projects to apply the theories learned in class (chapter 12) or educate others (chapter 2), or to write a Wikipedia article (chapter 19).

Perhaps the most significant concern for philosophers interested in EL is that, while it offers valuable contributions to philosophy classes, it is logistically difficult to implement. Most philosophers have learned philosophy in a very traditional setting; they have not seen EL implemented in philosophy classes in their undergraduate or graduate education and have a hard time imagining how it might work. Seen in this light, using EL assignments is a risk. It's also time consuming. Is it riskier or more time-consuming than delivering lectures one has perfected over years? Probably. However, compared to creating novel classroom activities or preparing new readings, it might not be. It all depends on what EL activity one wants to use and the support and resources available for EL at one's university. Many authors in this book present detailed ideas about how to set up the EL experiences they describe to make it easier for readers to set up similar EL experiences in their classes. Many of these authors would be happy to share their course materials. There are also a number of online resources that offer syllabi, assignments, grading forms, tips, and other resources. Here are just a few examples:

- The American Association of Philosophy Teachers is dedicated to the advancement of the art of teaching philosophy, and this includes experiential learning. To this end the organization sponsors a biennial workshop/conference on teaching philosophy and a teaching fellows program.
- The American Philosophical Association, the philosophy profession's umbrella organization, provides resources for philosophy teaching and outreach in the profession.
- Campus Compact, an organization dedicated to service learning in higher education, has resources for teachers and students. Their website includes many resources for those interested in doing service learning with their students. It also includes some syllabi of philosophy classes that incorporate service learning.
- Engaged Philosophy: Civic Engagement in Philosophy Classes gives faculty and students tools to implement activist or service projects in philosophy classes—assignment guidelines, sample projects, research resources, as well as testimonials and data supporting civic engagement results.
- Learn and Serve: America's National Service Learning Clearinghouse hosts a very useful database of research and teaching methods.
- Philosophical Horizons emphasizes diversity and underprivileged populations and serves the Mark Luttrell correctional facility and schools that are the least likely to have the resources to implement Philosophy for Children (P4C) into their curriculum.
- PLATO (Philosophy Learning and Teaching Organization) is a national organization that advocates and supports introducing philosophy to pre-college students.
- Public Philosophy Network is an online social network for philosophers, community-based practitioners, policy makers, and other constituents interested in thinking critically about public issues.
- Teach Philosophy 101 presents free, user-friendly strategies and resources for faculty members and graduate assistants who teach philosophy courses, especially at the introductory level.
- Teaching Children Philosophy archives lesson plans submitted by students from multiple institutions as well as sample courses, resources, and videos.
- Volgistics houses resources, communication tools, and some finished products to link people engaged in civic education around the world.

Another logistical difficulty some philosophers may draw attention to is finding financial support to do EL activities with their students. Funding is certainly required for some activities, such as studying abroad, and sometimes to a lesser extent for pre-college philosophy or service learning activities. But it is not required for others: civic engagement/activist projects (such as those described in chapter 8) and collaborative writing (e.g., those described in Hubbs's chapter), for example, do not usually require any monetary investment. Furthermore, there are solutions to the financial problem; for study abroad, for example, students are often required to pay their own way. Some universities have funding available for study abroad or for other EL activities through their office of study abroad, the center for civic engagement, the dean's office, teaching center, diversity center, or special grants.

Others worry about the lack of reward and recognition of EL work in the tenure and promotion process. We think this concern is justified at universities that primarily value research and publication in top philosophical journals. At most other colleges—including ours—innovative pedagogical methods count toward tenure and promotion. Many universities are increasingly placing value on high-impact practices[11] such as those described in this book. Some universities are even requiring their undergraduate students to fulfill a civic engagement or service learning requirement,[12] and many encourage students to study abroad. This suggests, then, that such universities value innovating teaching that helps to meet these requirements. In fact, some philosophers, like Jeremy Wisnewski (chapter 6), are pressured by their universities to incorporate some of the high-impact practices described in this book to increase retention, and so professors take on EL activities at their institution's request; for this, they are rewarded with funding or recognition toward tenure and promotion.

Finally, some philosophers worry that their home university does not attract the types of students needed to participate in EL or does not offer an environment supportive of EL. However, as the chapters in this book demonstrate, EL can be done in a wide variety of settings: at community colleges, liberal arts colleges, state schools, schools in urban and rural settings, schools with small classes, schools with very large classes, etc. While it is helpful for one's university to have a center or office that promotes EL (or civic engagement, service learning, or community-based learning), it is not necessary. Those interested in study abroad can also work with their university's study abroad office and consult with faculty teaching foreign languages and anthropology for a shared group travel opportunity. In fact, it is often valuable to work with faculty from other fields on various programs (e.g., education, social work, behavioral sciences for service learning and civic engagement; anthropology, languages, and many other social sciences for study abroad). Several chapters (16, 17 and 20) detail the importance of interdisciplinary collaboration with faculty members outside of philosophy, arguing that this can enhance the philosophical goals of a course.

IV. AN OVERVIEW OF THE CHAPTERS

The essays in this book have never been published before. The first part of the book, "Philosophical Reflections on Experiential Learning," includes seven chapters that give sustained treatment of the various philosophical theories that frame experiential learning and show how they can be applied in specific classes.

Michael Burroughs's chapter focuses on EL and the practice of pre-college philosophy. He begins the chapter with an overview of EL theory and various philosophical theories of education, showing that philosophers ranging from Plato and Aristotle to Rousseau and Dewey have regarded EL as a central component of education. He then argues that philosophy with children is an important way in which philosophers can engage in EL; doing philosophy with children allows philosophers to move beyond the academy into their communities and schools, challenging them to find the value of philosophy for children and adolescents as well as K–12 education more generally.

While Burroughs focuses on the history of EL from Plato to Dewey, Karen Hornsby and Wade Maki, in Chapter 2, survey the development of various EL theories since Dewey as well as recent scientific and educational research about how people learn. They then argue that three components are essential to the creation of successful EL pedagogy: structured scaffolding, measured cognitive dissonance, and repeated reflection activities. They end the chapter by describing the EL structure and classroom activities of their Business Ethics courses in order to show how they connected the essential elements of EL theories to their pedagogical practices.

While these first two chapters describe EL activities that take place outside of the classroom, Maurice Hamington and Minerva Ahumada show in the next two chapters that students can also have transformative experiences that impact their learning inside the classroom. Maurice Hamington draws on feminist care ethics to argue that care is an embodied activity whereby acts of care are performed. Those physical performances result in habits of care that build caring knowledge and provide the conditions for empathetic understanding. He concludes that EL is an essential element of how ethics should be taught if ethics is intended to be more than a game of normative adjudication. His course takes on two interwoven features: dramaturgical EL activities and theory readings that provide a cognitive framework for analysis. The dramaturgical exercises engage the corporeal and visceral aspects of caring. Students experience a high degree of personal engagement through EL and attentiveness to bodily activity, which the students say is life-altering. Minerva Ahumada then describes complex in-class activities that require substantial interaction between the students in a night class at a community college. She draws on John Dewey to design opportunities for her students to reflect and analyze their concrete involvement in the world and their connection to the ethical theories studied in class. These in-class EL opportunities are especially useful for those who are, for various reasons, restricted to working with students in the classroom.

Jeremy Wisnewski argues in Chapter 6 that the critical-theoretic model of EL (as exemplified by thinkers like Dewey, Freire, and Hahn) can be applied in any philosophy course. He discusses how he uses both traditional EL and critical-theoretic EL in two philosophy courses he teaches: a travel abroad course to Greece and Turkey and a first-year seminar that requires students to impersonate Socrates. He argues that EL is useful in cultivating critical reasoning skills and fostering independence of thought (two essential goals of for any philosophy course), and that these are also prerequisites for responsible citizenship. Thus, philosophy is a discipline uniquely suited to integrate experiential learning activities that aim at broad institutional goals such as critical thinking and responsible citizenship.

In chapter 7, Dan Yim complicates the standard story of the mind that undergirds the Socratic project of self-knowledge. In the course he describes, which focuses on understanding the social dynamics of race and gender, he shows students how empirical studies reveal the way our minds are replete with hidden biases and harbors the tendency to stereotype people in ways that are socially harmful and unfair. Yim argues that the distinctive value of EL pedagogies is their potential to bring these tendencies into the light and develop a more layered portrait of agency and mind. Ultimately, says Yim, the right kind of EL experiences can help to bring awareness of implicit biases related to race and gender, if not ultimately change them.

Although philosophers are not known for their empirical studies, empirical data is needed to show that the EL activities we use in our classes actually work the way we believe they do. Susan Hawthorne, Monica Janzen, Ramona Ilea, and Chad Wiener collaborated to conduct one such study, which was funded in part by an American Philosophical Association grant. They used pre- and post-course surveys, a qualitative analysis of students' final reflections, and standard course evaluations to assess the efficacy of the civic engagement assignments in achieving student learning outcomes in three courses on three campuses. From the data obtained, they conclude that the project and regular course content jointly improve student-perceived achievement in citizenship, communication, critical thinking, and practical skills.

Unit II of the book contains twelve examples of philosophy classes that successfully incorporate EL. Philosophy, as traditionally practiced and taught, is a solitary discipline. Many of the chapters in this unit show how students can work in groups to develop the skills prized by philosophers. The EL activities described here create innovative curricular methods that also genuinely contribute to student transformation and personal development.

In Chapter 9 Brian Glenney argues that an effective form of EL for undergraduate independent study courses is to focus student learning with a single research goal: submitting an article for presentation in a professional conference or publication in a professional journal. He describes two such independent study courses and argues that learning emerges organically in this pedagogy by simulating the discovery of ideas. Using Kuhn's theory of conflict and discovery as a framework, Glenney develops the notion of "emergent learning," where chaotic/disorderly learning conditions led to both professional presentations and publications. Both courses relate to a project to change the ubiquitous "disability" symbol (the International Symbol of Access) from a static to an active depiction of people with disabilities, with the first course leading to the genesis of a street art campaign and the second evolving the project to state-sponsored advocacy.

Many people care about animals, food, and social justice issues. But their actions do not match their beliefs because they are unanchored by intimate personal knowledge of animals' lives, farming, or poverty. In Chapter 10, Kathie Jenni describes a seminar in animal ethics that includes volunteering at animal rescues. The course aims to ground compassion and action for animals in careful moral reasoning and empathic understanding of their lives. In Chapter 11, Megan Halteman Zwart also shows the importance of facilitating student experiences with social justice issues by focusing on site visits and service learning. Like Jenni, Zwart shows that connecting students to a broad vision of philosophy as a way of life challenges their beliefs and provokes the integration of the theoretical and practical. In both cases, forming personal relationships and experiencing pertinent facts first-hand have a transformative effect on the students, changing their worldview and counteracting the powerlessness students can experience while passively studying systemic social injustice. Though this process may initially cause distress as students confront challenges to their beliefs, ultimately, it can promote harmony between belief and action.

Although many teachers get students involved in their communities, civic engagement does not need to take place off-campus. In Chapter 12, Sharon Meagher shows a different EL model that can be adapted to a wide variety of philosophy courses, especially those dealing with social justice issues: the campus educational fair or teach-in. For her feminist philosophy class, Meagher's students work together to develop a campus fair where they learn by teaching, sharing their newly acquired knowledge of key theoretical principles and practices with the rest of the university community.

Chapter 13 and Chapter 14, by Ericka Tucker and Katherine Kirby respectively, show how EL can address global justice. Each of Tucker's students chooses a semester-long internship with a local organization working on issues of global justice, while Kirby and her students study global justice by traveling to Guyana. Both of them show that pairing difficult theoretical materials with EL activities provides the kind of educational experience that can lead students to read the course materials differently and to ask more informed questions about theories of global justice. Those interested in study abroad classes will want to read Kirby's discussion of the potential dangers inherent in international service in developing countries. Kirby argues that careful philosophical grounding, coupled with prioritization of local organizations' wisdom, will avoid these dangers and prove to be transformative for both students and community partners as a result of the face-to-face engagement.

In Chapter 15, Joe Cole is also concerned with global issues, specifically, the ethics of war. Cole describes a course on Pacifism and Just War Theory that uses EL activities to prepare students for designing and implementing a final project involving community engagement. In addition to covering theoretical debates and case studies, his class includes conflict resolution methods and self-care techniques to manage the stresses of studying war. This combination leads to a class that provides students with an integrated experience of intellectual study, personal development, and community engagement.

As Tucker and Jenni describe in chapters 10 and 13, partnering with local nonprofits can be a very effective way to engage students in the community and provide them with transformative experiences. In Chapter 16, Donna Turney describes coteaching a first-year seminar with a colleague in psychology, with the goal of partnering with a local nonprofit that serves people with intellectual disabilities. The college students greatly benefited from this interaction, by asking incisive questions and making important critiques about course readings on the mind, knowledge, and disability. Meeting community needs became more of a priority, and the experience changed her understanding of teaching philosophy; the course also transformed the lives of all participants involved in the class.

The last section of the book focuses on new directions in EL in philosophy. In Chapter 17, Alexandra Bradner focuses on one of the new sub-disciplines of philosophy: experimental philosophy. Bradner describes in great detail how students can work on controlled studies to locate recurring correlations between factors of interest to the philosophical canon. This type of EL is not easy to execute; however, since students generated scientifically valid studies by working closely with members of the psychology department and the institutional review board to design, run, analyze, and present original X-Phi studies, experimental EL philosophy courses could become the new cutting edge in philosophy education.

Chapter 18 by Gregory Clark and Chapter 19 by Graham Hubbs both describe classes in which all the enrolled students work together. Clark describes a university-level course in which students learn to think philosophically about practices by: 1) engaging in practices (archery, writing, philosophy), 2) reading thick descriptions of practices, and 3) reflecting on practices philosophically. Hubbs's focus is different; his students work together to write collaboratively. By writing a Wikipedia article on the topic of their seminar class, collective intentionality, they engage with the world beyond the classroom, improve their writing, and learn how public knowledge is produced. This, in turn, helps them to be more aware—and when appropriate, critical—of the sources of knowledge on which we all rely in our daily lives. The last chapter, by Robin Zebrowski, also focuses on a new direction in EL opportunities in philosophy: the use of campus museums. Zebrowski shows that class projects involving museums can help students and can help us rethink our approach to teaching philosophy, changing our own ideas about the content we teach.

V. CONCLUSION

We hope to have given the reader an exciting taste of what follows. In conclusion, though, we would be remiss if we did not mention the fact that doing experiential learning is deeply rewarding to the instructor. EL changes the classroom dynamic between the student and teacher: the instructor gets off the stage and becomes a facilitator or coach, helping to bring forth new ideas, plans, and actions, encouraging students to do something they believed they could not do. And while doing EL requires more organization, creativity, and risk, on the days that students work on their projects, it is less preparation. It is rewarding to watch the students succeed, and disheartening to see them fail, but in both cases they learn something significant. Campus and community partners become invested in the students, and if the instructor is lucky, the university and the community will recognize her efforts. For those instructors who are looking for a way to enliven their philosophy courses, we hope the chapters here will be helpful.[13]

NOTES

1. Two useful books along these lines are Schick (2012) and Baggini (2007).
2. It's worth noting that the term *experiential learning* is not ours—it's the term used in education today. In fact, the term *experiential learning* may strike some philosophers as a bit of a bogey, given that *all* types of classroom experiences are experiential in the sense that students have experiences. The terms *reflective learning*, *applied learning*, or *deep learning* might have been better candidate terms to articulate these notions, but experiential learning seems to have been chosen because it broadly captures all of these notions. The term *experiential learning* and the abbreviation EL are used interchangeably throughout the book.
3. See information collected by the Association of American Colleges & Universities at https://www.aacu.org/resources/high-impact-practices.
4. For an elaboration of this point, see Part 4.
5. See, for example, Kunkel (1983), Liu (2000), and Wallace (2000).
6. Labs are taken to be the *sine qua non* of science education, because they are the primary opportunity for students to understand, at the level of practice, what they are learning in theory. They also remember substantially more with the hands-on experience.
7. Kirby suggests, referencing the work of Emmanuel Levinas, that abstract thought cannot reorient students to others; one needs a nonrational encounter that allows one to recognize another's needs, as opposed to (for example) fulfilling one's own service goals.
8. These two objections bring to the fore a critical question: what is the goal of teaching philosophy? If there are multiple goals, can they be realized

simultaneously? For our aims here, it is unnecessary to answer this question. We instead recognize that professors often have different goals in teaching philosophy to their students, and that they must decide based on a wide range of considerations. Our goal here is to revisit the goal of teaching philosophy and reflect on current educational practices.

9. For a longer discussion of the problem of forced voluntariness in a philosophy classroom, see Fitzgerald 263–265.
10. Haste and Hogan describe many varieties of civic participation: they summarize the roles of citizenship broadly as "voting, helping, and making one's voice heard" across a wide range of issues and motivations, and argue that young people (at least in Britain) understand good citizenship in this broad definition (Haste and Hogan 473).
11. See numerous examples collected by the Association of American Colleges & Universities at https://www.aacu.org/campus-model/3325.
12. Over 250 college and university presidents signed the *Presidents' Fourth of July Declaration on the Civic Responsibility of Higher Education*, a call for institutions of higher learning to recognize their role in revitalizing our democracy.
13. We are grateful to Justin Weinberg, Monica Janzen, Marilea Bramer, and Kerri Farrow for their feedback on earlier drafts of this chapter.

WORKS CITED

Abes, Elisa, Golden Jackson and Susan Jones. "Factors that Motivate and Deter Faculty Use of Service-Learning." *Michigan Journal of Community Service Learning* (Fall 2002): 5–17.

The American Association of Philosophy Teachers. Accessed March 24, 2015. http://philosophyteachers.org/.

The American Philosophical Association. Accessed March 24, 2015. http://www.apaonline.org/.

Association of American Colleges & Universities. "High Impact Practices." Accessed March 24, 2015. https://www.aacu.org/resources/high-impact-practices.

———. "Campus Models and Case Studies." Accessed March 24, 2015. https://www.aacu.org/campus-model/3325.

Ash, A. L., P. H. Clayton, and M. P. Atkinson. "Integrating Reflection and Assessment to Capture and Improve Student Learning." *Michigan Journal of Community Service Learning*, 11.2 (2005): 49–60.

Baggini, Julien. *Do You Think What You Think You Think?* New York: Plume, 2007.

Bosley, Deborah, and JoEllen Jacobs. "Collaborative Writing: A Philosopher's Guide." *Teaching Philosophy* 15.1 (1992): 17–32.

Campus Compact. "Philosophy Syllabi." Accessed March 24, 2015. http://www.compact.org/category/syllabi/philosophy.

Celio, C.I., J. Durlak, and A. Dymnicki. "A Meta-Analysis of the Impact of Service-Learning on Students." *Journal of Experiential Education* 34.2 (2011): 164–81.

Engaged Philosophy. "Civic Engagement in Philosophy Classes." Accessed March 24, 2015. http://www.engagedphilosophy.com/.

Fitzgerald, Patrick. "Service-Learning and the Socially Responsible Ethics Class." *Teaching Philosophy* 20.3 (1997): 251–67.

Foos, Cathy Ludlum. "Fluid Boundaries: Service-Learning and the Experience of Community." *Beyond the Tower: Concepts and Models for Service-Learning in Philosophy*. Ed. David C. Lisman. Washington, DC: American Association for Higher Education, 2000: 101–12.

Giebel, H. M. "In Defense of Service Learning." *Teaching Philosophy* 29.2 (2006): 93–109.

Hammond, C. "Integrating Service and Academic Study." *Michigan Journal of Community Service Learning* 1.1 (1994): 21–8.

Haste, Helen and Amy Hogan. "Beyond Conventional Civic Participation, Beyond the Moral-Political Divide: Young People and Contemporary Debates about Citizenship." *Journal of Moral Education* 35.4 (2006): 473–93.

Kirby, Katherine E. "Encountering and Understanding Suffering: The Need for Service Learning in Ethical Education." *Teaching Philosophy* 32.2 (2009): 153–76.

Kolb, David, *Experiential Learning: experience as the source of learning and development*. Englewood Cliffs: Prentice Hall, 1984.

Kuh, G. *High Impact Educational Practices: What They Are, Who Has Access to Them, and Why They Matter*. Washington, DC: American Association of Colleges & Universities, 2008.

Kunkel, Joseph. "Introductory Philosophy as a 'Service Course.'" *Teaching Philosophy* 6.1 (1983): 1–11.

Learn and Serve: America's National Service Learning Clearinghouse. Accessed March 24, 2015. http://www.servicelearning.org/.

Liu, Goodwin. "Knowledge, Foundations, and Discourse: Philosophical Support for Service Learning." *Beyond the Tower: Concepts and Models for Service-Learning in Philosophy*. Ed. David C. Lisman. Washington, DC: American Association for Higher Education, 2000: 11–34.

Nguyen, A. Minh. "Study Abroad's Contribution to Critical Thinking and World Citizenship." *Think: Philosophy for Everyone* 11.31 (2012): 27–40.

Philosophical Horizons. Accessed March 24, 2015. http://www.memphis.edu/philosophy/philhorizons.php.

Philosophy Learning and Teaching Organization (Plato): Engaging Young Philosophers. Accessed March 24, 2015. http://plato-philosophy.org

"Presidents' Fourth of July Declaration on the Civic Responsibility of Higher Education." Accessed March 24, 2015. https://www.internationalconsortium.org/about/presidents-fourth-of-july-declaration.

Public Philosophy Network. Accessed March 24, 2015. http://publicphilosophynetwork.ning.com/.

Schick, Theodore. *Doing Philosophy: An Introduction to Philosophy Through Thought Experiments*. New York: McGraw-Hill, 2012.

Teach Philosophy 101. Accessed March 24, 2015. http://www.teachphilosophy101.org/.

Teaching Children Philosophy. Accessed December 29, 2014. http://www.teachingchildrenphilosophy.org/wiki/Main_Page.

Valentine, Eugene J. "Service-Learning as Vehicle for Teaching Philosophy." *Beyond the Tower: Concepts and Models for Service-Learning in Philosophy*. Ed. David C. Lisman. Washington, DC: American Association for Higher Education, 2000, 139–166.

Vogelgesang, L. J., and A. W. Astin. "Comparing the Effects of Community Service and Service Learning." *Michigan Journal of Community Service Learning* 7 (2000): 25–34.

Volgistics. Accessed March 24, 2015. http://www.volgistics.com/.

Wallace, John. "The Use of a Philosopher: Socrates and Myles Horton." *Beyond the Tower: Concepts and Models for Service-Learning in Philosophy*. Ed. David C. Lisman. Washington, DC: American Association for Higher Education, 2000, 69–90.

Part I

Philosophical Reflections on Experiential Learning

2 Practicing Philosophy

Philosophy with Children and Experiential Learning

Michael D. Burroughs

I. INTRODUCTION

Experiential learning in contemporary education takes many forms, ranging from organized service learning and internships to outdoor education and fieldwork. Disciplines such as education, medicine, forensic science, and engineering (to name a few) abound with experiential learning opportunities. There is an established line of thought that one cannot become a competent educator, medical doctor, scientist, or engineer by theory alone. By contrast, philosophy students rarely participate in organized experiential learning within or beyond the classroom, and professional philosophy is characterized, in part, by a prioritization of theory over practice and personal experience.[1] But experiential learning is not as foreign to philosophy as is often assumed; numerous canonical philosophers—including Plato, Aristotle, Rousseau, Dewey, and others—have regarded experiential learning (in diverse forms) as a central component of education. These philosophers reserve a privileged role for educational experiences that, in addition to reason or dialectic, can contribute to the development of children into virtuous adults and citizens. In addition to these early roots of experiential learning, contemporary subareas of philosophy—such as applied ethics and experimental philosophy—call for philosophical training that engages with empirical research alongside traditional conceptual and theoretical questions.

In this chapter I will discuss an additional area of philosophy—philosophy with children[2]—and its points of intersection with experiential learning theory. Since the 1970s philosophy with children programs have substantially increased in the United States and internationally, many of which are housed in philosophy departments and represented in the discipline's professional associations.[3] These programs (and the philosophy with children movement more generally) have provided philosophers with increased opportunities to practice philosophy in schools and in turn, to engage in philosophical and experiential learning.[4] Employing accounts of experiential learning theory and their role in the history of philosophy of education, I will focus on philosophy with children as a prominent example of contemporary possibilities for philosophical and experiential learning. I will situate this movement within the educational and philosophical traditions of experiential learning, discuss the work of philosophers in K–12 schools, and argue that professional philosophy would benefit from including increased experiential learning opportunities and greater resources to support philosophical praxis.

II. EXPERIENTIAL LEARNING THEORY

In his now-canonical work *Experiential Learning: Experience as the Source of Learning and Development*, David Kolb notes that experiential learning theory derives from a tradition of philosophical and psychological scholarship—including the work of John Dewey, Kurt Lewin, Jean Piaget, and Kurt Hahn—that regards learning as an "emergent process" with ideas, concepts, and knowledge formed in and modified through experience (26). Learning as *process* is set in opposition to traditional rationalist conceptions of learning as *acquisition* of fixed ideas and pre-established knowledge that, in turn, are documented through measurable learning outcomes (Kolb 26). In traditional models of education—models that remain influential in K–12 and postsecondary education—learning is characterized by a transmission and accumulation of facts and skills (Kolb 26). By contrast, experiential learning theory places an emphasis on "direct engagement, rich learning events and the construction of meaning by learners" (Andresen, Boud, and Cohen 207). Vital learning experiences involve personal engagement with a learning environment, reflection, and adaptation based on new knowledge (Andresen, Boud, and Cohen 207; Itin 93; Kolb 26, 36). In turn, this provides a conception of knowledge that is subject to transformation, "continuously created and recreated, not an independent entity to be acquired or transmitted" (Kolb 38).

For the experiential educator and student, learning is not the "special province" of a particular human faculty, whether reason, memory, or perception. Rather, learning is a *holistic* process that, when practiced well, engages the "whole person" (physical activity, senses, emotions, and intellect) through vital learning experiences (Andresen, Boud, and Cohen 210; Beard and Wilson 2). These experiences are not limited to a single location such as the school; experiential learning occurs throughout life, in all realms of human experience, and is theorized most broadly as the process of human adaptation to the internal and external dimensions of lived experience. As Kolb writes:

> Learning is *the* major process of human adaptation. This concept of learning is considerably broader than that commonly associated with the school classroom. It occurs in all human settings, from schools to the workplace, from the research laboratory to the management board room, in personal relationships and the aisles of the local grocery. It encompasses all life stages, from childhood to adolescence, to middle and old age. Therefore, it encompasses other, more limited adaptive concepts such as creativity, problem solving, decision making, and

> attitude change that focus heavily on one or another of the basic aspects of adaptation. (32)

Given that experiential learning is a lifelong process, students do not enter classrooms as "blank slates"; they possess a multitude of previous learning experiences as well as ideas, concepts, and knowledge in various stages of formation. In turn, this conception of the student informs a reconsideration of traditional teacher and learner roles. Experiential learning is regarded as a "transactive process between an educator and student" such that the learner is no longer exclusively positioned as a recipient of knowledge from the teacher. As opposed to *the* epistemic authority in the classroom, the experiential educator is a *facilitator* and cocreator of the learning process with students (Andresen, Boud, and Cohen 209; Beard and Wilson 2). This means that the educator does not focus on providing students with fixed ideas or pre-established knowledge to be reproduced on a test. Rather, the teacher facilitates education by structuring a productive learning environment and providing ongoing possibilities for reflection and reconstruction of experience and ideas. The goal here is to provide learners with the opportunity to "analyse their experience by reflecting, evaluating and reconstructing it (sometimes individually, sometimes collectively, sometimes both) in order to draw meaning from it in the light of prior experience" (Andresen, Boud, and Cohen 207). As such, experiential learning theory has grown in opposition to traditional power dynamics in the classroom and has affinities with democratic and learner-centered conceptions of education.

III. HISTORICAL ROOTS OF EXPERIENTIAL LEARNING IN PHILOSOPHY

To what extent has experiential learning theory been of interest to philosophers? Although a full answer to this question is beyond the scope of this chapter, a number of illustrative examples reveal that at least some elements of experiential learning—education based in vital experiences in the world, through diverse forms of activity, and beyond a sole focus on cognitive and rational learning processes—are part of the Western philosophical tradition.[5] These aspects of experiential learning are often considered in relation to children and their development. For example, if we turn to Plato and Aristotle's discussion of moral education we find numerous examples of experiential learning *qua* habituation of children. Moral education begins with forms of imitation and habituation for the child, vital experiences that dispose her to take pleasure in virtue and pain in vice.[6] As Plato writes:

> Education [is] the initial acquisition of virtue by the child, when the feelings of pleasure and affection, pain and hatred, that well up in his soul are channeled in the right courses before he can understand the reason why. (*Laws* 42; 653a)

For Aristotle, too, prior to education through reason and dialectic the "soul of the student needs to be prepared by habits for enjoying and hating finely" (168; 1179b25). Thus, it is "all-important" that the child "acquire one sort of habit or another, right from . . . youth" such that her habituation to virtue becomes "second nature" (Aristotle 19; 1103b22–25, 103; 1147a21–22). This change in the child's nature is accomplished through a mode of experiential learning, namely, musical education (*mousike*). Focusing on the use of song, rhythm, and harmony to habituate the child's soul to moral ends, Plato writes:

> Because rhythm and harmony permeate the inner most element of the soul, affect it more powerfully than anything else, and bring it such grace, such education makes one graceful if one is properly trained, and the opposite if one is not . . . since he [the well-educated child] feels distaste correctly, he will praise fine things, be pleased by them, take them into his soul, and, through being nourished by them, become fine and good. What is ugly or shameful, on the other hand, he will correctly condemn and hate while he is still young, before he is able to grasp the reason. (*Republic* 84; 401d5–402a3)

It is through engagement with carefully structured experiences—stories, games, and songs—that the child begins her education and becomes virtuous.[7]

Rousseau offers an additional example of experiential forms of learning in the Western philosophical canon. In *Emile, or On Education* the education of the child begins in the form of an "education of things," a "natural" choice of method stemming from Rousseau's conception of the development of "original dispositions" in the child through experience of her environment:

> We are born with the use of our senses, and from our birth we are affected in various ways by the objects surrounding us. As soon as we have, so to speak, consciousness of our sensations, we are disposed to seek or avoid the objects which produce them, at first according to whether they are pleasant or unpleasant to us, then according to the conformity or lack of it that we find between us and these objects, and finally according to the judgments that we make about them on the basis of the idea of happiness or of perfection given us by reason. These dispositions are strengthened as we become more capable of using our senses and more enlightened; but constrained by our habits, they are more or less corrupted by our opinions. Before this corruption, they are what I call in us *nature*. (39)

As with Plato and Aristotle, Rousseau is interested in marshaling lived experience as an educational tool prior to the advance of reason in the child. By nature the child receives an experiential education from birth as she senses and responds to objects in her environment. As the child ages, her experiential education advances as well—judgment, reason, imagination, and sentiment develop naturally through an encounter with new relations of objects and the need to acquire requisite forms of knowledge and skill to master them (Rousseau 203). As Rousseau argues, to foster this early education we need only follow "the order of nature" by exposing the child to the experience of her environment, her own needs, and in turn, her own motivation to learn by satisfying them (85, 96, 80–81, 166).

IV. DEWEY AND EXPERIENTIAL LEARNING

We now see how the roots of the concept of experiential learning are illustrated in some of the most important texts in the Western philosophical canon—from *Republic* and the *Nicomachean Ethics* to *Emile*. In particular, Plato, Aristotle, and Rousseau discuss aspects of experiential learning and their influence on the moral and intellectual development of children. But Dewey's progressive and constructivist philosophy of education articulates a conception of experiential learning that has had a broad impact on educational theory and schooling more generally. Dewey's commitment to experiential learning is clear in his most prominent works on education, including *Democracy and Education* and *Experience and Education*. Discussing the preeminent role of experience in education, Dewey writes:

> An ounce of experience is better than a ton of theory simply because it is only in experience that any theory has vital and verifiable significance. An experience, a very humble experience, is capable of generating and carrying any amount of theory (or intellectual content), but a theory apart from an experience cannot be definitely grasped even as theory. It tends to become a mere verbal formula, a set of catchwords (*Democracy and Education* 80).

For Dewey, there is an "organic connection" between the process of learning and personal experience, and thus, theory alone is not a sufficient basis for education (*Experience and Education* 25).[8] At least two concepts are key for understanding Dewey's emphasis on the role of experience in education: the *principle of the continuity of experience* (or the *experiential continuum*) and the *interaction* of objective and internal conditions of experience. These concepts are also germane to establishing points of connection between philosophy, experiential learning theory, and philosophy with children.

The principle of continuity of experience holds that "every experience both takes up something from those which have gone before and modifies in some way the quality of those which come after" (Dewey, *Experience and Education* 35).[9] The educational value of this principle, Dewey contends, appears once we use it to identify educative and mis-educative experiences (*Experience and Education* 33). Whereas some forms of experience (educative experiences) will lead to *growth* by broadening the field of possible educational experiences and by engaging the interests and capabilities of learners, other experiences (mis-educative experiences) will prevent or hinder interest in growth (Dewey, *Experience and Education* 45, 36, 25–26).[10] The fundamental focus of the experiential educator, then, is to introduce learning experiences that "live fruitfully and creatively in subsequent experiences" (Dewey, *Experience and Education* 28, 33, 35). It is the *business of the educator* "to see in what direction an experience is heading" and to organize the conditions of educative experiences so as to lead to continuing growth in students (Dewey, *Experience and Education* 38, 40, 45, 50, 75, 79):

> A primary responsibility of educators is that they not only be aware of the general principle of the shaping of the actual experience by environing conditions, but that they also recognize in the concrete what surroundings are conducive to having experiences that lead to growth. Above all, they should know how to utilize the surroundings, physical and social, that exist so as to extract from them all that they have to contribute to building up experiences that are worthwhile. (Dewey, *Experience and Education* 40)

In order to meet this responsibility, the educator must harness the *interaction* of objective and internal conditions of educational experience (Dewey, *Experience and Education* 42). That is, the educator must be aware of her students' attitudes, needs, interests, and capacities (internal conditions) alongside objective conditions—the learning environment, bodies of knowledge from past experience, and educational resources—that can productively meet internal conditions and in turn, lead to growth.[11] Although she cannot control conditions internal to the student, objective conditions can be the subject of planning and regulation by the educator.[12] She can create a learning environment that is conducive to learners' "reconstruction of experience," forming and acting upon ideas, observing resulting conditions, and utilizing lessons learned to navigate and expand future experience (Dewey, *Experience and Education* 87–88).

Dewey provides insight into a number of important elements of experiential education, elements that remain influential in contemporary educational and experiential learning theory. Following Dewey, in order to foster educational growth, both the learning environment (the structured environment in which learning will take place) and the needs, attitudes, and interests of the student (internal conditions of learning) should be taken into account by the educator. Dewey notes that the shortcomings of traditional forms of schooling lie in prioritizing certain objective conditions (specifically, pre-established bodies of knowledge) to the exclusion of the current motivations, attitudes, and interests of students. The result is an educational experience that is alienating to many students insofar as it does not provide internal motivation toward learning. Thus, although all education involves some form of experience, broadly construed, not all educational experiences are of equal value. The best forms of educational experience are vital in nature—they engage the interests and attitudes of students, provide them with independence and responsibility as learners, and in turn, provide a path to continued learning through additional experiences.

My philosophical work with children has been influenced by this "vital" conception of education and the related belief that philosophy can be a catalyst for this experience in K–12 classrooms. As a philosophy graduate student at the University of Memphis I cofounded *Philosophical Horizons*, a philosophy outreach program for children in Memphis City Schools. Through my work with children in Memphis (as well as additional years of philosophical practice with school children in Maryland, North Carolina, Pennsylvania, and Belize, Central America) I recognized the intersection of philosophy and experiential learning, both for myself and for participating children. The experience of visiting local schools and engaging in classroom discussions with children—a practice I have continued each semester for over a decade—has taught me a great deal. The enthusiasm of children, their openness to philosophical questioning, and their capacity for philosophical thought and expression (among other things) has led me to question philosophical norms and consider the expanded possibilities of philosophical practice beyond academia. In my experience, children often are philosophers—persons who ask and are quite capable of exploring philosophical questions, concepts, and ideas. When given the space and support to do so, many children will seek out opportunities for engaging in philosophy with their teachers and peers.

In response, we as professional philosophers and students have the opportunity to support the inclusion of philosophical experience in K–12 education, which can also lead us to interrogate philosophical norms regarding the nature of philosophy, prevailing conceptions of the "philosopher," and the broader value of philosophical practice for our communities and schools. Although I cannot address all of these items here,[13] in the remaining sections of this chapter I will expand on the relationship between philosophy with children and experiential learning, including discussion of the practice of philosophy in K–12 settings, its experiential value for faculty, undergraduate, and graduate student practitioners, and its importance for the discipline of philosophy more generally.

V. PHILOSOPHY WITH CHILDREN AND EXPERIENTIAL LEARNING

As noted above, there is a growing movement toward increased experiential learning opportunities in contemporary philosophy. Service and experiential learning components have increased in philosophy classrooms and forms of "publicly engaged philosophy"—including philosophy outreach and philosophy with children programs—now have a place in many graduate philosophy programs.[14] At this point, however, I want to focus on philosophy with children as a philosophical practice that is deeply tied to experiential learning methods and aims. Philosophy with children has developed into a robust movement within the discipline, supported by professional philosophers, K–12 teachers and administrators, and students alike. The experiential impact of this practice is bidirectional; through philosophy with children professional philosophers (and other practitioners) acquire unique forms of philosophical and pedagogical experience and in turn, participating children and adolescents engage in the experience of philosophical exploration and dialogue that is often lacking in K–12 curricula.

Let us briefly recall some of the fundamental elements of contemporary experiential learning theory: it is an *emergent* process, a *holistic* process, and shifts power dynamics between teacher and student. In their work with young philosophers, practitioners of philosophy with children utilize a pedagogical style that is influenced by experiential learning theory, including the educational philosophy of John Dewey. In *How We Think* Dewey discusses the need to establish an education with "*conditions* that will arouse and guide *curiosity*" and set up "connections in things experienced" such that students will be motivated to contribute suggestions, ideas, and resolutions to challenges encountered in their learning environment (56–57). These educational aims—to spark curiosity, present challenging problems, and encourage collaborative problem solving—are also central to philosophy with children and the *community of philosophical inquiry*. As Matthew Lipman describes it, a community of philosophical inquiry is a structured learning environment in which:

> students listen to one another with respect, build on one another's ideas, challenge one another to supply reasons for otherwise unsupported opinions, assist each other in drawing inferences from what has been said, and seek to identify one another's assumptions. A community of inquiry attempts to follow the inquiry where it leads rather than be penned in by the boundary lines of existing disciplines. A dialogue that tries to conform to logic, it moves forward indirectly like a boat tacking into the wind, but in the process its progress comes to resemble that of thinking itself. (*Thinking in Education* 20–21)

In practice the community of inquiry takes diverse forms. Many (though not all) philosophy with children programs are led by graduate and undergraduate philosophy students. These students volunteer with partner schools, visiting K–12 classrooms to facilitate philosophy discussion sessions with young philosophers (often in collaboration with a partner K–12 classroom teacher). These sessions can range from class discussions on a weekly or monthly basis to semester-long philosophy courses, but in either case, philosophy with children practitioners attempt to establish a community of inquiry with K–12 students. While sitting in a circle with students the facilitator will generally introduce a prompt (a text, question, idea, etc.) to encourage initial questioning and discussion within the group. As students begin to engage in dialogue on the chosen prompt, they are encouraged (and gradually learn) to raise claims, arguments, and counterarguments and seek to construct knowledge and additional questions for exploration as a community. When working with young children (K–4) the community of inquiry might begin with the generation of philosophical questions in relation to characters or problems raised within works of children's literature or through facilitated discussion of artwork created by the class. When working with older children and adolescents, this process could begin with the discussion of primary philosophical texts, film, and many other prompts. The fundamental aim in each case is to use educational resources (functioning as objective conditions) to foster collaborative dialogue between participants (facilitator and K–12 students) on a philosophical question, problem, or concept.

The educational value of this process is, in most cases, not determined by traditional learning outcomes (such as better scores on a standardized test or examination).[15] Rather, success or progress is understood in terms of developments in the community such as the identification of a new dimension of knowledge, an important philosophical distinction, or even the formulation of a previously unconsidered question (Lipman et al., *Philosophy in the Classroom* 111). In addition, success is located in the establishment of a learning environment that allows for a shift away from traditional power dynamics between teacher (or graduate/undergraduate student facilitator) and student. Lipman describes the teacher-student relationship in a community of inquiry as follows:

> The relationship between teacher and students has th[e] character of face-to-face dialogue. It is at once a community exhibiting both apprenticeship and mutual respect and a workshop in which traditional skills are passed on from one generation to another. (*Thinking in Education* 25)

Whereas the traditional educational paradigm includes the transmission of knowledge to the student by the teacher with the latter in an authoritative role as *the* epistemic authority in the classroom, philosophy with children takes a markedly different approach. The learning process is negotiated by the community of inquiry and thus, is the shared responsibility of both teacher and students. Akin to experiential learning practitioners, the philosophy with children teacher (or facilitator) is not the sole epistemic authority, and students are expected to take important roles in the learning process.

In my experience, children are not immediately familiar with this shift in teacher-student power dynamics or its significance as an educational approach. In many elementary and secondary schools children learn to accept a *one-way* mode of communication in the classroom: the teacher speaks and the student listens. The K–12 teacher or philosopher attempting to change this form of communication (and conceptions of the student and learning underlying it) must recognize its influence on young learners and their passive role in the learning process. Forms of "philosophical scaffolding" must be introduced to counter the one-way mode of communication and encourage students to be active, questioning participants in group discussion. This will include providing space for young philosophers to formulate questions that will then be the basis of class dialogue, helping students to make connections between ideas and points formulated by the group during discussion and, as much as possible, allowing students to determine the direction of dialogue through their own contributions and interests.

VI. THE IMPORTANCE OF PHILOSOPHY WITH CHILDREN

For professional philosophers (as well as graduate and undergraduate philosophy students) there are a variety of motives for practicing philosophy with children. Some philosophers seek out opportunities to serve the communities in which they live or have a particular interest in teaching young children philosophical skill sets. But an additional motivation for practicing philosophy with children lies in collaborating with young philosophers in the experience of philosophical questioning, curiosity, and exploration. That is, philosophy with children is distinct from other forms of philosophical practice in that it is motivated, in part, by a primary kind of *philosophical experience*, namely, the open questioning and exploration of philosophical ideas and concepts that is often found in childhood. Gareth Matthews notes his attempt to recall this original form of philosophy in his university classes:

> I first became interested in the philosophical thought of young children by worrying about how to teach introductory courses in philosophy to college students. Many students seemed to resist the idea that doing philosophy could be natural. In response to their resistance I hit on the strategy of showing them that as children many of them had already done philosophy. It occurred to me that my task as a college philosophy teacher was to reintroduce my students to an activity that they had once enjoyed and found natural, but that they had later been socialized to abandon. (*Philosophy & the Young Child* vii)

Philosophy with children serves as an opportunity to return to the vital experiences—of questioning, curiosity, and exploration of philosophical concepts and questions—that underlie and ultimately motivate major areas (e.g., ethics, metaphysics, epistemology) of the discipline. As in many experiential learning practices, philosophy with children provides an educational space that begins with the experiences of the learner and progresses as students and the facilitator draw meaning from these experiences through dialogue and philosophical investigation in a community of inquiry.

For many philosophers this experience also provides an experiential constraint on their own teaching practices in higher education; mastering the pedagogy of philosophy with children can contribute to our ability to be better teachers for adults in university classrooms.[16] And given the absence of pedagogy training in many philosophy graduate programs learning to shape an effective learning environment with young students can be valuable professional development. Through experiential learning in the K–12 classroom the practitioner comes to understand how to develop and deploy a *learner-centered pedagogy*. As Dewey notes, educators must recognize that students are immersed in present concerns and learn most successfully when a "vital connection" is maintained between educational content and their current experiences (*Democracy and Education* 44). By including the learners' "vital energy" and "powers and purposes" the practitioner of philosophy with children can make central areas of philosophy and skill sets accessible to students (Dewey, *Experience and Education* 45).

Practicing philosophy with children requires this learner-centered approach; practitioners must make philosophical problems, concepts, and the practice of dialogue clear to developing students without formal philosophical training. The practitioner must also learn to focus on essential and, at the same time, inviting elements of philosophical concepts and questions. Thus, a discussion of ethics and the good life will not begin with a lecture but perhaps center instead on ethically relevant questions relating to *friendship* (e.g., "What makes someone a *good* friend?" and "Are friends important for a *good* life?") or *fairness* (e.g., "How do you know when a classroom rule is *fair* or *unfair*?"). A discussion of epistemology and metaphysics will not begin with discussion of Locke, Hume, or Kant, but perhaps with questions relating to *dreams* and *reality* (e.g., "Are your dreams *real* in any way?" and "How do you *know* when you are or are not dreaming?").[17] In these instances, learning is no longer defined by student mastery of preselected bodies of information, but rather, learning through personal experience and social interaction in the classroom become central elements of a philosophical education. Appeal to these kinds of questions—raised with discussion prompts, rooted in philosophical concepts, and based in children's life experiences (of friends, rules, dreams, etc.)—can engage the interests of young philosophers and provide a pedagogical foundation for robust philosophical discussion in K–12 and university classrooms alike.

In addition, experiential learning *qua* philosophy with children can introduce philosophers to previously unconsidered, yet significant, philosophical questions. In *The Philosophy of Childhood* Gareth Matthews describes philosophy as, in part, "an adult attempt to deal with the genuinely baffling questions of childhood" (13). As discussed above, there is a sense in which practicing philosophy with children brings the professional philosopher or student practitioner back to a primary experience of questions, concepts, and ideas that motivate major areas of study in philosophy. Moreover, there are philosophical questions that directly arise through experiential learning in the K–12 classroom (or otherwise, remain largely inaccessible). For example, philosophical work with children can present the facilitator with questions relating to the nature of philosophy, as well as the place of the discipline beyond higher education. Although generally reserved for higher education in the United States, practicing philosophy with children can lead to central questions as to the proper scope of philosophy (e.g., "Is philosophy a subject that should be taught at all ages?" and "How would philosophy need to adapt to be relevant to populations beyond the academy?") as well as normative assumptions regarding who is (and who can/cannot be) a philosopher (e.g., "Are children philosophers, or should this term be reserved for adult professionals?" and "What does it mean to be a *philosopher*?"). Those engaging in dialogue with children are also faced with questions relating to agency in childhood and our understanding of the adult-child distinction more generally (e.g. "What is a child?" "On what bases do we classify adults and children as distinct kinds of people?" and "What forms of agency, capabilities, and/or responsibilities are unique to children and adults?"). Finally, and perhaps most importantly, philosophy with children requires philosophers to move beyond the university into the different learning environment of K–12 schools and more generally, into the communities in which they live. This move—and the transition of the philosopher to publicly engaged work—can open new opportunities for philosophical engagement with pressing issues relating to ethics, education, and social justice.

VII. CONCLUSION

I began this chapter with an overview of experiential learning theory and its relationship to philosophical theories of education. In diverse forms, both contemporary and historical philosophers have embraced experiential learning methods. The connection between philosophical pedagogy and experiential learning is most pronounced in the work of John Dewey. Following Dewey we can envision ways in which a philosophical education can also be experiential, involving vital learning experiences, collaboration between students and teacher in the production of knowledge, and the creation of a learning environment that is conducive to continuing growth.

Moving forward from Dewey's educational philosophy and contemporary experiential learning theory, I argued that philosophy with children serves as a significant opportunity to combine experiential and philosophical practice. Since the 1970s the philosophy with children movement has provided numerous experiential and educational benefits for K–12 schools, teachers, and students. In addition, philosophy with children can benefit the pedagogical and philosophical work of professional and student philosophers alike. Doing philosophy with children provides an opportunity to move beyond the academy into our broader communities and schools. We are then challenged to consider the value of our practice, not exclusively in terms of publications in academic journals, conferences, and institutions of higher learning, but also for children, adolescents, and K–12 education in our communities. These challenges have pushed me to expand and enrich my philosophical practice, to make my work accessible for young and old philosophers alike, and to return to fundamental philosophical experiences and questions that underlie much of our professional work. As evidenced by the continuing growth of philosophy with children programs in the United States, I am not alone in facing these productive challenges. Given the benefits of philosophy with children and the "vital" education it can provide for its practitioners and participants, we should continue to support its advancement and legitimation as a valuable practice, alongside other traditional forms of philosophical work in the academy. In doing so, we will contribute to a valuable form of professional development, an important means for university-community engagement, and further, an additional path for enriching our experience as philosophers.

NOTES

1. There are relevant exceptions. For examples of experiential and service learning components in contemporary philosophy courses see Donovan 2008, Nissani 1995, Fitzgerald 1997. Also see Lisman 2000. Additional citations for articles on philosophy, service learning, and experiential learning, can be found at http://www.engagedphilosophy.com/publications/.
2. I use the term *philosophy with children* to refer to a wide range of philosophical practice with children and adolescents in K–12 schools and related educational settings. *Philosophy for children* (or P4C) is also a common term used to refer to these practices. However, philosophy for children can also refer to a specific curriculum and pedagogy for philosophical work with children developed by Matthew Lipman and the Institute for the Advancement of Philosophy for Children in the 1970s. I use the more general designation—philosophy with children—to include Lipman's work, as well as the work of many other practitioners who do not use the P4C curriculum. For detailed discussion of this curriculum see Lipman 1980.
3. To name only a few, graduate philosophy departments at the University of Memphis, the University of North Carolina at Chapel Hill, New York University, the Pennsylvania State University, and Columbia University have graduate student–led philosophy with children programs. Professional associations such as the American Philosophical Association Committee on Pre-College Instruction in Philosophy and the Philosophy Learning and Teaching Organization (PLATO) provide resources and support for philosophers interested in practicing philosophy with children. The PLATO website can be found at http://plato-philosophy.org.

4. For discussions of practicing philosophy with children in K–12 schools see Wartenberg 2014; Lone 2012; Haynes and Murris 2012; Haynes 2008; Goering, Shudak, and Wartenberg 2013; and Lipman 1980.
5. It is important to avoid anachronism in making a comparison between a contemporary concept (*experiential learning*) and the work of past philosophers. My claim here is not that the philosophies of education presented by Aristotle, Plato, and Rousseau contain this contemporary concept as such. Rather, I put forward the minimal claim that harnessing vital, educative experience—apart from education through reason and dialectic—is an important element of their conceptions of education and in turn, has influenced contemporary understanding of and approaches to experiential learning.
6. "They [children] must imitate right from childhood what is appropriate for them—that is to say, people who are courageous, temperate, pious, free and everything of that sort" (See Plato's Republic 81; 399c1–2).
7. For Aristotle, the final product of moral education—the practically wise adult (*phronimos*)—develops and becomes virtuous, in part, through practical experience. Describing the aims of moral education and the end of the practically wise agent, Aristotle writes, "knowing about virtue is not enough, but we must also try to possess and exercise virtue, or become good in any other way" (168; 1179b). That is, to be virtuous is not simply to have a theoretical understanding of virtue but also to possess virtues of action and undergo the forms of experience (habituation, imitation, and practice) that lead to their formation.
8. Dewey maintains "there is an intimate and necessary relation between the processes of actual experience and education" (*Experience and Education* 20).
9. Describing this process in detail Dewey writes: "The basic characteristic of *habit* is that every experience enacted and undergone modifies the one who acts and undergoes, while this modification affects, whether we wish it or not, the quality of subsequent experiences . . . From this point of view, the principle of continuity of experience means that every experience both takes up something from those which have gone before and modifies in some way the quality of those which come after" (*Experience and Education* 35).
10. Dewey uses the examples of a "spoilt child" and an "expert burglar" to illustrate mis-educative experiences: "No experience is educative that does not tend both to knowledge of more facts and entertaining of more ideas and to a better, a more orderly, arrangement of them" (*Experience and Education* 82).
11. Dewey defines the interaction of internal and objective conditions of experience as a *situation* (*Experience and Education* 42). It is the duty of the educator to determine "that environment which will interact with the existing capacities and needs of those taught to create a worth-while experience" (*Experience and Education* 45).
12. Examples of objective conditions include "what is done by the educator and the way in which it is done, not only words spoken but the tone of voice in which they are spoken . . . equipment, books, apparatus, toys, games played . . . the materials with which an individual interacts, and, most important of all, the total *social* set-up of the situations in which a person is engaged" (*Experience and Education* 45).
13. I consider these topics in more detail in my papers "Reconsidering the Examined Life: Philosophy and Children" and "A Different Education: Philosophy and High School."
14. For relevant references and program examples see footnotes 1 and 3 above.
15. However, there are numerous studies that do measure and document positive learning outcomes for philosophy with children classes and student groups. For a review of relevant empirical literature see Trickey and Topping 2007.
16. For example, see Schapiro 2013.

17. Numerous works of children's literature are particularly useful for raising these and other philosophical concepts with children. See footnote 4 above for relevant resources, as well as Thomas Wartenberg's web site *Teaching Children Philosophy*: http://www.teachingchildrenphilosophy.org/wiki/Main_Page.

WORKS CITED

Andresen, Lee, David Boud, and Ruth Cohen. "Experience-based Learning." *Understanding Adult Education and Training*. Ed. Griff Foley. Sydney: Allen & Unwin, 1995. 207–19.

Aristotle. *Nicomachean Ethics*. Trans. Terence Irwin. Indianapolis: Hackett Publishing, 1999.

Beard, Colin, and John P. Wilson. *Experiential Learning: A Best Practice Handbook for Educators and Trainers*. 2nd ed. London: Kogan Page, 2006.

Burroughs, Michael D. "A Different Education: Philosophy and High School." *Philosophy in Schools: An Introduction for Philosophers and Teachers*. Eds. Sara Goering, Nicholas Shudak, and Thomas Wartenberg. New York: Routledge Press, 2012. 179–89.

———. "Reconsidering the Examined Life: Philosophy and Children." *Negotiating Childhoods*. Eds. Lucy Hopkins, Mark MacLeod, and Wendy C. Turgeon. Oxford, UK: Inter-Disciplinary Press, 2010. 191–200. Web.

Dewey, John. *Democracy and Education*. Hollywood, FL: Simon & Brown, 2011.

———. *Experience and Education*. New York: Simon & Schuster, 1938.

———. *How We Think*. New York: Heath, 1933.

Donovan, Sarah K. "Teaching Philosophy Outside of the Classroom: One Alternative to Service Learning." *Teaching Philosophy* 31.2 (2008): 161–77.

Engaged Philosophy: Civic Engagement in Philosophy Classes. Accessed December 9, 2014. http://www.engagedphilosophy.com/publications/.

Fitzgerald, Patrick. "Service-Learning and the Socially Responsible Ethics Class." *Teaching Philosophy* 20.3 (1997): 251–67.

Goering, Sara, Nicholas Shudak, and Thomas Wartenberg, eds. *Philosophy in Schools: An Introduction for Philosophers and Teachers*. New York: Routledge, 2013.

Haynes, Joanna. *Children as Philosophers: Learning Through Enquiry and Dialogue in the Primary Classroom*. 2nd ed. New York: Routledge, 2008.

Haynes, Joanna, and Karin Murris. *Picturebooks, Pedagogy, and Philosophy*. New York: Routledge, 2012.

Itin, Christian M. "Reasserting the Philosophy of Experiential Education as a Vehicle for Change in the 21st Century." *The Journal of Experiential Education* 22.2 (1999): 91–8.

Kolb, David. *Experiential Learning: Experience as the Source of Learning and Development*. Englewood Cliffs: Prentice-Hall, 1984.

Lipman, Matthew. *Thinking in Education*. 2nd ed. Cambridge, UK: Cambridge University Press, 2003.

Lipman, Matthew, Ann Margaret Sharp, and Frederick S. Oscanyan. *Philosophy in the Classroom*. 2nd ed. Philadelphia: Temple University Press, 1980.

Lisman, David C., ed. Beyond the Tower: Concepts and Models for Service-Learning in Philosophy. Washington, DC: American Association for Higher Education, 2000.

Matthews, Gareth B. *Philosophy & the Young Child*. Cambridge, MA: Harvard University Press, 1980.

———. *The Philosophy of Childhood*. Cambridge, MA: Harvard University Press, 1994.

Mohr Lone, Jana. *The Philosophical Child*. Lanham: Rowman & Littlefield, 2012.

Nissani, Moti. "An Experiential Component in Teaching Philosophy of Science." *Teaching Philosophy* 18.2 (1995): 147–54.

Philosophical Horizons. Accessed December 9, 2014. http://www.memphis.edu/philosophy/philhorizons.php.

Philosophy Learning and Teaching Organization (Plato): Engaging Young Philosophers. Accessed December 9, 2014. http://plato-philosophy.org.

Plato. *Laws*. Trans. Trevor J. Saunders. New York: Penguin Books, 1970.

———. *Republic*. Trans. C.D.C. Reeve. Indianapolis: Hackett Publishing, 2004.

Rousseau, Jean-Jacques. *Emile*. Trans. Allan Bloom. New York: Basic Books, 1979.

Schapiro, David. "Engaging Students—of Any Age—in Philosophical Inquiry: How Doing Philosophy for Children Changed the Way I Teach Philosophy to College Students." *Philosophy in Schools: An Introduction for Philosophers and Teachers*. Eds. Sara Goering, Nicholas J. Shudak, and Thomas E. Wartenberg. New York: Routledge, 2013. 168–76.

Trickey, S., and K.J. Topping. " 'Philosophy with Children': A Systematic Review." *Research Papers in Education* 19.3 (2007): 365–80.

Wartenberg. Thomas E. *Big Ideas for Little Kids: Teaching Philosophy Through Children's Literature*. 2nd ed. Lanham: Rowman & Littlefield, 2014.

Wartenberg, Thomas E. "Teaching Children Philosophy." Accessed December 9, 2014. http://www.teachingchildrenphilosophy.org/wiki/Main_Page.

3 A Short History of Experiential Learning and Its Application to Business Ethics

Karen Hornsby and Wade Maki

The belief that all genuine education comes about through experience does not mean that all experiences are genuinely or equally educative.

—John Dewey, *Experience and Education*

The idea of learning by doing is not new—apprenticeships, driver's training programs, and medical residencies all operate on the model of learning through experience. Observation and modeling alone, however, cannot produce the significant learning experiences needed to prepare our students for successful futures in today's global society. Given the millennial student's fifteen- to twenty-minute attention span (Middendorf and Kalish 2), their "No Child Left Behind"–acquired predilection to performance rather than learning-focused outcomes (Trolian 5), and their technology-embedded, multitasking deportment (McCoy 6), what pedagogical methods might foster intentional, lifelong learners? This chapter will survey the development of various experiential learning (EL) theories and then critique components of these theories for philosophy EL classroom activities. In our view, three components are essential to the creation of successful experiential learning pedagogy: structured scaffolding, measured cognitive dissonance, and repeated reflection activities. We will then examine recent scientific and educational research about how people learn for application in contemporary university contexts. Finally, we will discuss the experiential learning structure and classroom activities of our Business Ethics courses in order to show how we connected the essential elements of EL theories to our pedagogical practices.

I. SURVEY OF EXPERIENTIAL LEARNING THEORIES

In order to provide a broader understanding of experiential learning, this section provides a historical overview of eight contributions to the theoretical landscape of EL. After presenting this chronology, we will discuss commonalities found in these theories and then evaluate the essential components for designing successful experiential learning activities in a philosophy classroom.

The nineteenth-century philosopher William James proposed a "radical empiricism" where truth is shaped by both objective sensory data and subjective interpretation of these data through one's thoughts, memories, and experiences. In James's account, learning requires controlled, intentional reflection—thinking about one's thought process—or what we now call *metacognition*. For James (1890), "introspective observation is what we have to rely on first and foremost and always" (185). This continuous didactic between the mind and the material world refined by reflection established a foundation for experiential learning.

Although James recognized that recurrent reflection was essential to learning, John Dewey (1938) is generally credited for connecting experience to formal classroom learning. In his evaluation of "traditional" educational practices, designed to impart "bodies of information and skills" to a new generation, with "progressive" practices, focused on the learner's interests and impulse without educator guidance, he characterizes these pedagogies as "mis-educative" because both omit a "sound philosophy of experience" (40). Dewey argues that "there is an intimate and necessary relation between the processes of actual experience and education" and establishes a framework for a new type of education where learners interact with a dynamic experiential continuum (7). Within this framework, Dewey stresses the educator's responsibility for ensuring experiential activities that 1) align with student capabilities and 2) foster student engagement and the production of new ideas. Thus on Dewey's account, experiential learning is an intentionally organized, generative, continuous spiral of learner-reconstructed knowledge.

To differentiate types of constructed knowledge, Kurt Lewin (1946) coined the term "action research" in comparing "research that produces nothing but book" to "research leading to social action" (202–3). In his work about group dynamics, Lewin noted that problem solving was best accomplished through "a spiral of steps, each of which is composed of a circle of planning, action, and fact-finding about the result of the action" (206). Although Lewin never used the term *experiential*, he asserted that interaction of a person's "life space" with "external stimuli" shapes development (*Field Theory in Social Science: Selected Theoretical Papers* 8). Later, Jean Piaget's constructivist theory of learning further contributed to the refinement of experiential learning theories by connecting cognitive development to evolutionary biological development. Learning, or what Piaget calls "adaptation," involves an ongoing dialectic process between "accommodation" and "assimilation." For Piaget, when new experiences confront our previously established beliefs, we adjust beliefs to accommodate this new experience, or if the new experience fits with our already established beliefs, we assimilate the new experience as further validation of this mental construct. On Piaget's (1952) account, "The principle goal of education is to create men who are capable of doing new things, not simply repeating what other generations have done" (80).

These concepts continued to gain traction as educational theorists began to emphasize the context of education, not just the process. Equally important to producing creative, inventive, knowledgeable learners is the teacher-student dynamics of the learning process. In his seminal work, *Pedagogy of the Oppressed*, Paulo Freire (1970) challenged the passive "banking" concept of education where "the teacher issues communiques and makes deposits which the students patiently receive, memorize, and repeat" and instead advocated a dialogical problem-solving method of education (58). The vertical banking model views students as "objects of assistance", while the horizontal, problem-posing method transforms students into "critical co-investigators in dialogue with the teacher" (81). The educative process involves critical conversations about perceptions of reality and what Freire calls praxis or "reflection and action upon the world in order to transform it" (51). Through this authentic experiential inquiry, the "problem-posing education affirms men and women as beings in the process of *becoming*" (84). For Freire, learning is a cyclical process of discourse about lived experiences, critical reflection on already acquired knowledge, which then generates new knowledge.

Integrating the foundational ideas of Dewey, Lewin, and Piaget, David Kolb offers a cyclical experiential learning theory model of cognition centered in experience. For Kolb (1984), "Knowledge is continuously derived from and tested out in the experiences of the learner" (27). Responsible for popularizing the term *experiential learning*, Kolb's distinct theory of learning through reflection on doing has transformed modern higher education pedagogy. Viewing his theory of experiential learning as a holistic integration of perception and experience combined with behavioral and cognitive learning theories, Kolb conceptualizes knowledge in a state of flux—constantly shaped and reshaped by experience. Kolb's model of learning involves four modes: concrete experiences, reflective observation, abstract conceptualization, and active experimentation. On this dynamic cycle, learners enter the process at different modes based on their adaptive and fluctuating learning styles.[1]

Expanding on Kolb's reflective component of experiential learning, Graham Gibbs offers the inclusion of what he called a "de-briefing sequence" that extends the rational reflective process into affective contemplation. Gibbs's six-stage reflective cycle includes: description, feelings, evaluation, analysis, conclusion, and an action plan. Unlike Kolb's model where the learning process can begin at any stage of the cycle, Gibbs's view of learning starts from the experience description but is an ongoing, repetitive process. Widely adopted by professional education programs, especially as a pedagogy in nursing curriculums,[2] both Kolb's and Gibbs's experiential learning models are designed to help students challenge assumptions, explore new ideas, promote self-improvement, and link theory to practice.

Although reflection is a key component in all of the previously discussed experiential learning theories, David Schön's (1987) work on *reflective practice* expands these models by positing two types of reflection, which are jointly required for experiential learning. *Reflection-on-action* involves the learner's conscious review and evaluation of past practices with the goal of future improvement. Conversely, *reflection-in-practice* is a type of thinking while doing where learners examine their experiences and responses as they unfold. In this experiential process, learners reflect on prior knowledge informed by their experiences to create new understanding. As Schön describes, "The practitioner allows himself to experience surprise, puzzlement, or confusion in a situation which he finds uncertain or unique. He reflects on the phenomenon before him, and on the prior understandings which have been implicit in his behavior" (68).

The below graphic illustrates a comparison of the experiential learning theories of Kolb, Gibbs, and Schön.

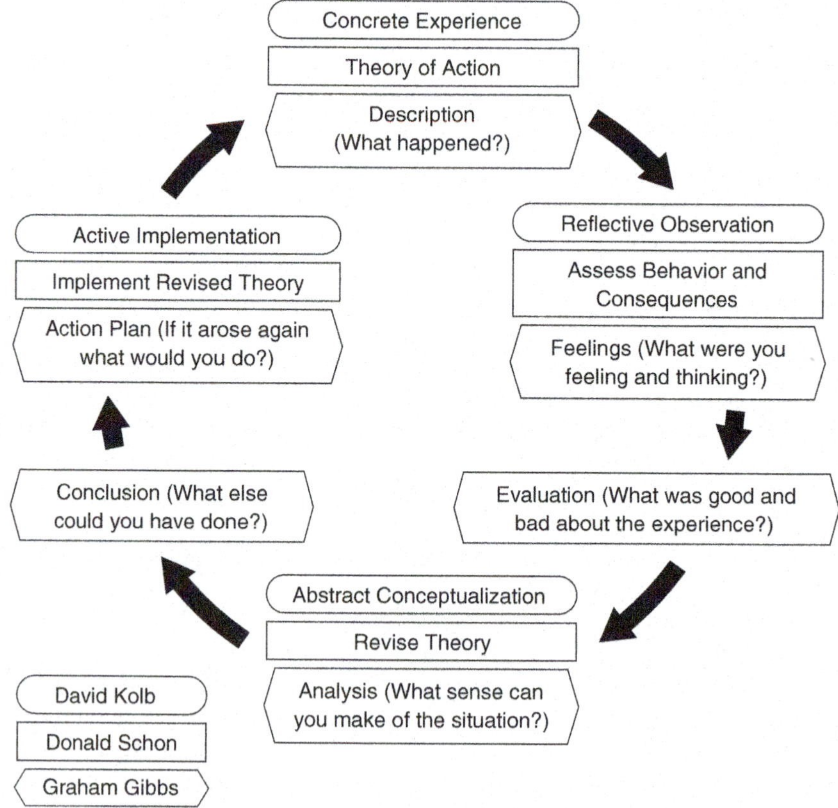

Figure 3.1 Experiential Learning Cycles

What features are shared in these eight experiential learning theories that we might apply in our philosophy classrooms? Alice and David Kolb characterize the commonalties of experiential learning theories into six overarching principles of experiential learning:

1. *Learning is the creation rather than the transmission of knowledge.* Learning is more than the passive, uncritical regurgitation of transmitted information or content knowledge. Learning requires students to critically reflect on new information, individually construct their own understanding, and take ownership of their knowledge.
2. *Learning is a process that requires scaffolding.* Learning involves nurtured development of students' ideas and competencies. Classroom activities strategically designed to provide ongoing feedback and to elicit periodic reflection promote learning.
3. *All learning is relearning to achieve a type of epistemological coherency.* Students' beliefs, values, and preconceptions continually test and accommodate new ideas. Learning occurs through a type of reflective equilibrium where knowledge is regularly refined to achieve consistency. Knowledge is dynamic and perpetually changing based on new experiences.
4. *Conflicts, disharmony, and tension of ideas drive the learning process.* Cognitive dissonance between students' commonly held beliefs and new information creates an intellectual uncomfortableness. This disharmony sparks reflection where learners reexamine and revise existing frameworks.
5. *Learning occurs through reasoned reconciliation of conflicting ideas.* The dialectic process of accommodating new experiences with prior knowledge promotes the synergetic construction of new knowledge. Learning is enhanced through social negotiation of ideas where students offer support for their views and consider alternative perspectives.
6. *Learning is a holistic adaptation to the world.* Learning requires more than cognition; it unifies one's thoughts, feelings, behaviors, and perceptions into a cohesive person.

While these principles emphasize the importance of new experiences and learner-constructed knowledge, the role of foundational knowledge to successful experiential learning must not be overlooked. Experiential learning is more than the mere application of a concept to a real-world scenario; it constitutes the integration of *knowing* and *doing* in "an ongoing interactive process in which both knowledge and experience are repeatedly transformed" (Hutchings & Wutzdorff 7). Most central to experiential learning is the process of reflection. Reflection is what turns experiences into learning. But in the educational process, this contemplative activity is often overlooked. Acknowledging this common omission, John Duley remarks, "The skill of experiential learning in which people tend to be the most deficient is reflection" (611). Max van Manen suggests that as reflection is practiced, the depth and the breadth of reflection will gradually increase. To express this progression of the contemplative process, van Manen advances three "levels of reflectivity" that focus on different content. The first level, *technical rationality*, emphasizes the application of existing knowledge to reach specific goals. With this level of reflectivity, a student does not evaluate the knowledge but rather works to demonstrate competency in meeting the objective. In van Manen's second level of *practical rationality*, the learner's focus is on "analyzing and clarifying individual and cultural experiences, meanings, perceptions, assumptions, prejudgments, and presuppositions" in relation to educational goals and principles. Classroom activities designed for this level of reflectivity might evaluate the merits of competing approaches or articulate initial biases and preconceptions or the authenticity of the activity. The highest level, *critical reflection,* focuses on ethical, political, and socio-economic implications of the educational process. This holistic deliberative process considers what knowledge is of value and to whom and questions implicit frameworks (226–7).[3] Only the higher two levels of reflectivity are important to deepening the experiential learning process.

In designing experiential learning activities for our philosophy courses, we find three components are essential: structured scaffolding, measured cognitive dissonance, and repeated reflection activities. We disagree with Kolb's view that experiential learning may begin at any stage of the cycle. In our judgment, classroom exercises are best organized around a specific concrete event beginning with a description of the context (Figure 3.1 top). The learning process requires orderly, guided inquiry that directs students' focus. Since experiential learning instruction is unfamiliar to most college students matriculating in from K–12 classrooms focused on standardized test outcomes, students must become comfortable with this more holistic approach of knowledge construction. Classroom activities designed to incrementally increase difficulty while gradually fading instructional reinforcement encourage students' adjustment to experiential learning. When EL learning activities are too open-ended or overly challenging, students become frustrated and unreceptive to critical coinquiry methods. Embedding periodic opportunities for students to reflect on and record their progression of learning is undoubtedly the most crucial element of EL design. As van Manen demonstrates, reflection is a skill that requires repetition for developing proficiency. To foster reflective competency, students must practice thinking about their experiences. We give some examples of how we do this in our Business Ethics course in the final section. Regular, varied reflection activities[4] help build students' proficiency and comfort with metacognitive exercises. Recent contributions from neuroscience, cognitive psychology, and education research about the learning process provide additional explanation for why experience is crucial to facilitating learning that lasts.

II. SCIENTIFIC AND EDUCATIONAL RESEARCH ON LEARNING

In addition to new developments in classroom education over the last several decades, findings from science of learning research have also informed classroom instruction and assessment practices. In this section we will lay out some of the critical findings regarding brain activity during the learning process so that we can better understand why experiential learning is so important. Neuroscience has confirmed that learning is a lifelong process where the plasticity of the brain allows changes in size and activity at any age. The brain's nerve cells, or neurons, have short tree-like projections called dendrites. For an experience to translate into a lasting memory, the dendrites must be activated. The pedagogical challenge is to discover how to stimulate students' dendrites' development activity, thus creating larger, denser neural networks and brain growth. Many of our strongest neural networks are formed by stimulating or challenging experiences (Wolfe 138). Insofar as experiential learning activities are challenging and stimulating, then these lessons physically alter and adapt the brain. As noted by the National Research Council, "Learning changes the structure of the brain. . . . These structural changes alter the functional organization of the brain; in other words, learning organizes and reorganizes the brain" (115). Gibbs's addition of feelings in the experiential learning cycle is also grounded in the cognitive sciences. Cognitive neuroscience research studies involving brain imaging in humans show that when the brain's amygdala experiences emotional reactions, it stimulates memory-formation activity in the brain (Phelps 34). Thus incorporating stimulating, engaging, multisensory activities into the classroom promotes the cognitive activity needed for learning.

In *The Art of the Changing Brain*, James E. Zull links findings from neuroscience research to Kolb's theory, postulating that the physical changes that occur in the brain's structure in the learning process align with the experiential learning cycle model. More recently, Zull (2011) claims "growth of the mind is arguably the most fundamental goal of all education" and "experiential learning builds a complex brain—one that looks more like a 'mind' " (*From Brain to Mind* 13, 23). Yet neuroscience has also shown that dendritic pruning occurs if synapses become inactive; in other words, the brain operates on a "use it or lose it" principle. For learning to last, classrooms need to provide ongoing "mental aerobic" experiences that challenge students to reorganize, adjust, and construct ideas. When new information is used or practiced, the neural networks establish a trail or "long-term potentiation" making information recall easier and creating long-term memories (Ratey and Galaburda). Neuroscience has clearly demonstrated that "the one who does the work does the learning" (Doyle 63). But research has also shown that "distributed practice" involving multiple study sessions over time is necessary to form lasting memories. To optimize learning and the creation of long-term memories, learners need to find the "sweet spot" as processing information too frequently "leads to impotent reminding" whereas too little cognitive work leads to reduced learning (Benjamin and Tullis 244).[5] Research conducted by educational psychologists Ference Marton and Roger Säljöl on students' learning processes led to the creation of a distinction between deep versus surface learning. *Deep learning* involves the critical reflection on new ideas, connecting these ideas to prior concepts and principles, which results in long-term retention and the transferability of concepts in solving new problems. *Surface learning* is characterized by memorization, regurgitation, and recitation without an ability to apply this information or connect it to prior knowledge. Deep learning focuses on the active construction of meaning whereas surface learning focuses on the uncritical acceptance and reproduction of information.[6] This body of scientific research thus establishes that experiential learning activities designed for dispersed, repeated application of new ideas promotes deep learning that lasts.

By knowing how students learn, educators can guide learners' integration of knowledge and academic experience. Yet in the oftentimes content-focused academy, some students who master difficult theoretical courses are unable to transfer this disciplinary knowledge into the workplace. This missing synthesis of knowledge to the everyday world is a frequently voiced concern about the educative process in today's universities. Many students seek out a college education with hope of a better, higher earning future. Yet educational practitioner Margit Watts cautions, if our colleges continue to ignore "the importance of enabling students to make connections across the curriculum and to their lives, we fail miserably in our mission to educate" (100). Similarly, educational anthropologist David Thornton Moore describes the tension between the experience-based learning that students desire and the professional community utilizes and the "marginal and rather second-class status" it occupies in the educational process. Calling it the "the paradox of experiential learning in higher education" he sees this as a fundamental disconnect between "the academy and the rest of the world" (1–2). To ensure students' successful transition into civic participation and careers and as community partners, experiential education needs to become an integral part of the curriculum, not just a course-by-course additive.[7] Affirming the call for expansive integration of experiential learning, noted educational researcher Marcia Mentkowki asserts that instructors need to provide ongoing opportunities for "real-life applications of concepts" that challenge students to connect "knowing and doing, theory and practice" (230).

In addition to seeking college graduates adept at applying what one has learned in the classroom to occupational contexts, what are the other skills that employers prioritize? The National Association of Colleges and Employers (2014) recently surveyed over one thousand employer members about the skills they most value in new hires. The two traits companies ranked highest are the ability to make decisions and solve problems. In a survey from the American Association of Colleges and Universities (2013) employers indicated the "demonstrated capacity to think critically, communicate clearly and solve complex problems" is more important than a candidate's undergraduate major. The capacities for continued new learning and application of knowledge to real-world settings were also cited as critical to a candidate's success (1). Given the impact of experiential learning on student cognitive development and employer priorities, philosophers need to pay careful attention to their classroom practices. Let us consider an experiential learning design for a Business Ethics classroom, which could be easily adapted for other philosophy courses, and the theoretical support for these activities.

III. EXPERIENTIAL LEARNING IN A BUSINESS ETHICS COURSE

Educational research concludes that experiential learning physiologically, psychologically, and pedagogically fosters deep, long-lasting learning.[8] How might we integrate this student-centered method of teaching into our philosophy classrooms? The level of guidance educators should provide students in the experiential learning process is often disputed. Those who favor a "minimally guided approach" argue for allowing learners to discover or construct knowledge for themselves. Advocates of this approach claim guidance that "embeds learning strategies in instruction interferes with the natural processes" and impedes learners' ability "to construct new situated knowledge" (Kirschner, Sweller and Clark 76). Critics of the minimal approach claim that learning is about more than mere discovery; learning requires students to cognitively manipulate information in ways that result in long-term memories. Conversely, "direct instructional guidance" provides learners with explanations of concepts, exposure to procedures, and potential strategies for learning compatible with how the brain learns. Proponents of this approach argue direct guided inquiry assists novice learners, who lack prior relevant knowledge, with the information needed to construct new ideas. The direct approach also harmonizes with the cognitive architecture of the brain by facilitating shifts between the usage of long-term and working memories. As previously discussed in Section I, we advocate scaffolding students' learning through direct instructional guidance as this method helps learners organize their knowledge and allows for reexamination of any misconceptions.

The North Carolina Piedmont region in which we live demonstrates a firm commitment to ethical business practices. In 2009 student teams from a Business Ethics course at the University of North Carolina (UNC) Greensboro began serving as ethics consultants to nominees for the annual Piedmont Business Ethics Award (PBEA). These awards recognize businesses that exemplify a strong commitment to excellence and to the highest standards of civic and social responsibility, integrity, and ethical conduct. In subsequent years, hundreds of business ethics students from six area colleges and universities have participated in this experiential learning project.

Nominated businesses may request student teams to assist in preparation of their entry materials; these requests are then assigned to participating universities. In what follows, we describe the pedagogical framework of the PBEA project at two universities, North Carolina Agricultural & Technical State University (NC A&T) and UNC-Greensboro, using a model that incorporates structured scaffolding, measured cognitive dissonance, and repeated reflection activities.

To prepare for the PBEA project, students in the Business Ethics courses at our two institutions are assigned numerous applied ethics cases, various companies' codes of ethics, as well as classic philosophical readings in ethics. These course readings are combined with training on the PBEA process, presentations by student consultants from previous years' classes, and guest speakers from prior award-winning businesses. The experiential learning project is structured in a collaborative learning format. After each university is assigned its client nominees, students select their preferred business and sign up to work on a four-member consultant team. Assignments for this project are individually graded but designed to create positive interdependence—where working together is individually and collectively beneficial to the team.[9] Before beginning any work on this project, as part of the repeated reflection process, students individually complete an initial reflective journal. The prompt for this written response asks students what they expect from the project, their initial views about business ethics, and any concerns or reservations they have about the consultant role.

The community-based portion of the experiential learning project is comprised of four components: initial client vetting, site visit, entry packet, and creative artifacts. For the initial vetting process, teams conduct a background review of their chosen nominee. To provide structured scaffolding, student teams are assigned "practice businesses" that have been crafted to reveal various methods of research and types of information to explore. The results of the practice business vetting are discussed in class along with various strategies for effective probes. After the rehearsed review, teams then conduct background research to learn about their clients and the company's public record. This investigation pursues both positive stories to bolster the company's narrative as well as problem areas (any discrimination, environmental, labor, customer complaints, or lawsuits) that might need to be addressed in the entry packet. The goal of this vetting is to increase student teams' knowledge about their businesses and to identify any problem nominees. A report of what the student teams find is submitted to the PBEA judges, who are drawn from the business, academic, public service, and media sectors, and serves as the basis for the team's initial conversation with the client.

Teams next deliver a five-minute class presentation about their client and what they plan to do on the site visit. Class members ask questions, offer suggestions (which provides measured cognitive dissonance), and glean ideas from other teams' strategies. Prior to the site visit, teams create a blog (within the university's learning management system) that provides client information, a site visit plan, interview questions, and each team member's responsibilities on the visit. The student teams craft interview questions in advance, and these queries are designed to draw out the ethical principles, training, and culture of the business with the goal of capturing the company's ethical narrative. Teams then conduct a site visit where they tour the business, interview employees and managers, and collect materials for creative artifact construction.

After the site visit, student teams update their blogs with information about what they learned, how the visit went, and photos of the team at the business. Students then construct an individual post-site visit reflective journal (repeated reflection) that addresses the project in general, what was learned on the site visit, any surprises or problems, and connections they see with assigned course materials. Teams next submit a draft PBEA entry packet for the client. These drafts are reviewed by the instructors for composition, completeness, and alignment with judging criteria. The team then submits a revised draft to their client business. Nominated companies make final edits and submit the actual entry. Student teams also compile required creative artifacts, including: a company logo, digital photos, and a short promotional video. Once the entry packet is submitted to the company, student teams give a second classroom presentation focused on what they learned about ethics from the experiential learning activities with the client. The final requirement of this project is a reflective memo to the instructor. Students are instructed to discuss what they learned, what worked, what might be improved, and advice for future student teams; in addition, they are invited to reflect on their original journal posts and compare their expectations about the project with their actual experiences and to individually rate their team members' contributions.

Classroom pedagogical activities for this project are designed to deepen experiential learning. Student assessment exercises in the Business Ethics courses are crafted for ongoing meta-cognition throughout the PBEA project. The community-based events are scaffolded by individual reflective essays, team blog updates, team class presentations, and final project memo assignments. Students found the real-world application of ethical theory extremely valuable as it helped them better understand the importance of ethics. Several team members of this experiential learning project leveraged these community relationships into internship opportunities, professional references, and mentors. Compared to our traditional discussion-based Business Ethics courses, students who participated in the PBEA project displayed *deep* rather the *surface* learning. Reaffirmation of the importance of ethical principles through community-based interactions transformed students' focus from an extrinsically grade-focused goal to an intrinsic appreciation of ethics.

From the repeated reflections, we learned that many of our students were extremely nervous about taking on the professional role of a PBEA ethics consultant. Their journals revealed apprehension, a lack of perceived expertise, and hostility toward team activities. Students' reflective writings completed after a structured scaffolding activity displayed more confidence and an appreciation of group members' unique contributions. The cognitive dissonance from the in-class presentations and team blog updates generated lively, productive discussions prior to team site visits and the PBEA ceremonial luncheon. This experiential learning project that recognizes companies' outstanding ethical commitment is a national award sponsored by the Society of Financial Service Professionals (FSP). Educators seeking to replicate this project might initiate collaboration through local FSP chapters within their communities.[10]

The goal of this chapter has been to show how we integrated numerous dimensions of experiential learning pedagogy into our Business Ethics courses. We began by considering various experiential learning (EL) theories and then identified three components that we view as essential to the creation of successful EL pedagogy: structured scaffolding, measured cognitive dissonance, and repeated reflection activities. We then reviewed recent scientific and educational research about how people learn to show why experiential learning is so important in today's classrooms. Finally, we demonstrated how experiential learning theory is integrated into classroom activities of our Business Ethics courses. We recognize that designing an active, experiential learning classroom environment is challenging and sometimes frustrating and generally requires sacrifice of content breadth to attain learning depth. In these "swampy lowlands" of educational practice, where "problems are messy and confusing" is where we find the questions "of greatest human concern" (Schön, "Knowing-in-Action" 28). But these "pedagogy of the real" marshes also create the laboratories of engaged learning required to prepare our students for twenty-first-century successes (Garcia 32).

NOTES

1. Kolb's Learning Styles Inventory (LSI) is different from the Myers-Briggs personality inventory or VARK sensory modality preferences as the LSI is grounded in the experiential theory of learning, although Kolb argues that there is a correlation between one's personality and one's learning style.
2. For example, see Bulman and Schutz—especially Chapter 9, Newnham 114–15, and Ekebergh.
3. These levels of reflectivity have frequently been wrongly attributed to Jesse Goodman and called "Goodman's levels of reflection." For example see, Pearce 25–28, Jasper 72–77, and Orland-Barak. Yet Goodman in "Reflection and Teacher Education" clearly credits van Manen with this hierarchy of reflection.
4. A great resource that provides numerous activities with explanatory instructions is "Reflective Activities: Service-Learning's Not-So-Secret Weapon" available at http://mncampuscompact.org/clio/wp-content/uploads/sites/2/2014/07/Reflection-Activities-for-All-Classrooms.pdf

5. These temporal boundaries on learning processes also impact optimal class length and design of students' schedules to promote learning. The brain needs time to process new learning experiences and to strengthen neural networks. Back-to-back classes or three-hour seminar formats actually impede the brain's physiological processes of learning (see Tambini, Ketz, and Davachi).
6. Strategic learning is a third approach of student engagement in the learning process and overall success. This approach blends surface and deep learning while mediating competing demands and desires of employment, caring for others, and socializing. The student adopting a strategic approach balances effort to achievement to maximize outcome.
7. The transitional gap between college and careers is less pronounced in pre-professional programs (accounting, engineering, nursing, etc.) where the concepts, principles, and processes of learning in the classroom are often closely related to needed work-related skills.
8. For a comprehensive explanation of these various types of experiential learning, see Chapter 1 of Moore.
9. Cooperative learning involves structured coordination of experiential activities in a classroom environment where teams remain constant for a substantial period and group learning activities are regularly implemented. Cooperative learning activities require the integration of five principles: positive interdependence, face-to-face promotive interaction, individual accountability, social skill development, and reflective group processing (see Johnson, Johnson and Smith; and Millis and Cottell).
10. The national website for this award is http://businessethicsawards.org. Educators attempting to establish new awards processes in their community might find the structure used for the PBEA award helpful. http://www.piedmontethics.com

WORKS CITED

Association of American Colleges and Universities & Hart Research Associates. "It Takes More Than a Major and Student Success: Employer Priorities for College Learning." *Liberal Education* 99.2 (2013): 22–29.

Benjamin, Aaron S., and Jonathan Tullis. "What Makes Distributed Practice Effective?" *Cognitive Psychology* 61.3 (2010): 228–47.

Bulman, Chris, and Sue Schutz, eds. *Reflective Practice in Nursing*. Hoboken: John Wiley & Sons, 2013.

Business Ethics Awards. "National Capital Business Ethics Awards.". http://businessethicsawards.org.

Dewey, John. *Experience and Education*. New York: Macmillan, 1938.

Doyle, Terry. *Helping Students Learn in a Learner-Centered Environment: A Guide to Facilitating Learning in Higher Education*. Sterling, VA: Stylus Pub, 2008.

Duley, John S. "Field Experience Education." *The Modern American College*. Ed. Arthur W. Chickering. San Francisco: Jossey-Bass, 1981. 600–13.

Ekebergh, Margaretha. "Lifeworld based Reflection and Learning: A Contribution to the Reflective Practice in Nursing and Nursing Education." *Reflective Practice* 8.3 (2007): 331–43.

Freire, Paulo. *Pedagogy of the Oppressed*. New York: Continuum, 2000.

Garcia, Angela C. "The Pedagogy of the Real: Teaching "Animals in Society" to Undergraduates through Doing Research and Dissemination the Results. *Radical Pedagogy* 11.2 (2014): 31–59.

Gibbs, Graham. *Learning by Doing: A Guide to Learning and Teaching Methods.* Oxford: Further Education Unit at Oxford Polytechnic, 1998.

Goodman, Jesse. "Reflection and Teacher Education: A Case Study and Theoretical Analysis." *Interchange* 15.3 (1984): 9–26.

Halcrow, Katie. "Reflective Activities: Service-Learning's Not-So-Secret Weapon." http://mncampuscompact.org/clio/wp-content/uploads/sites/2/2014/07/Reflection-Activities-for-All-Classrooms.pdf.

Hutchings, Pat, and Allen Wutzdorff. *Knowing and Doing: Learning Through Experience.* San Francisco: Jossey-Bass, 1988.

James, William. *The Principles of Psychology.* New York: Dover Publications, 1950.

Jasper, Melanie. *Beginning Reflective Practice.* Cheltenham: Nelson Thornes, 2003.

Johnson, David R., Roger T. Johnson, Karl A. Smith, and Edwina L. Stoll. *Active Learning: Cooperation in the College Classroom.* Edina, MN: Interaction Book Co., 2006.

Kirschner, Paul. A., John Sweller, and Richard E. Clark. "Why Minimal Guidance During Instruction Does Not Work: An Analysis of the Failure of Constructivist, Discovery, Problem-Based, Experiential, and Inquiry-Based Teaching." *Educational Psychologist*, 41.2 (2006): 75–86.

Kolb, Alice Y., and David A. Kolb. "Learning Styles and Learning Spaces: Enhancing Experiential Learning in Higher Education." *Academy of Management Learning & Education* 4.2 (2005): 193–212.

Kolb, David A. *Experiential Learning: Experience as the Source of Learning and Development.* Englewood Cliffs, NJ: Prentice-Hall, 1984.

Lewin, Kurt. "Action Research and Minority Problems." *Journal of Social Issues* 2 (1946): 34–46.

Lewin, Kurt, and Dorwin Cartwright. *Field Theory in Social Science: Selected Theoretical Papers.* New York: Harper & Brothers, 1951.

Marton, Ference, and Roger Säljöl. "On Qualitative Differences in Learning: Outcome and Process." *British Journal of Educational Psychology* 46 (1976): 4–11.

McCoy, Bernard. "Digital Distractions in the Classroom: Student Classroom Use of Digital Devices for Non-class Related Purposes." *Journal of Media Education* 4.4 (2013): 5–14.

Mentkowski, Marcia. *Learning That Lasts: Integrating Learning, Development, and Performance in College and Beyond.* San Francisco: Jossey-Bass, 2000.

Middendorf, Joan, and Alan Kalish. "The Change-up in Lectures." *The National Teaching Learning Forum* 5.2 (1996): 1–5.

Millis, Barbara J., and Philip G. Cottell. *Cooperative Learning for Higher Education Faculty.* Phoenix, AZ: Oryx Press (1998).

Moore, David T. *Engaged Learning in the Academy: Challenges and Possibilities.* New York: Palgrave Macmillan, 2013.

National Association of Colleges and Employers. *Job Outlook 2015.* Bethlehem: NACE, 2014.

Newnham, John. To Reflect or Not? Reflective Practice in Radiation Therapy. *Journal of Radiotherapy in Practice* 1 (1999): 109–16.

Orland-Barak, Lily. "Portfolios As Evidence of Reflective Practice: What Remains 'untoldCloseCurlyQuote'." *Educational Research* 47.1 (2005): 25–44.

Pearce, Ruth. *Profiles and Portfolios of Evidence.* Cheltenham: Nelson Thornes, 2003.

Phelps, Elizabeth A. "Emotion and Cognition: Insights from Studies of the Human Amygdala." *Annual Review of Psychology* 57 (2006): 27–53.

Piaget, Jean. *The Origins of Intelligence in Children.* New York: International Universities Press, 1974.

Piedmont Business Ethics Award. http://www.piedmontethics.com.

Ratey, John J., and Albert M. Galaburda. *A User's Guide to the Brain: Perception,*

Attention, and the Four Theaters of the Brain. New York: Pantheon Books, 2001.
Schön, Donald. A. "Knowing-in-Action: The New Scholarship Requires a New Epistemology." *Change* 27.6 (1995): 26–34.
———. *Educating the Reflective Practitioner: Toward a New Design for Teaching and Learning in the Professions*. San Francisco: Jossey-Bass, 1987.
Tambini, Arielle, Nicholas Ketz, and Lila Davachi. "Enhanced Brain Correlations during Rest are related to Memory for Recent Experiences." *Neuron* 65.2 (2010): 280–90.
Trolian, Teniell L., and Kristin S. Fouts. "No Child Left Behind: Implications for College Student Learning. *About Campu*, 16 (2011): 2–7.
van Manen, Max. "Linking Ways of Knowing with Ways of Being Practical." *Curriculum Inquiry* 6 (1977): 205–28.
Watts, Margit M. "Taking the Distance Out of Education." *New Directions for Teaching and Learning* 94 (2003): 97–103.
Wolfe, P. *Brain matters: Translating Research into Classroom Practice*. Alexandria, VA: ASCD, 2001.
Zull, James E. *The Art of Changing the Brain: Enriching Teaching by Exploring the Biology of Learning*. Sterling, VA: Stylus Pub, 2002.
Zull, James E. *From Brain to Mind: Using Neuroscience to Guide Change in Education*. Sterling, VA: Stylus Pub, 2011.

4 Performing Care Ethics

Empathy, Acting, and Embodied Learning

Maurice Hamington

> *Our classrooms ought to be nurturing and thoughtful and just all at once; they ought to pulsate with multiple conceptions of what it is to be human and alive. They ought to resound with the voices of articulate young people in dialogues always incomplete because there is always more to be discovered and more to be said. We must want our students to achieve friendship as each one stirs to wide-awakeness, to imaginative action, and to renewed consciousness of possibility.*
>
> —*Maxine Greene (1995, 43)*

Experiential learning can represent much more than a new method for teaching philosophy. This chapter is about experiential learning and caring. One way to interpret experiential learning is as recognition that *how* one comes to knowledge impacts the very nature of that knowledge and thus the relationship between the knower and the known. Similarly, when one authentically engages the other as in a caring relationship, one's knowledge of the other doesn't just grow; it is transformed.

Care ethicists have articulated the way in which caring relationships are transformative. They suggest that our relationships are the centerpiece of morality; abstraction and rules are inadequate to capture human morality.[1] Beyond ethics, I further contend that caring relationships impact *who we are* and *what we know* as well as what we value. An example of the significance of relational understanding can be witnessed in changing national attitudes toward same-sex marriage. In the decade between 2003 and 2013, the United States experienced what the Pew Research Center describes as "among the largest changes in opinion on any policy issue over this time period." In 2003, 58 percent of Americans opposed and 33 percent favored same-sex marriage. However, by 2013 the circumstances had reversed and 49 percent favored and 44 percent opposed such unions. What is significant about this remarkable shift are the reasons given for the change. The top rationale for those who described changing their minds on this issue, representing one-third of all who altered their position, is that they came know someone who is gay (Pew 2013). In other words, the moral rules or context surrounding same-sex marriage did not change nor did the perceived consequences, or the virtues associated with an ethical person. Certainly the religious injunctions against same-sex relations did not change. However, relational awareness and knowledge did change, resulting in shifts of empathetic imagination. The deep proximal knowledge that comes through relationship altered the framework of the knower and the known, the caregiver and the cared for, and forced reflection on self-identity and relationship.

This popular shift of opinion speaks to the power and transformative potential of experiential relational learning, particularly when it comes to ethics. Moral variables in the abstract (i.e., the rights of gays) are far less compelling than direct experience of how a moral issue impacts known others (i.e., gay acquaintances, friends, family). Relationship can be a great teacher. The basis for struggling with normative concerns requires more than rules or formulas. Experiential relational learning provides the context, nuances, and textures of those involved in a given situation that are necessary to navigate normative complexities. More importantly for this project, every iteration of experiential learning attended to, whether that experience is intentional or serendipitous, represents an occasion to build the skill and capacity to better confront the next morally charged circumstance. In other words, every opportunity to care is a chance to build the skills to be a more caring person. Furthermore, realizing that moral injunctions against same-sex marriage are artificial constraints on the growth and development of human love relationships in our society may provide the basis for translating that realization to other analogous circumstances. If I, through my relationships with others, can see the folly of prohibiting same-sex marriage, might that process of empathetic expansion also imaginatively apply to others for whom I might have experiential distance? The homeless? Immigrants? Experiential learning aims at personal engagement and discovery that raises the stakes in the personal investment with knowledge. Just as it is easy to ignore the challenges of "distant" others, it is easy to overlook the significance of a science experiment that one only reads the results of. Abstraction is a form of distance that can be mitigated through experiential learning.

In this chapter, I address an intentional effort at collaborative learning about care that engages hand, heart, and mind. What follows is the description of a philosophy course that I taught that holistically applied the principles of experiential learning as outlined by Alice and David Kolb's six-proposition framework:

1. Learning is best conceived as involving students in an interactive process.
2. Learning is optimized when a student can test personally held ideas.
3. Learning flourishes when it transcends modes such as thinking/feeling and action/reflection.
4. Learning succeeds when it is holistic, involving multiple methods of engagement.

5. Learning works best when it responds to the environment.
6. Perhaps most radical of all, experiential learning suggests that in the learning knowledge is created rather than simply transmitted. Knowledge is thus constructive (2005, 194).

The Kolbs' sixth proposition has significant epistemological implications that are consistent with the notion of "embodied care." The premise of embodied care is that our bodies capture and hold important knowledge about morality—what it is to care for one another—that is not always easily communicated through language (Hamington 2004). Muscle memories of the subtleties needed to offer a caring hug, look, touch, or comportment of the body are largely unarticulated. They are learned through social interaction. We develop a myriad of caring habits through experiencing the care of others or observing others engaged in care. These habits of care effect knowledge creation (Dalmiya 2002). The more mature or developed are the social intelligences that go into caring interaction, the more one can understand, empathize, and thus learn from others. Of course, like any physical ability, individuals have different levels of proficiency in their habits of care. Furthermore, these habits of care are dynamic: they change and evolve as individuals navigate life experiences. One premise of this article and the course discussed herein is that we can attend to and learn habits of care. Sally Harrison-Pepper describes the potential for embodied learning in the college classroom:

> Students' bodies contain vital tools for learning, and experiential activities simply help students to use their bodies and minds in meaningful and memorable ways. I have discovered, in using such experiential learning modes, that when students are physically engaged, deep learning occurs—a kind of learning that can activate key transformational moments. Performance theory and performative pedagogy locate and provide such learning opportunities in a broad spectrum of courses and educational settings (1999, 142).

In the iterations of caring performances, we transform our self-identity, our relationship to knowledge, and our moral interactions.

What follows is based on my experience of teaching a unique undergraduate philosophy course, Performance, Phenomenology, and Feminist Ethics (PPFE for short). PPFE is an upper-division undergraduate semester-length course cross-listed with honors, philosophy, theatre, and women's studies. The course grew out of the notion that feminist care ethics represents a paradigm shift in thinking about ethics. Rather than another abstract normative theory of moral decision making in the mold of principle-based or utilitarian ethics, care is a relational approach to morality that values context and empathetic connection. Furthermore, I have argued elsewhere that care is very much an embodied activity whereby acts of care are performed

(Hamington, 2010). Those physical performances can result in habits of care that build caring knowledge in the body and provide the conditions for empathetic understanding of others. In this manner, caring has epistemic and identity implications, as well as ethical significance. Iterations of actions combined with self-observation and reflection seep into one's self-understanding. *This embodied and performative definition of care ethics offers a significant challenge to the premise that ethics can be limited to a learned set of rules, rights, and rubrics, thus making a form of experiential learning essential to the process.* Rather than an abstract normative concept, morality can only be appreciated through inhabiting and attending to diverse experiences of care. Furthermore, caring can also be practiced and habituated through dramatic rehearsal. In other words, experiential learning is not simply a better way to teach ethics, but it also represents an essential element of how ethics must be taught if it is intended to be more than a game of normative adjudication.

Consistent with Kolb and Kolb's framework, PPFE is organized to provide cognitive reflection of selected works of feminist care theorists as well as on philosophical research regarding identity and phenomenology. The course devotes substantial class time to dramaturgical exercises designed to engage the corporeal and visceral aspects of caring. Students in this course experience a high degree of personal engagement through experiential learning and attentiveness to bodily activity. Specific learning outcomes for the course include:

- Examine the ways in which ontology, epistemology, and ethics influence one another, particularly in regard to caring.
- Attend to and appraise the body's influence on morality.
- Distinguish the major philosophical influences on theories of performativity.
- Debate the merits of a performative approach to moral identity.
- Examine the ways in which philosophy and dramaturgical theory can be integrated.

With these goals in mind, the "work" of the course took on two interwoven tracks: dramaturgical experiential learning activities and readings of theory that provided a cognitive framework for analysis. The activities and the readings informed and infused the experience of one another.

I. EXPERIENTIAL LEARNING ACTIVITIES

> *We need to practice and develop skills that help us to be successful at understanding others and gaining further insight into our own perspective.*
>
> —*Barbara J. Thayer-Bacon (2000, 107)*

The course includes fourteen dramatic exercises—approximately one per week (or half of all class time) in which every student participates. Each week of class includes exercises that complement assigned readings. Given that students in the class did not necessarily have acting experience, and because students in a philosophy course (or most college classroom courses) do not anticipate having to move and perform in front of one another, the exercises at the beginning of the course ease participants into the physical work of the course. At first students engage in simple meditative and internally focused activities and then incrementally move toward greater self-disclosure, risk, and interaction. This gradual approach fosters trust and individual confidence. Each exercise is followed by significant debriefing discussions that address the physical aspects of morality and allow students to integrate the course readings with what they have just experienced.

The experiential learning activities for the class are adapted from existing dramaturgical exercises used in the development of actors. Many of the activities are modified versions of the exercises developed by Augusto Boal, a Brazilian theater director, politician, and activist best known for creating the Theatre of the Oppressed (1985). His work exhibits a keen awareness for how theater could be a means for engaging people in active work, rather than passive spectatorship of entertainment, to alter social and political circumstances through personal exploration (1995 and 2002). In other words, Boal viewed the Theatre of the Oppressed as an exercise in experiential learning. Boal integrated social and aesthetic theory in his approach to performance and incorporated the philosophical tradition in his analysis of dramatic history.

Improvisational and method acting themes were also included in the course exercises. A number of authors have supported the notion that dramaturgical exercises can engender empathetic development; however, Susan Verducci explicitly claims that in the process of character development, theatrical training can support the skills of caring. She views the actor's job as understanding the situation, relationships, and dispositions of the character in order to create a believable performance. For Verducci, these are the same qualities that individuals need to build the empathetic skills in order to be effective care givers. Verducci contends that this development of care can serve a transformative purpose: "With practice and guidance, one hopes that students will cultivate not only their capacity to empathise, but the habit of doing so. Ideally, students would develop a way of being in the world that centres on the connections between their own lived lives and those of others" (Verducci 2000, 97). Even as a spectator, theatre has the potential to enrich one's moral imagination (Woodruff 2008, 20), but as a participant, or what Boal refers to as "spect-actor" (1985, 144–5), the depth of immersion in the activity creates an intense level of engagement whereby one inhabits the material. PPFE aimed at putting this idea to the test combining action with intentional reflection.

What follows is a very brief synopsis of the exercises employed in the course:

- *Body Awareness*. The initial exercise in the course is a simple closed-eye meditation on one's own body. This meditation sets the tone that this course will integrate visceral and cognitive experience to explore embodiment.
- *Sculpture Exercise*. This is the students' first foray into the risk of performance as they pair up to sculpt one another into objects that others in the class can guess.
- *Emotional Sculpture*. Building on the last exercise, students again pair up for body sculpting but this time the focus is on displaying emotions.
- *Push Not to Win*. This nonverbal exercise focuses upon bodily cooperation. In pairs, students push on one another's hands with varying degrees of force with a goal of not falling forward or backward.
- *Body Mimicking*. This exercise asks students to engage in a bit of acting for the first time by mimicking the language and behavior of someone they knew.
- *Gender Exercise*. This exercise explores "othering" by having students act out a gender display other than their own.
- *Bus Stop Exercise*. This exercise takes students to a new level of dramatic engagement by having them extemporaneously engage one another as a character with an appropriate backstory, as if they were waiting on a bench for a bus.
- *Bus Stop Plus Care Exercise*. Building on the previous exercise, students are asked to explicitly listen to one another in a caring fashion.
- *Decision-Making Exercise*. This exercise asks students to play out a scenario of ethical decision making as if they were characters in a case study.
- *Nonvisual caring*. Rather than the visual and tactile emphasis in the exercises thus far, students are asked to care for one another only using their voices and language through a telephone call scenario.
- *Self-disclosure*. In a simple conversational exercise, students are asked to pair up and share an upcoming event, including their feelings about that event.
- 30 Days *Exercise*. This is the only passive exercise in the class where the students watch an episode of Morgan Spurlock's television show, *30 Days* (Spurlock 2005), a short-lived series that explored the interpersonal power of proximal knowledge.
- *Character acting*. This exercise involves no actual acting but rather the preparation for acting as students are divided into small groups of three and each member of the group is given a slip of paper describing a character they would be asked to play, such as "an adolescent who is grieving because of the recent death of a childhood dog."

- *Baby Exercise*. Modeled on the *Roots of Empathy* program (Gordon 2009), this exercise involves a young couple bringing their baby to class and then having the class observe parent-child interactions.[2]

What makes for dynamic experiential learning is that the debriefing or the reflection upon the exercises is just as significant as the exercises themselves. In each case, the activity is followed by extensive critical examination—not to create better actors but rather to investigate the whole experience in terms of knowledge creation, interpersonal insight, and caring habit formation. These discussions integrate critical reflection on course readings as well.

During the semester students read twenty-four articles or book chapters grouped by topic addressing concepts such as embodiment, phenomenology, performativity, care ethics, freedom and ontology, epistemology, empathy, character acting, education, intersectionality, care of the self, aesthetics, somaesthetics, and play. The philosophers that students read draw from continental, American, and feminist traditions, as well as a few scholars from disciplines outside of philosophy. PPFE course materials were intentionally selected to illuminate the experiential learning from the dramaturgical exercises. For example, the students read a selection from Judith Butler's work on performative gender identity (1988). In subsequent class discussions, they apply the concept of iterative identity development to their self-understanding of moral character, drawing upon the physical experiences in the dramaturgical experiences of the course. The bus stop exercise described above, because of its explicit instructions to add a caring demeanor for the second attempt, is particularly good fodder for such discussions, although all the exercises are woven into the theory-based conversations. In this manner, theory carries a unique living dimension in the course. Given the emphasis on attending to the body, micro habits of caring, such as touch, voice tone, and bodily comportment as witnessed in the exercises, are brought to the forefront. However, aggregate experiences or macro habits of caring as perceived by the caregiver and cared-for are also addressed.

PPFE student assessments consist of both traditional and nontraditional approaches. Students are given a midterm, final examination, and periodic quizzes to assess comprehension of materials. Highlighting the values of experiential learning, students are asked to keep a journal of their growth of understanding in regard to care ethics and their visceral responses to the activities of the course. Leaving room for student choice, course participants are given the option of either a written final project, such as a traditional research paper, or an original performance that communicates an application and analysis of performative care. Given the comfort developed in the course with physical performance, the vast majority of the students choose to present their final projects with some form of visual representation, often with physical movement of some sort.

II. OUTCOMES AND IMPLICATIONS: TEACHING ETHICS VERSUS MORAL EDUCATION

> *We do not have a dichotomy of creating either a feel-good classroom or a challenging one, but the reality that intellectual challenges are more likely to be taken seriously if we trust those who are challenging us.*
>
> —*D. Kay Johnston (2006, 51)*

Despite having intentionally designed the course for interaction, PPFE exceeded my expectations for the level of student engagement. Conceptually, the ethical and ontological theories have the complexity appropriate for a graduate course, but undergraduate students found themselves so involved in the experiential aspects of the course that they fully committed to understanding the difficult material required. They developed a personal stake in the learning, and it was contagious. Students opened up to one another in unexpected ways. Although self-disclosure is explicitly not mandatory for the course, the level of interpersonal comfort prompts very personal revelations. One student discussed the pain and discrimination she felt upon revealing her sexual orientation to her high school coach. Two other students, one Latina and the other African-American, made a presentation on partner abuse that they experienced and how that abuse intersected with their racial identity. In the process of learning about care and risking of themselves in the dramaturgical exercises, the students begin to care deeply about one another. This was evident in how they attended and treated one another before and during the course. Perhaps the experience of this course supports the notion that experiential learning is best conducted in an atmosphere of care.[3] The final projects, such as the ones mentioned above, included stunning analyses and processing of life events that often left students weeping.

One implication of this course is that treating ethics as if it were an abstract rubric to be learned and simply applied to real-world circumstances lends itself to an incomplete notion of morality. Ethics is more than rules, and learning ethics is more than a cognitive exercise. Experiential learning is not merely an enhancement to pedagogical methods, but it is essential for a robust understanding of morality. The process of learning about ethics is comingled with the content of ethics. Another implication of this course is that it is difficult to divorce ontology from ethics. Learning about one self—one's embodiment, one's relationality, one's habits of existence—leads to new perspective on ethical behavior best described as care.

Traditional approaches to teaching philosophical ethics take a propositional knowledge approach: ethics is a bounded body of knowledge to be learned and applied to various situations or issues. This describes a cognitive process. What the experience of PPFE suggests is that cognitive development can be greater if students have an interpersonal, visceral, and physical experience of the meaning of morality. The "playfulness" of the course exercises is not a diversion or a distraction but central to intellectual inquiry. Instead of learning *about* ethics, students practice and reflect on *being* their relational selves, which ultimately implicates morality.

As I stated above, I contend that care theory is much more than a traditional normative ethical philosophy. Care theory has a postmodern character in its resistance to strict categories of understanding. This course demonstrates that learning about ethics is tied to learning about oneself and one's relationship to others. Care is very much a theory of *being* (as indicated earlier in the discussion of habit formation) rooted in a relational ontology.[4] Academia has typically used a system of well-defined disciplines and curricular divisions to transmit ethics education. The experiential aspects of PPFE allowed the course to transcend the categories of ethics, epistemology, and ontology in an organic manner. Experiential learning of this sort is holistic in its communal engagement of mind and body. This form of experiential learning, one that attends to physical relationality, creates a tremendous opportunity for forming a caring community as part of a learning community. This is consistent with what we have described as the epistemological dimension of care. Knowledge creation and caring creation are interrelated endeavors.

The experiential learning of the sort described here supports a breaking down of the distinction between studying ethics, usually considered an abstract cognitive endeavor, and moral education, understood as an effort toward personal moral growth. Nel Noddings describes a framework of four major components for moral education that is well suited to experiential learning: *modeling, dialogue, practice*, and *confirmation* (2000, 15–21 and 2007, 226–234). These elements are not surprising and yet have a great deal of efficacy as demonstrated by PPFE. If caring is not modeled in the classroom then ethics can become an abstract concept to be studied and discussed. *Modeling* care creates a classroom environment where engagement with care theory can flourish. *Dialogue* reflects the responsiveness of care to particular individuals. Particularism is a crucial aspect of care ethics that stems from listening and responding to the voice and context of individuals. *Practice* gets to the heart of the experiential aspects of the course. As Noddings describes, "If we want to produce people who will care for another, then it makes sense to give students practice in caring and reflecting on that practice" (2007, 228). Finally, confirmation represents the support we give one another in achieving the moral ideal. *Confirmation* is affirmation, encouragement, and challenging one another to be better caring individuals. Philosophers are typically tasked with teaching ethics rather than engaging in moral education. Some of that is due to concerns over politics and subjectivity: whose moral education is taught? If care can be valorized as essential to human society and its progress, then perhaps care as a moral ideal can elicit more widespread support as a framework for ongoing moral education. Such an approach further elides the boundary between moral education and teaching ethics.

Furthermore, the experiential learning approach taken in PPFE is consistent with empowering students to be active agents in their education with implications for becoming active agents for social change. Paulo Freire famously contended that traditional academic methods employed a "banking" model that framed education as passive transmission of information. For Freire, this model supported social oppression by supporting passive inquiry. Freire offers "praxis" as an alternative pedagogical framework. He defines praxis as "reflection and action upon the world in order to transform it" (1997, 33) Freire goes on to claim, "apart from inquiry, apart from the praxis, individuals cannot be truly human. Knowledge emerges only through invention and re-invention, through the restless, impatient, continuing, hopeful inquiry human beings pursue in the world, with the world, and with each other" (1997, 53) Similarly, the aforementioned Augusto Boal criticized traditional theatre as creating a passive audience who merely witnesses the play unfold, thus supporting a passive citizenry that merely watches injustice unfold. Boal created the Theatre of the Oppressed, which is an approach to drama whereby the divide between audience and actor is mitigated such that audience members create the play as it goes. The Theatre of the Oppressed shifts the passive spectator paradigm: "The theatre of the oppressed has two fundamental principles: 1) To help the spectator become a protagonist of the dramatic action so that s/he can 2) apply those actions s/he has practiced in the theatre to real life" (Boal and Epstein 36). The experiential and relational learning of PPFE allowed much of the knowledge to emerge from the embodied interactions in class. Although the course represents a structured experience, and thus is not entirely extemporaneous, students engaged in self-discovery that gave them tools to confront familiar and unfamiliar others in further inquiry.

The testimony of one student is indicative of the cognitive and affective dimensions of learning about care in this course:

> As an introvert who is plagued by shyness, I am typically the least vocal in any of my courses and try to skate though with little acknowledgment and minimal participation. When I learned of Dr. Hamington's exploratory course, Performativity, Phenomenology, and Feminist Ethics, which was rumored to involve dramatic exercises through acting and movement, it quite honestly sounded like a personal nightmare, and I had no intention of enrolling. . . . In the beginning of the term the dramatic exercises made me feel exceptionally uncomfortable for a multitude of reasons, including not wanting to be tactile with strangers and the inability to take role playing seriously.
>
> During the first exercise we were asked to sculpt one of our classmates into an emotion—any emotion—and I remember feeling

> paralyzed to the point where after several minutes had passed and all of my classmates had successfully maneuvered their partners' limbs and faces into "excitement!," "sadness," and "surprise!," I pleaded with my partner to "just sculpt yourself into however you're feeling." I'm sure she chose "annoyed" with a hint of "confused." Other exercises included a role-playing situation in which we had to navigate how to choose between two loved ones who needed emotional support at the same time, and another role-playing scenario where strangers interacted with one another while waiting at a bus stop. Through the embodiment of these fictional characters, these activities were often met with laugher and silliness but also with raw emotionality and genuine care.
>
> PPFE required me to step so far outside my comfort zone that some days I felt disembodied as a spectator of myself participating in activities, tactility, and emotionality that I've never allowed myself to experience, particularly in front of others. Without the dramatic exercises the theories we explored would not have been as deep or as easy to internalize, as they acted as a vehicle for tangibility and understanding. . . . My experiences as part of PPFE fostered my abilities to be vulnerable, push boundaries, act on empathy rather than letting it consume me, and mostly, feel comfortable and able to understand and act accordingly to the ever-evolving complexities and challenges we face as embodied beings. The most significant takeaway from the experiences in PPFE for me were learning how to empathize with myself and realizing that without self-reflexivity and empathetic action there are limits to how we perform care for ourselves and the beings that surround us. (Banayad 2014)

This description came several years after the student took the course. I suspect that the physicality of the course contributes to the retention of ideas and raises the significance of the experience learning among other academic experiences.

Given the enmity and divisiveness in the world that leads to misunderstanding and violence, can we afford to go on teaching ethics as an abstract method of adjudication? Experiential learning of the sort described here provides the opportunity to deeply and holistically engage students in what it is to be caring human beings of hand, heart, and mind. Today's postmodern world reveals complex and deeply interconnected oppressions. We need an approach to morality that has the liminality to work in the in-between spaces: between the personal and the political, between the one and the many, and between interiority and alterity. If we agree that who we are, what we know, and what we value are interconnected and relationally based, then embodied and performative care offers a means for exploring the connection while journeying toward personal and collective moral progress. In this framework, experiential learning is an indispensable partner.

NOTES

1. For example, prolific care ethicist Nel Noddings claims, "Moral decisions are, after all, made in real situations; they are qualitatively different from the solutions of geometry problems" (1984, 30).
2. For a more detailed description of the exercises see, Hamington 2012.
3. Of course the elements of a caring classroom are far from definitive and are made more challenging by the proliferation of online and hybrid courses. The fact that the topic of this experiential course was care theory only made the need for a caring atmosphere more compelling.
4. Mary Daly favored a philosophy of "be-ing" understood as a verb rather than a noun to reflect the individual's active existential participation in a manner that transcends individuality (1984, 2). The notion of an active ontology supports the principles of experiential learning as a process of dynamic self-development.

WORKS CITED

Banayad Connie. [student in the course] e-mail correspondence. December 10, 2014.

Boal, Augusto. *Theatre of the Oppressed*. Trans. Charles A. and Maria-Leal McBride. New York: Theatre Communications Group, 1985.

———. *The Rainbow of Desire: The Boal Method of Theatre and Therapy*. Trans. Adrian Jackson. London: Routledge, 1995.

———. *Games for Actors and Non-Actors*. 2nd ed. Trans. Adrian Jackson. London: Routledge, 2002.

Boal, Augusto and Susana Epstein. "The Cop in the Head: Three Hypotheses." *The Drama Review* 34.3 (1990, Autumn): 35–42.

Butler, Judith. "Performative Acts and Gender Constitution: An Essay in Phenomenology and Feminist Theory." *Theatre Journal* 40.4 (1988): 519–31.

Dalmiya, Vrinda. "Why Should a Knower Care?" *Hypatia* 17.1 (2002, Winter): 34–52.

Daly, Mary. *Pure Lust: Elemental Feminist Philosophy*. Boston: Beacon Press, 1984.

Freire, Paulo. *Pedagogy of the Oppressed*. Trans. Myra Bergman Ramos. Revised ed. New York: Continuum, 1997.

Gordon, Mary. *Roots of Empathy: Changing the World Child by Child*. New York: The Experiment, 2009. www.rootsofempathy.org.

Greene, Maxine. *Releasing the Imagination: Essays on Education, the Arts, and Social Change*. San Francisco: Jossey-Bass, 1995.

Hamington, Maurice. *Embodied Care: Jane Addams, Maurice Merleau-Ponty, and Feminist Ethics*. New York: Routledge, 2004.

———. "The Will to Care: Performance, Expectation, and Imagination." *Hypatia* 25.3 (2010, Summer): 675–95.

———. "A Performative Approach to Teaching Care Ethics: A Case Study." *Feminist Teacher* 23.1 (2012): 31–49.

Harrison-Pepper, Sally. "Dramas of Persuasion: Performance Studies and Interdisciplinary Education." *Theatre Topics* 9.2 (1999): 141–56.

Johnston, D. Kay. 2006. *Education for a Caring Society: Classroom Relationships and Moral Action*. New York: Teachers College Press.

Kolb, Alice Y., and David A. Kolb. "Learning Styles and Learning Spaces: Enhancing Experiential Learning in Higher Education." *Academy of Management Learning & Education* 4.2 (2005): 193–212.

Noddings, Nel. *Caring: A Feminine Approach to Ethics and Moral Education.* Berkeley: University of California Press, 1984.

———. *Educating Moral People: A Caring Alternative to Character Education.* New York: Teachers College Press, 2000.

———. *Philosophy of Education.* 2nd ed. Boulder: Westview Press, 2007.

Pew Research Center. "Growing Support for Gay Marriage: Changed Minds and Changing Demographics." March 20, 2013. Accessed March 1, 2014. http://www.people-press.org/files/legacy-pdf/3–20–13%20Gay%20Marriage%20Release.pdf.

Spurlock, Morgan. "Straight Man in a Gay World." [television show] *30 Days.* 2005. Aired July 6, 2005.

Thayer-Bacon, Barbara J. *Transforming Critical Thinking: Thinking Constructively.* New York: Teachers College, 2000.

Woodruff, Paul. *The Necessity of Theater: The Art of Watching and Being Watched.* New York: Oxford University Press, 2008.

Verducci, Susan. "A Moral Method? Thoughts on Cultivating Empathy through Method Acting." *Journal of Moral Education* 29:1 (2000): 87–99.

5 Dewey and Collaborative Experiential Learning Indoors

Minerva Ahumada

Experiential learning is generally envisioned as the practice of creating experiences that link the classroom with the external environment: students going on trips to museums, parks, or historical landmarks; students doing internships, engaged in projects with their community, or shadowing a professional in an area that will help the student better understand what her future profession might entail. But I teach at a community college, which affords most students little opportunity to work on projects outside of class. Nevertheless, I believe that students can benefit from experiential learning *inside* the classroom, so I began examining this concept more carefully by turning to John Dewey, whose writings allowed me to better address what I saw as a weakness in my ethics class. In this chapter I will examine the criteria that, according to Dewey, underline the experiences that are quintessential to the idea of EL. I will do this by establishing the relevance Dewey assigned to certain types of experience and by explaining how the criteria he established are kept alive in the work of Jennifer Moon and David and Alice Kolb. This understanding of the concept of experience has enabled me to transform a previously assigned collaborative project into an experiential learning venture in an urban setting that affords few logistical opportunities to meet with students outside the classroom.

I. SETTING THE STAGE: NIGHT CLASSES AT LAGUARDIA

Ethics and Moral Issues (HUP 104) at LaGuardia Community College aims to introduce students to classical moral theory and to have them analyze their role in society.[1] Because the only prerequisite for this class is that students are ready to take English 101 (that is, that they are not in pre-college English classes), the class mostly enrolls students who have never taken a philosophy class before and who are at very different stages in their college education; therefore the course must cover some of the basic historical and disciplinary knowledge students need in order to be able to fully engage with moral theory.

Some of the texts students read include Plato's *Euthyphro*, and excerpts from Aristotle's *Nicomachean Ethics*, Immanuel Kant's *Prologomena to Any Future Metaphysics*, and John Stuart Mill's *On Utilitarianism*. Students must learn how to carry on a clear exegesis of these texts, while also being able to come up with criticisms for each theory. Students are also required to respond to case studies and write essays that test their interpretation and application of the works discussed in class. This class in particular reads and analyzes Ariel Dorfman's play *Death and the Maiden*. This play serves as our jumping point for our discussions of ethics and for the essays written during the semester.

My desire to include EL was rooted in a tension in the nature of the class itself: while students engage in deep ethical reflection when responding to a case study, their answers may not be genuine in the sense that they truly represent what they would do when facing an ethical conundrum. Some students have mentioned the way in which they curb their responses, trying to gauge what might be the best possible course of action, and do not really put forth effort to decide what they *would do* in a given situation. The difference between these two possibilities is relevant for anyone teaching an ethics class. And while I like the thought experiment approach to ethics, it seems that EL can offer more practical and concrete experiences for students to test their ethics. However, most of the information I found about how to incorporate EL to an ethics class referenced having students participate in community projects. While these projects are indeed worthwhile experiences, students who are taking night classes are not an easy match for said projects. I needed to find a way to bring experience *into* the classroom.

II. ACT 1: DEFINING EXPERIENCE AND EXPERIENTIAL LEARNING

Although an experience is commonly seen as something we undergo or encounter, not all experiences we encounter are conducive to learning. Therefore, the linkage between *experience* and *learning* should already make us cautious of what we name *experience*. By adopting the concept of experiential learning, we are already claiming that experience is a domain of human interaction from, in, and through which learning *can* happen. In order to better understand this allegiance, one must understand what is meant by *experience* in a fuller sense.

Dewey's *Experience and Education* defines what experiences are and which ones are worth including in an educational setting because he sees a strong connection between the value of experience and progressive education. Dewey, as well as many other philosophers of education, sees traditional education as the practice in which a student is called to simply receive and recall the knowledge that is being presented to her by her teachers. In contrast, progressive education places higher value on actively involving the student in the process of learning. Dewey argues that progressive education—if planned and executed correctly—can be superior to traditional education because it follows the same principles that are inherent in our acceptance of democracy: "the principle of regard for individual freedom and for decency and kindliness of human relations" (34). Traditional education, which Dewey acknowledges can achieve limited success, disregards the individual as a free and complete agent and sees her only as a disembodied vessel that can absorb predigested information. In acknowledging that a student is a subject who can make decisions, think rationally, and establish relations with others, Dewey asserts in the classroom an interaction that is akin to how we expect that same student to behave as part of a democratic society—now in her role of citizen, by exercising "mutual consultation" and establishing "convictions reached through persuasion" (34); the progressive classroom prepares the student for behaviors that are expected outside the classroom as part of a progressively democratic society because it allows her to better examine life.

Two pedagogical principles differentiate progressive education from traditional education, according to Dewey: the experiential continuum and interaction. Dewey calls the principles of continuity and interaction "the longitudinal and lateral aspects of experience" (44) as experiences do not just succeed one another, but there is always a carryover, something that we take from one experience to the next; therefore practitioners of progressive education must remember that they want to offer learning opportunities that can be linked to what the learner will encounter in her life in the future. Dewey sees experience demarcated by epistemological principles. Because our life is a constant succession of experiences, we must learn to analyze, criticize, and separate these experiences from one another.

The experiential continuum, in Dewey's philosophy, is understood as the way in which "every experience enacted and undergone modifies the one who acts and undergoes, while this modification affects, whether we wish it or not, the quality of subsequent experiences" (35). For example, the questions my mom asked me after we read a story together still influence the questions I ask myself after every novel I read. The experience creates a lasting effect onto which every new experience builds on. This, according to Dewey, "suggests that experience is cumulative and that the types of experiences people learn from are those that generate habits" (35). So each experience changes—refines, modifies, rearranges—the past and prepares us in a different way toward the future; classroom settings must help students form that continuum, so their experiences won't be disjointed, rarified, or in the worst-case scenario, irrelevant. This cumulative aspect affects not only the experiences but also the subject, who develops new habits and strategies.

The continuum of experience is joined by the principle of interaction, which "is going on between an individual and objects and other persons" (Dewey, 43); this suggests that students need to interact with each other to have a more significant learning process. Dewey mentions that when we claim that "individuals live in a world" we mean by this that they are not as "pennies are 'in' a pocket" (43), that is, as objects who have no connection to one another; Dewey encourages interaction among students, so that they can feel they can offer information that is valuable even when it has not been certified by the professor.[2]

Both principles underline the criteria that ground an experience as worthwhile: an experience that will propel the student into an unknown future with knowledge that is valuable and applicable, extracted through consultation with those who also live in our world. For Dewey an experience is helpful because it connects to the future in some concrete way. Therefore, if the student cannot comprehend the way in which the experience is relevant for her learning process, then the experience was not carefully selected. This is one of the problems with traditional ways of learning such as memorization, where a student cannot foresee how this method and information will prove helpful and relevant in her future.

Naïveté and good intentions might make teachers see any experience to which they expose students as a good learning opportunity. However, Jennifer Moon, in her book *A Handbook of Reflective and Experiential Learning: Theory and Practice*, points out that Dewey warned that experiences are not "good." Moon says,

> Experiential learning tends to have an aura of 'good' around it [. . .]. Some of this comes from the enthusiastic but often simplistic writings on the topic. Clearly what is learnt from experience cannot be neither 'good' nor positive to the learner. Dewey (1997) makes this point through his distinction between education and experience: 'some experiences are mis-educative. Any experience is mis-educative that has the effect of arresting or distorting growth of further experience' (107).

Therefore, educators need to carefully and purposefully select an experience that will allow for growth, interaction with the world and those in it, and reflection.

With a better understanding of what Dewey deemed experience that leads to learning, I amended my collaborative projects assignment and reorganized them under David Kolb's cycle of learning. In "Learning Styles and Learning Spaces: Enhancing Experiential Learning in Higher Education," David and Alice Kolb explain that EL "portrays two dialectically related modes of grasping experience—Concrete Experience and Abstract Conceptualization—and two dialectically related modes of transforming experience—Reflective Observation and Active Experimentation" (194).

Concrete Experience is understood to be the task that is presented to students in the classroom, and it must be, Kolb establishes, one that demands an active involvement. Reflective Observation requires the participants of the experience to take a step back and analyze the practices, behaviors, and attitudes that were present in it. This task can be overlooked because of its simplicity, but it is extremely important that EL practitioners provide time, space, and vocabulary to discuss the experience selected.

The learner's initial reflection allows her to better interpret and understand the experience. Abstract Conceptualization allows practitioners of EL to discuss previous experiences that might be related to the one at hand, as well as theories and previous knowledge that might be helpful to better analyze and comprehend this new experience. The last stage in Kolb's cycle is Active Experimentation. At this stage EL is interested in lasting knowledge, which is achieved through planning, developing predictions, or engaging in case studies. EL seeks to apply the discoveries that were made in the aforementioned stages so that the learner can establish longitudinal connections.

To add an experiential dimension to my class, so students could better assess their own ethical commitments, agency, and expectations, I needed to find a situation we could concretely assess and dissect. This situation needed to fulfill Dewey's criteria of a worthy experience and the work and needed to be guided using Kolb's cycle. Due to logistical constraints, it needed to be done inside the classroom. It is with this idea in mind that I made the collaborative project in class an experiential learning project.

III. ACT 2: COOPERATIVE LEARNING AS EXPERIENTIAL LEARNING

As previously mentioned, Ethics and Moral Issues aims to introduce students to classical moral theory and to have them analyze their role in society. In order to fulfill the course description and its learning objectives, I have students work in small groups, using cooperative learning (CL), to critically engage with philosophical theories. Having students work in small groups has proven successful in developing students' analytical skills and to get them involved in philosophical analysis of texts. The new challenge was to provide a setting where students could learn more not only about philosophy but also about the way in which they were interacting with others while working in small groups. Because of CL's emphasis on roles, rules, and responsibility, the work done through this pedagogical strategy seemed to provide a perfect link to EL.

Cooperative learning is defined by David W. Johnson et al, in *Cooperation in the Classroom,* as "the instructional use of small groups so that students work together to maximize their own and each other's learning" (5). Cooperative learning (CL) differs from group projects in its intentionality, the mentality that all members of the group must be equally responsible and knowledgeable at the end of the task, and that the grade earned is "mutually caused by oneself and one's colleagues" (Johnson and Johnson 5). Johnson et al developed the acronym PIGS Face to underline the five different components that serve as the intentional basis to work in cooperation in an effective way:

P—**Positive Interdependence:** each one of the members of the group is given a specific task or role.

I—**Individual and Group Accountability:** every member of the group knows that for them to succeed, there cannot be members of the team who do not contribute to the task.

G—**Group Processing:** the group comes up with goals and decisions that will lead them to successfully achieve their task.

S—**Social Skills:** students are expected to develop respectful ways in which they can communicate with each other.

Face—**Face-to-Face Interaction:** students engage with one another in order to clarify concepts or to explain to one another what they are studying in order to make sure that each member of the group clearly and accurately understands their topic.

In class, the inclusion of CL in the classroom already moves students to the center, as they are assigned texts that they will analyze both individually and in their groups.[3] The projects we use in class also present groups with a common goal (the analysis of a text or the interpretation of a situation), which requires the collaboration of everyone in the classroom. While the use of CL in class had always been quite successful, linking it to EL allowed students to think about the way in which they acted in the group and not just about the presentation they had produced.

In order to participate in Kolb's experiential learning cycle, students were asked to produce two presentations using CL during the semester. The first presentation became the Concrete Experience under analysis and became linked to Reflective Observation and Abstract Conceptualization. The second presentation gave the class the opportunity to engage with Active Experimentation as students were asked to enact and analyze the concepts they had derived from their first project.

IV. ACT 3: EXPERIENTIAL LEARNING IN THE CLASSROOM

From day one students are made aware of the two CL projects they will carry out during the semester. During the third week of classes—which is when the first project begins—the acronym PIGS Face and its expectations are introduced and discussed. Students know that they are expected to work on their projects during class time, so that they do not have to struggle with coming up with alternate times to meet.

Although EL is not explicitly introduced at this time, students are asked to think about why they are working in a cooperative fashion; their answers highlight the two most important reasons for this decision: 1) they will have to directly engage with texts, therefore probing their philosophical skills; 2) they will interact with one another and this sort of interaction can be related to the theme of the class.

Linking CL and EL (CE and RO and AC)

Students' first CL project requires them to develop a brief presentation on an excerpt dealing with the origins of morality.[4] These presentations dovetail the reading and analysis of Ariel Dorfman's play *Death and the Maiden*. As a class, we analyze the "transformation" that took hold of Dr. Roberto Miranda, once a humanitarian doctor who is now accused of having raped and tortured Paulina Salas. Each team is assigned an excerpt on the origins of morality—using the philosophies of Mencius, Aristotle, and Sigmund Freud among others—and to develop a presentation in which they explain their philosopher's argument. After the presentations, students will write an individual essay in which they analyze Miranda's change through one of the presentations given in class. Although this essay is not graded as part of the project, it allows us to better incorporate the work done by students in their presentations, to have students listen attentively to one another, and to elicit questions at the end of each presentation.

Students are given three sessions of class (4.5 hours of class time) to work with their peers analyzing their assigned reading and turning that understanding into a presentation for their classmates. The project is staged as follows:

1) In preparation for the first group meeting, students are asked to submit notes on their assigned philosopher via e-mail before class.
2) In the first class session, students begin discussing their assigned philosopher. The professor hands back the students' notes with feedback. At the end of the session students provide a working draft of the interpretation of the philosopher.
3) In the second session, a small cycle of drafts–feedback between group and the professor takes place. At this point, the professor now plays the role of a facilitator who addresses and assesses the needs and progress of each group. Although the facilitator needs to encourage students to engage with the text, she also needs to be aware that most students feel anxious about being responsible for the accurate understanding of the text.[5] Groups turn in a proposed outline for their presentation.
4) On the third CL session, students are expected to have an approved outline for their presentation and to use that outline to finish their visual aid—a PowerPoint, Prezi presentation, etc.—that they can use in their presentation. All teams, regardless of when they are presenting, are expected to submit their finished visual aids at the end of the session.
5) Students present their work on the philosopher at the following class meeting. Students are given twenty minutes for their presentation and ten minutes for Q&A.

After the presentations, the class discusses their interpretation of Miranda's transformation and the philosophers they used. On this day, as a class, we discuss the way in which they engaged with their peers in their project. Students discuss the expectations and challenges they had; we also discuss the goals of CL and the way in which their work could be improved.

In EL terms, their project becomes the Concrete Experience under scrutiny. Students *look* at the work they did in order to analyze it and learn from it. Students reflect not only on the way in which the project was staged but also on practical experiences they had during their collaborative work sessions. Mostly, students talk about how they need to rely on one another more and the fact that they can't miss any of these sessions because if they do, the group gets truly affected and scheduling a makeup session outside of class is nearly impossible. Most students discuss how important it was to have someone in their group who encouraged them to express their opinions or who seemed more confident on the topic. This session grants us the opportunity to decompress after what has been an intense couple of weeks of work and to agree on what is feasible to expect when doing these sorts of projects. Students create a set of principles based on this thorough reflection, thus linking the Concrete Experience to Abstract Conceptualization through Reflective Observation. These agreements are extremely important because they are grounded on the students' experiences and expectations and they will become the basis for how we conduct ourselves in the second CL activity students have.

Active Experimentation

For their second project students are assigned to teams of four.[6] Each team is assigned a set of primary sources related to a normative theory: Kantian ethics, utilitarianism, feminism, existentialism, moral sentimentalism, or intersubjectivity. The staging of the process is similar to the one described above except that, because the texts are lengthier and more complex, groups have fifteen hours to work on this project. Groups are expected to develop a clear understanding of the theory that was assigned to them and to create an online presentation for their peers. The staging includes:

1) Each student is asked to read their team's assigned sources individually and to submit a set of notes about their reading. The notes must contain relevant quotes from the text, a summary of their understanding of the reading, and questions they have after their first interaction with the text. Students are asked to turn in their individual notes before they meet with their teammates.
2) During their first meeting with their teammates, and based on the parameters they previously crafted, students design a plan that will help them achieve the goals this project has: which roles need to be created? Who is in charge of taking notes? Who can create the visual aid required? How will they record their presentation and upload it to the course's online management site?[7]

3) The professor returns to the role of facilitator to engage in a cycle of drafts–feedback that takes place informally during class and formally after class when the professor goes over the draft the students submitted for the day.
4) After the first two weeks of CL, students are asked to write an individual paper in which they assess the way in which Paulina Salas treated Roberto Miranda in *Death and the Maiden* using the theory they have been studying. This is done in order to corroborate that all members or the team are gathering a clear understanding of the theory they have been studying.[8]
5) Once students have received feedback as groups and individually, they are cleared for working on the online presentation of their assigned theory. Students develop an online class in which they inform their peers of the main tenets their theory has, as well as of some of its applications and criticisms.[9]
6) Once all presentations have been uploaded, each team is assigned a "workshop" session. During workshop days two teams answer their peers' questions about their online presentation. For example, students prepare by watching the online presentation on Kantian ethics and utilitarianism at home. When class meets, the team in charge of Kantian ethics does a five-minute introduction of their theory, and we devote the other forty minutes of their session to Q&A. Students who watched the online session ask questions that help them clarify their understanding of the theory as well as its application.

After the presentations, students are asked to fill out a self-evaluation and co-evaluation form. This form is based on the analysis and reflection done in class after the first round of presentations. The expectations are based both on the elements of CL and on the expectations and understanding that the students gathered during their first interaction with CL, their Abstract Conceptualization. Students assess, for example, whether they and the members in their group came to class prepared, by having done the readings and taking notes that reflected the critical analysis of the texts; students also assess whether they and their peers listened and encouraged participation of the members of their group. Students assess each one of these questions using a one-to-five scale, where five is the best. Their scores are averaged, and students earn a grade for self-evaluation and a second one for co-evaluation (this one based on all the grades they received from their peers).

Students' grades for their project on normative theories represents 35 percent of their final grade. Students are graded both individually and as a group. The presentation, workshop day, drafts submitted, and outline are given a grade for the whole team. Each student's notes—the ones submitted before the CL began—are graded individually; the self-evaluation and co-evaluation are also graded individually.[10]

Connecting Experiences: Agency

Experiences, as indicated before, are not "good" on their own; they also do not simply grant us with immediate knowledge. Reflection, argues Dewey and practitioners of EL, helps open up experience into its worthy components. Because of this, the last activity we do in class in relation with the project is a reflection on what students think about the way in which they cooperated and collaborated with others (thus relating the activity to Concrete Experience and Reflective Observation in Kolb's cycle). Students write down their answers, and then we have a discussion as to how we behave when engaging with others and the way in which this project showcases our ethical engagement. Students discuss the responsibility they experienced while doing this project and the way in which other responsibilities (such as classes, work, familial situation, etc.) seemed to threaten or thwart their participation in the project. They also discuss the way in which they learned from one another and the sort of community that they formed.

As part of this reflective activity, students are asked to write down ways in which this project might extend beyond the classroom. For example, they talk about the way in which clearly defining the responsibilities and expectations of each participant in this project contributed to the sort of work they produced. Some students mentioned that they applied some of the concepts they learned in this project to the work they are doing with other people (therefore furthering an element of Active Experimentation).

This last reflection becomes extremely significant for EL as it is up to each student to reflect on her role during the collaborative work and to identify what sort of learning has happened throughout the project. Discussions include not only the significant learning they have done with regard to the theoretical components of the class but also the attitudes and behaviors that students had and whether or not they can be deemed as ethical. Through this project students not only develop their critical and analytical skills, but they also engage in practical discussions of what it means to lead a good life in the company of others and their role as ethical agents.

V. CURTAINS DOWN: EXPERIENCE, PRACTICE, ETHICS

The incorporation of EL into Ethics and Moral Issues allowed students to reflect on their own agency and involvement not only in their learning but also in their dealings with others. While collaborative projects can be highly successful in having students contribute with others, EL's emphasis on reflection and analysis presented the class with opportunities to be more intentional about the way in which they work in groups, thus allowing students to connect the learning happening in the classroom to their lives outside of the classroom.

In *Experience and Education* Dewey highlighted the important ways in which experience can be brought into the classroom in order to provide students with a better approach to learning. By selecting experiences that require students to interact with their peers in order to engage in consultation and reach agreements that allow them to better integrate their skills and knowledge, classrooms can be transformed into sites where students are not seen as "pennies in a pocket" but free agents who can reflect on the way in which they are educated and the way in which the classroom is connected to their concrete experience outside colleges and universities. One of the goals Dewey had that is acknowledged by practitioners of EL is that experience links and seamlessly integrates classroom teachings with the real world—its actual state and future possibilities.

EL's success is grounded in the intentionality involved in choosing to have a certain type of reflective experience; in the idea that students can generate their own learning; in allowing space in the classroom for meaningful reflection and analysis; and in the value placed on interaction. If these elements are carefully curated, it won't matter if the experience students are exposed to happens in the classroom. As I have shown here, it can be the result of a staged collaborative project—or a field trip.

NOTES

1. This course investigates the nature of morality and its place in human experience. Among the questions posed and discussed are: is morality simply relative to specific cultures? What are criteria for right and wrong? What is moral agency? Does love have a place in the moral life? Students are encouraged to explore how morality functions in their own lives (Catalogue of Courses 2012–2013, 146)
2. Dewey's principle of interaction challenges, in a similar way, what Paulo Freire deemed "the banking model of education" as the students who are asked to regurgitate knowledge do not effectively interact in the world of education.
3. One should note that because CL moves the student to the center, it also changes the role the professor has as she becomes a facilitator to the students—she responds to their needs, whether these are content-based or logistical.
4. Our textbook is Peter Singer's *Ethics* reader.
5. At LaGuardia, especially, students might also be nervous because English is their second language and philosophical texts are especially challenging for this population. Since it is an honors class, these students also experience anxiety because some of them are in taking their first honors course and they deem their peers to be excellent communicators and impressively smart students.
6. I usually assign students to groups after the final withdrawal date has passed; this way I have a better idea as to how many students are still in the class. The number of students enrolled in class determines the number of theories covered in class.

7. In order to have students reflect on the kind of work they are doing, all the groups are new. There are no two people who worked together in the previous presentation.
8. Students receive feedback on this paper and are asked to discuss their papers with the rest of their team; this is done so that they can clarify their understanding of the theory and to make sure everyone has a similar understanding. This step is very helpful in clarifying aspects of the theory that have not been appropriately understood. For example, a common problem students working with utilitarianism face is that they do not fully incorporate the idea of "community" or "greatest number" to their utilitarian calculations.
9. The reason why students are asked to create the online presentation is so that we can flip the classroom and instead of using class time to provide factual information, students study these presentations outside of class and then come to the session with questions about the presentation. Flipping the classroom this way allows students to have more time to react to the information they have been presented with. This is the equivalent to the structure used in NYSWIP where the papers are circulated in advance so that the session is not used to present the paper but to engage in meaningful discussion of the ideas presented.
10. The breakdown of the 35 percent is as follows: Individual Notes 3.5; Drafts 4.0; Outline 5.0; Presentation and Workshop 15.0; Self-evaluation 3.5; Co-evaluation 4.0. Although students write two essays related to these presentations, those are graded as part of a different requirement for class (Essays).

WORK CITED

Dewey, John. *Experience and Education*. New York: Free Press, 1997.

Johnson, David, Roger Johnson, Edythe Johnson Halubec. *Advanced Cooperative Learning*. Denver: Interaction Book Co., 1987.

Kolb, Alice and David Kolb. "Learning Styles and Learning Spaces: Enhancing Experiential Learning in Higher Education." *Academy of Management Learning & Education* 4.2 (June 2005): 193–212.

Moon, Jennifer. *A Handbook of Reflective and Experiential Learning: Theory and Practice*. New York: Routledge, 2004.

6 Philosophy, Critical Pedagogy, and Experiential Learning

J. Jeremy Wisnewski

I. INTRODUCTION

The aim of this essay is to examine some ways in which philosophy instruction can and does involve experiential education. The most obvious context where this is so is in study abroad courses. I discuss my own experience teaching ancient philosophy (on two occasions, in 2009 and 2011) during a monthlong January term in Greece and Turkey. A second, more traditional context is an on-campus first-year seminar course entitled The Socratic Project, in which students are tasked, among other things, with impersonating Socrates. This is a course I taught three times from 2008 to 2011. Given a suitably nuanced understanding of experiential education, I suggest, both of these courses can be seen as falling under the heading of experiential learning. More controversially, I argue that philosophy courses in general can integrate components of experiential learning and that philosophy departments have nothing to fear from the movement to engage in more experiential learning in the classroom.

Prior to 2009, I was a skeptic about the ability to engage in experiential learning in philosophy courses. I was certainly aware that particular philosophy courses could engage in some *kinds* of EL—by writing representatives in Congress about policy issues, protesting the School of the Americas, or otherwise acting on those arguments encountered and examined in applied ethics and political philosophy courses. My skepticism centered on how *other* philosophy courses might also fit under this rubric. Our standard "chalk and talk" approach to pedagogy seemed, at the time, difficult to abandon.

Hartwick College (my academic home) had recently been defined by the new president as a liberal arts college that focused on integrating experiential learning (EL) into the curriculum. Despite the fact that faculty had yet to agree on a definition of what was meant by EL at Hartwick, there was, and is even now, a large emphasis on fulfilling the president's vision. Indeed, candidates for tenure are asked about how their teaching fits into the president's model, and faculty are routinely encouraged to incorporate elements of EL into our courses. This may well be a trend in the discipline.

My skepticism was perhaps exacerbated by the increased emphasis on EL at my college and a collective fear among academic philosophers—one that is probably justified—that philosophy departments are in danger of being assessed out of existence. I came to realize, however, that my skepticism—perhaps as is often the case with skepticism—was grounded in a very narrow view of what the term *experiential learning* actually meant.[1] Yet the urge for a narrow view of EL is understandable. The variety of models sometimes lends itself to skepticism about the very idea of EL due to worries about the seeming vacuity of a unique kind of learning that is distinguished by being "experience based," sometimes equated with mundane life practices removed from reflection about theoretical connections. As Tara Fenwick rhetorically asks: "What manner of learning can be conceived that is not experiential, whether the context be clearly educational or not?" (244).

But these worries—worries shared by many philosophers—can be met. The fact that *all* education, properly so-called, involves an experiential dimension does not entail that every kind of experience is equal in value or importance. While all education is experiential in some sense, we can nevertheless distinguish *kinds* of experiences that one can have, or foster, within the institutional context of higher education that may nurture compassion and "inspire curiosity, critical thinking, creativity, personal courage and an enduring passion for learning."[2]

II. CRITICAL THEORY AND EXPERIENTIAL LEARNING

Regardless of the definitions of EL one embraces, one common perception is that it requires getting outside of the classroom and into some type of field experience—be it doing field biology, field archaeology, or even internships in government offices or businesses. Engaging the world one encounters in other ways, not obviously connected to one's discipline, has also become recognizable as a model of EL. For instance, one might volunteer at a local charity, nursing home, teen center, or school; likewise, one might participate in activism of various sorts.

The Association for Experiential Education defines EL as "a process through which a learner constructs knowledge, skill and value from direct experience" (Itin 91). This process involves several key components that seem to be more or less orthodoxy. J. J. Stehno identifies the following features across divergent models of EL and education. EL includes "1) action that created an experience, 2) reflection on the action and experience, 3) abstractions drawn from the reflection, and 4) application of the abstraction to a new experience or action" (Itin 91). On the traditional model, EL thus involves an academic component, an action component that takes place outside of the classroom, and a structured reflective component. In other words, we do theory, then practice, and then we reflect on how theory was implemented in practice, remaining cognizant of connections between coursework and field experience. On this view, EL is defined in terms of specific out-of-classroom activities (field work, internships, political engagement, etc.) and reflections on those activities.

There is also, however, work supporting the view that EL does not require leaving the classroom.[3] What matters is the manner in which we approach pedagogy, not where it happens. In my own thinking about this alternative model of EL, one model of learning has been more useful than any other: the model of Frankfurt School-style Critical Theory. While infrequently discussed in these terms, the work of Paulo Freire, John Dewey, and Kurt Hahn fall squarely into this camp. Central to each of these thinkers is the view that education is a process by which we become competent democratic citizens. As Christian Itin explains, "all three are concerned with increasing the capabilities (self-efficacy) of individuals to participate in the democratic process (political awareness and action)" (93). This is accomplished by "developing a critical understanding" (93)—that is, an understanding that is both capable and willing to question the structures of power and privilege that largely structure social experience and organization.

Experiential education, on this model, is thus not concerned to simply construct experiences as part of a reflective exercise, but to develop "the competency of the learner to integrate what is being learned with the actions that are required" (Itin 93). While this can certainly occur in internships and field and lab work, such examples of EL are subordinate to the larger aim and purpose of education more generally. This aim is not to produce agents capable of reciting information (what Freire calls the "banking approach" to education). The aim, rather, is to raise "the critical consciousness of individuals through education so that they will be better able to participate in the democratic political process" (93). As Stephen Brookfield usefully articulates this idea, the "adult educator's task is to create conditions in which authentic dialogue and communicative discourse can occur" (24).

Behind this process, undeniably, is a devotion to a set of democratic values, as well as a conception of what is required of an educational system in a nation that hopes effectively to foster those values in its citizens. There are interesting philosophical questions about how these values might be defended, alongside some troubling practical questions about how any large-scale institution might successfully, and perpetually, embody such values. I will not address the practical worries, real though they are. Regarding the issue of values, I will simply note here that *all* educational choices embody values and that being explicit about these values amounts to a recognition that "education is a political process" (Itin 94). As Ira Shor has argued, "All forms of education are political because they can enable or inhibit the questioning habits of students, thus developing or disabling their critical relation to knowledge, schooling, and society" (13).

Much philosophy shares its aim with critical theory in general—to excavate and critique the commonly accepted ideas of our peers, academic and otherwise, in order to both better understand and more deliberately and effectively act in the world. But raising questions is by no means sufficient to a critical pedagogy. As we know all too well, questions can fall dead from our lips or be met by the blank stares of our students—that is, when they look up from their smartphones. So while philosophy is well-suited to the kind of EL advocated by Freire, Dewey, and Hahn, simply being a part of the discipline is not sufficient for achieving the goals of a critical-theoretic approach to experiential education.

There are several key elements in a critical pedagogy that various approaches all try to meet. It is generally agreed, for example, that the learning environment in EL must be *transactive* rather than merely interactive. That is, interaction between professor and student is in itself insufficient for EL. The idea captured in "transactive" approaches, as I understand it, is that the student is a cocreator of the educational process (Itin 94) rather than merely a recipient of it. Students "cocreate" their learning environments in the sense that the very content of one's learning is driven by active engagement in particular (but varied) activities rather than by the (traditional) activities of an instructor (lecturing, grading, and so on). An educator's role "becomes that of facilitating access to learning environments" of a particular kind (Allison and Pomeroy 93). Put otherwise, "educators create activities that provide opportunities for students to experience what it is like to interact with specific situations" (Carver 152). In this sense, such activities can be in the classroom or out of it. The location of the activity makes no difference to its character as *transactive*.

One common model for accomplishing the construction of such transactive environments is the "talking circle," something many philosophy professors already incorporate into their classrooms.[4] There is no denying that this is a good place to start, but there is doubt that this is sufficient. Brookfield, for example, has argued that "one of the chief arguments for using discussion—that it opens learners to considering carefully alternative perspectives and interpretations—is invalidated by [the] behavior of [many learners]" (24). Brookfield comes to this conclusion by reflecting on his own actions when involved in such situations, noting that, as a learner, he often simply waited for his turn to speak and measured his contributions in terms of their perceived outcomes (the respect of his teachers and classmates). Such approaches to participation in conversation actively thwart the very aim of such activities: students with this approach carefully construct their contributions to the conversation while *ignoring what others are contributing*.

What Brookfield's reflective analysis demonstrates, I think, is that there is no formulaic way to guarantee transactive experiences that promote the cultivation of critical thinking skills and hence also of conscientious citizens. There are *strategies*, but our strategies must be adaptable to the particular circumstances we face, and our implementation of these strategies must always be thoughtful. One (rather radical) way to approach cultivating critical awareness is by democratizing the classroom itself. Ira Shor reports on doing just this in a class on "utopias," where the themes, assignments, readings, and grades were all determined democratically by the *class itself*. He also outlines many useful ways to promote student awareness of power dynamics we see in society—including in the classroom. This can be accomplished in myriad ways, and Shor provides a number of useful examples.

Importantly, such critical-theoretic approaches *do not* attempt to teach students specific values. They aim, rather, to foster independence and critical acumen. In this sense, one can engage a critical-theoretic approach to experiential education *regardless* of the topic of one's course. Shor's democratic approach to syllabus construction, for example, could be utilized (in whole or in part) in *any* course. While this in-class activity (debating and trying to reach consensus concerning the syllabus) does not *directly* create conscientious citizens, it *does* foster those skills required for such citizenship—namely, critical thinking that is (largely) independent of the undue influence of those in power.

III. PHILOSOPHY IN AN EXPERIENTIAL KEY

Travel Abroad: Take One

On two occasions I have taken groups of students to Greece and Turkey. The course I taught was set up in the first instance as an ancient philosophy course with readings from the Pre-Socratics, Plato, and Aristotle. In the second instance, the course had a broader focus, including additional readings from Homer, Sophocles, Sappho, Euripides, Pindar, and others. The duration of the course was approximately twenty-one days. About half of the time was spent in Athens, with the rest of the time devoted to visiting a range of sites around Greece and Turkey. Sites visited included Mycenae, Epidaurus, Corinth, Olympia, Delphi, the closer Greek islands, Troy, and Istanbul. While in Athens, students visited the agora, the theatre of Dionysus, the site of Aristotle's Lyceum, along with a host of museums.

For each site, students were assigned readings that connected with the site in some way. In Olympia, for example, students read Pindar's *Olympian Odes*. While in the agora (and we went there several times during the trip), students discussed Plato's *Euthyphro*, *Apology*, *Crito*, and portions of *Phaedo*. One of the first tasks assigned to the students, when we entered the agora, was to find the Royal Stoa, the setting of Plato's *Euthyphro*. The assignment was, in a sense, a trick. The Royal Stoa are *outside* of the current agora park, across some railroad tracks, and cannot be accessed. They can be seen from within the current agora park, but one cannot walk among the ruins. This exercise seems to increase student interest in *Euthyphro* (judging from student feedback) while also presenting the reality of historical change and the relative newness of archaeological preservation.

We discussed the *Apology* in the central area of the Agora, where the trial of Socrates is said to have taken place in order to accommodate the large jury and the many spectators. Students are asked to write the prosecution's speech—to convince an audience that Socrates is in fact guilty of the charges brought against him. Finally, we discuss the *Crito* and *Phaedo* at the site of Socrates's death—the jail structure in the southwest corner of the agora. By the time we got to this dialogue, the students had a familiarity with the agora, as they had been there on several separate occasions.

By indexing readings to sites—even in sometimes tenuous ways, I'll admit—our discussions of Socrates and Plato took on a kind of existential dimension that is much harder to foster in a classroom. Being abroad provided an ideal opportunity to engage students in readings on the history of Ancient Greece as well, utilizing both ancient sources (like Thucydides and Herodutus) as well as contemporary ones (essays in the *Cambridge Companion to Archaic Greece*, for example). By situating our ancient readings in cultural and historical context, the class emphasized both the philosophical ideas we were exploring as well as the contexts that made these ideas come to life. We likewise went far outside of the canonical confines of philosophical texts. We read Pindar's *Odes* when visiting Olympia; we read portions of Homer when we visited Troy and Mycenae. Moreover, every effort was made to relate ancient texts to more recent writings and concerns. When we read Sophocles's *Oedipus Rex*, for example, we spent time considering the way the ideas in the play had been utilized in Freudian psychology.

The activities of this course fit the model of traditional EL: we read, engage in an activity (visiting a site, for example), and then reflect on the relationship between the reading and the activity. Some of the specific activities we engage in (finding the Royal Stoa, for example) obviously could not be carried out in a classroom. If we limit our notions of EL to a traditional model that emphasizes leaving the classroom, EL will be out of reach for a number of our courses, and perhaps for a number of our colleagues. Not everyone has the great fortune to be able to take students abroad, or to teach classes that otherwise lend themselves to traditional EL.

On the critical-theoretic model of EL, however, the location of a course is no hindrance to its ability to be *transactive* and hence experiential in the relevant sense. To take one example mentioned above, students must write the speech of Meletus, attempting to prove to a jury that Socrates was in fact guilty of the charges against him. The nature and quality of this assignment changes substantially when *the students themselves* become the jury, and the speech must be delivered to them. With a little coaching about jury behavior in Athenian culture, as well as about the protocols of the Athenian court system, the assignment quickly becomes an occasion to develop one's critical thinking and independence. The activity itself encourages students to think *outside of the text*: how will one convince *this* jury (the other students)? What arguments are likely to work? What can one get the jury to believe? The jury, for its part, must critically assess what is being said. Is the prosecutor saying something false about the historical Socrates? Has she done research that would justify her assertions, or is she simply inventing stories for the sake of conviction? Are the arguments presented worthwhile? If one further encourages students to do what it takes to win the case, including inventing historical "facts"—the ante is automatically raised. One *must* critically assess everything said, for anything said may well be untrue.

There is no doubt something very nice about watching students engage in this process in the *Agora* itself, at the site where Socrates had his trial. It is not the location, however, that makes the activity experiential. It could occur in the classroom or out of it, so long as the student is actively cocreating *the very thing being learned*—how to think critically about claims made by others. They are not initially *told* what is right or wrong in the speech. They must think for themselves. They are not *told* how to raise an objection. They must work out their own objections. When the activity is complete, of course, we meet and discuss the entire process, as well as how it might relate to our current political and social environment.

Being Socrates at Home: Take Two

On three separate occasions, I have taught a course called The Socratic Project as a seminar-style course restricted to first-year students. In the course, we raise questions of self-knowledge. We begin with Plato and Socrates, as one might guess, but we proceed to read Nietzsche, Freud, Marx, and some more contemporary material on the evolutionary explanation of beliefs and morality. For each major writing assignment in the course, I try to force students to interact in a meaningful way with the ideas of the course—again in a way that involves potentially transformative experiences alongside a healthy dose of good, old-fashioned critique. Assignments in the course included the following:

1. Impersonating Socrates for fifteen minutes somewhere on campus, outside of class, and then completing a follow-up assignment involving a second impersonation.
2. Writing the speech of the prosecution in Socrates's trial, as in the travel abroad class.
3. Psychoanalyzing one of our authors (most students choose to psychoanalyze Freud's texts).
4. Writing a Marxist critique of our curriculum.

All of these exercises, I believe, constitute examples of EL on the critical-theoretic model. I will focus my attention, however, on the first assignment: the impersonation of Socrates. The (abbreviated) assignment instructions read as follows:

> In this course, you will impersonate Socrates. To do this, we will divide into groups of three. Each member of a group will take a turn playing Socrates, while the other two record and observe the conversation. The

impersonation should last fifteen minutes—no matter how many people you need to talk to! Remember: Socrates was put to death for his behavior. Don't let it get that far! If people don't want to talk to you, do not try to force them. Explain that you're completing a class project. If they do not want to participate, you should leave them alone!

Report:

There are two components to your report:

1) You must provide me with access to your conversations. Audio and video recording devices are available through Media Services (in the library).
2) You should also provide an account of whether or not you think being "Socratic" can help us to live the examined life. Be sure to consider the claim that Socratic encounters might help *the person imitating Socrates*, as well as the view that these encounters might help those on the receiving end of Socratic questioning. (500 words)

The assignment is provided at the beginning of the semester in the syllabus and must be completed in the first six weeks of the course. A follow-up assignment is given toward the end of the semester, when students must *again* "be Socratic" but are asked to do so in a way that suits their individual personalities and requires them to take up topics they find interesting and important. The follow-up Socratic exercise also takes place in a public forum: Hartwick's First-Year Seminar Showcase, which occurs at the conclusion of the first semester. At the showcase, students from various first-year seminars present the work they have done and what they have learned during their courses. My students engage with representatives from these courses "Socratically," asking them questions about their work, trying to encourage an "examined life." Following this exercise, students are once again asked to write a report on whether or not their activities helped to facilitate an "examined life."[5]

Fifty-two students completed this exercise over three iterations of the course. Ninety percent of the students turned in video or audio recordings, with the number of students doing so increasing in each successive year. First reports on the exercise revealed a large number of students reporting that the experience of impersonating Socrates was a valuable exercise; second reports on the follow-up exercise showed 100 percent of students reporting some benefit from engaging in the exercise, and a smaller number reporting newly perceived benefits from *both* occasions of participating in the exercise.

As with any self-reporting activity, the results here are questionable. Students are certainly more likely to report positive outcomes in such exercises when they believe that such reports will result in higher grades. To combat this predictable result, the assignments were graded on a pass/fail basis. Nevertheless, such effects cannot be eliminated completely. Students may well (and some undoubtedly do) aim to cultivate favorable impressions with their faculty and hence may well report positive benefits when they think they experienced none.

For this reason, having the actual video footage is invaluable for assessing how students approached the exercise. Perhaps even more valuable, however, are *negative* reports. Approximately 30 percent of first reports received expressed skepticism that the exercise was worthwhile, with students citing a variety of perceived problems. Some complained that they learned nothing from the experience because they could not get people to participate in the questioning. A more common complaint was simply that engaging in the exercise did not help *the student* live an examined life (such complaints seldom considered whether or not Socratic questioning might help *others*). The positive reports also varied a good deal. A few students reported simply recognizing how difficult it is to be Socrates, something they regarded as worthwhile (seeing that Socrates was not simply "being a jerk," as one student put it, but was engaging in a kind of thoughtful questioning that required a huge amount of skill).

The second round of reports were even more valuable, particularly comparatively. Once students had reflected on why their previous attempts had failed (when they did) or had been less than fully successful, they were able to adapt their approaches to critical conversation. Crucial in doing this was the recognition that a good Socratic exchange could not involve randomly chosen topics.[6] Recognizing, moreover, that students were more likely to engage in meaningful dialogue about topics that actually *interested them*, and that the benefit of such dialogue could be mutual, produced more meaningful results. Finally, once students recognized that "being Socratic" need not mean being rude to others, or trying to refute them simply for the sake of refuting them, dialogue became less about some specified goal (refuting one's interlocutor; completing an assignment) and more about engaging in a particular kind of process. The original reflections students wrote informed their second Socratic impersonation and hence forced them to reconsider some of the benefits and drawbacks of Socratic questioning they had articulated in their initial reports. Because the entire process was repeated with a second Socratic impersonation and a second reflective component, in other words, the reflection on the experience was far more robust than it would have been *had the exercise ended* after the initial report was written.

Importantly, the Socratic impersonation fits *both* traditional and critical-theoretic models of experiential education. It meets traditional versions of EL because one must apply the method one has studied (Socratic questioning) to people outside of the classroom and then reflect on this application. In addition to the traditional theory-implementation-reflection approach to EL, the Socratic impersonation assignment also emphasizes the *practice* of critical thinking. It does this by charging students with *reasoning with others* (those they question) in a way that requires raising objections, providing reasons, and critiquing dominant views. The assignment meets the critical-theoretic version of EL by cultivating those skills necessary for active citizenship—namely, the ability to assess evidence, consider and raise objections, construct arguments, and critique dominant views—and to do all this in actual conversations. The assignment, like all critical-theoretic EL assignments, attempts to cultivate critical and independent thinking by creating experiences that demand the active use of these skills outside of traditional exams and essays. Given the open-ended nature of the Socratic assignment—the inability to know where a conversation will go or what an interlocutor might say—students must utilize their critical thinking skills in ways that simply cannot be captured in a lecture or even in a normal classroom discussion of a text, where deference is usually given to the instructor's power and point of view. As in the speech of Meletus, there is nothing special about *where* this assignment takes place. It could be in the classroom or out of it, depending on the constraints one places on who can be an interlocutor. What matters, rather, is fostering independent and critical thinking—skills that are essential to being a conscientious and responsible citizen.

I strove to create other assignments that also facilitated such cultivation, aiming as often as possible to ignore any supposed disciplinary boundaries. In another assignment (mentioned above), students used Marxist methods to analyze and critique our college's curriculum, general education requirements, facilities and services, and departmental structures and even their relationships with staff and faculty. The aim of this project was, again, to get students to think with greater depth and clarity about the institutional environment surrounding them—one that structures and shapes their education. This employs critical-theoretic skills without requiring leaving the classroom for some particular location. Students are tasked with applying theory to something that shapes their daily lives and experiences and extends well beyond the course content (in this case, Marxism). Such assignments, in my view, are sufficient to meet the goals of EL yet tame enough to avoid causing problems for those comfortable in a standard "chalk and talk" environment. Of course, there are many ways to instantiate EL that go well beyond the level of the assignment. My aim has been to highlight how the critical-theoretic model of EL makes room for EL even within the classroom.

IV. CONCLUSION

In many ways, my conversion to EL is an instance of EL through critical theory. Reading a smattering of articles on EL, participating in workshops, and designing syllabi intending to implement the vision of my college's president were not enough *of themselves* to bring about any particularly transformative experience. The motivation in such a case was too top-down. It was only when I *experienced* EL in action that I came to appreciate the content of some of the articles I had read.

In my view, what matters in a philosophy education is the development of imaginative and critical faculties. I, for one, do not particularly care if a philosophy major, after graduation, can recite Aristotle's four causes or Kant's categorical imperative. It is far more important, from my point of view, that our majors are more equipped to participate responsibly as citizens. I think philosophy as EL can advance this goal. Responsible citizens, in my view, are not necessarily those who advocate particular positions or views. Rather, responsible citizenship demands the cultivation of independence and critical acumen. In a political and social landscape where advertisement influences what we do and how we vote to a perhaps unprecedented degree, it is increasingly important to help students develop the ability to question the views they are exposed to, the arguments for those views, and the dogmas that tend to entrench them. Based on the model of experiential learning as transactive, interdisciplinary, and embodying critique, philosophy can fit the bill as much as it did when Socrates stood before his jurors on that fateful day in Athens some twenty-four hundred years ago.

NOTES

1. The divergent models of EL have been usefully explored by a number of authors (see, e.g., Fenwick). For publications specifically on *philosophy* and experiential education, as opposed to those on the varieties of models of EL across disciplines, one can consult www.engagedphilosophy.com.
2. From the Hartwick College Mission Statement.
3. See works by Friere, Hahn and Flavin, and Shor, as well as Brookfield's *The Power of Critical Theory*.
4. A talking circle involves arranging the class into a circle in order to facilitate discussion and interaction.
5. The second reflective component of the exercise was only implemented in the second and third iterations of the course.
6. Seeing footage of students asking other students randomly about the meaning of "piety" was often an occasion for laughter and always an occasion to witness failure.

WORKS CITED

Allison, Pete and Eva Pomeroy. "How Shall We 'Know'? Epistemological Concerns in Research in Experiential Education." *The Journal of Experiential Education* 23:2 (2000): 91–8.

Brookfield, Stephen. "Against Naïve Romanticism: From Celebration to the Critical Analysis of Experience." *Studies in Continuing Education* 20:2 (1998): 127–42.

———. *The Power of Critical Theory: Liberating Adult Learning and Teaching*. San Francisco: Jossey-Bass, 2005.

Carver, Rebecca. "Theory for Practice: A Framework for Thinking about Experiential Education." *Theory and Practice of Experiential Education*. Ed. Karen

Warren and Denise Mitten. Boulder: Association for Experiential Education, 2009.149–158.

Dewey, John. *Experience and Education*. New York: Free Press, 1997.

Engaged Philosophy: Civic Engagement in Philosophy Classes. www.engagedphilosophy.com.

Fenwick, Tara. "Expanding Conception of Experiential Learning: A Review of the Five Contemporary Perspectives on Cognition." *Adult Education Quarterly* 50.4 (2000): 243–72.

———. *Learning through Experience: Troubling Orthodoxies and Intersecting Questions*. Malabar: Krieger Publishing Company, 2003.

Friere, Paulo. *Pedagogy of the Oppressed*. New York: Continuum, 1970.

Hahn, Kurt and Martin Flavin. *Kurt Hahn's Schools and Legacy*. Wilmington: Middle Atlantic Press, 1996.

Itin, Christian. "Reasserting the Philosophy of Experiential Education as a Vehicle for Change in the 21st century." *The Journal of Experiential Education* 22.2 (1999): 91–8.

Shor, Ira. *When Students Have Power: Negotiating Authority in a Critical Pedagogy*. Chicago: University of Chicago Press, 1996.

7 Implicit Bias, Race, and Gender
Experiential Learning and Dual-Process Cognition

Dan Yim

Studying philosophy can be a transformative learning experience. I aim to articulate how experiential learning in philosophy courses can contribute to student development by examining and then challenging the conception of the self we tend to assume when teaching philosophy. My goal will be to show that if we complicate the standard story of the mind that undergirds the Socratic project of self-knowledge, we generate a conception of the self that shows it to be replete with hidden biases and the tendency to stereotype. If we acknowledge this, then we find that we need innovative curricular methods to genuinely contribute to student transformation and personal development.

In this chapter, I briefly describe how students typically understand their own agency and mental representations. I then show that there are good empirical reasons to challenge this story by presenting some of the psychological data on implicit bias and stereotyping that lead to a more layered portrait of agency and mind. Next I show how certain experiential learning pedagogies are highly effective in addressing these issues in the philosophy classroom. Recent social science research suggests that experiential learning techniques can modify persistent judgments such as implicit biases. While the chapter highlights methods that are particular to a course I teach called PHI220: Philosophies of Race and Gender, the justification and strategies are generalizable to a wide range of philosophy courses.

I. THE STANDARD CONCEPTION OF THE MIND

In the fifth century BCE, Socrates famously promoted the Delphic maxim to "know thyself." His philosophy is a call to pursue self-knowledge above all else. What seems to be a simple injunction to self-knowledge is part of the Socratic goal of rational self-mastery. To know oneself is to know one's interior life of beliefs, moral and intellectual virtues, vices, and habits—in short, to know one's own psychological and epistemic character. From that knowledge comes the power of responsible agency, of rational self-determination.

This power is distinctively human and therefore to the classical mind-set the most desirable state of a flourishing life.

Regarding intellectual virtue, the Socratic dictum means apportioning judgment to the best and most appropriate evidence. This involves knowing not just one's beliefs and evidential bases but also one's metacognitive habits. This requires vigilance against weak evidence and against the varieties of bias that affect the epistemic credentials of judgment. The irony of the demise of Socrates is that he was put on trial and then put to death by fellow Athenians who were operating on stereotypes of philosophers and biased, ill-justified associations about Socrates's character.

The story is a familiar way to initiate the philosophical imaginations of undergraduates, not only for its narrative power, but also for its emblematic value. Socrates's great injunction is alive and well in philosophy education today. Courses that introduce undergraduates to the study of philosophy still promote the virtues of rational self-mastery through self-knowledge. While the value of the educational project of rational self-mastery has endured the test of time, the psychological assumptions that license inferences about the acquisition of self-knowledge are drastically different. As is common in our species' investigation into matters of human behavior, things are more complicated than we thought.

This standard conception of the mind implies that a rational agent is transparent to herself with a unique authority on the contents of her own mind. In light of such a theory of mind, the traditional educational methodologies that promote the Socratic dictum to rational self-mastery of course include all the objectives pertaining to critical thinking. These traditional philosophical pedagogies and assessment methodologies function using the assumption that because the rational agent has special epistemic access to her own mind, a student merely needs to be able to describe and practice the properties of good thinking and rationality, and her beliefs and attitudes will be better justified. Once she understands the definitions of these virtues and vices, the application to her own mind will follow naturally.

II. THE COMPLICATED STORY

In recent years, these standard conceptions of the mind and decision-making have been complicated by psychological research revealing the complexity of our mental lives. A helpful way to initiate students into the complicated story of mind is to have them study the dual process theory of cognition.[1] Psychologists Keith Stanovich and Richard West have named these dual processes System 1 and System 2 (Stanovich and West 658), and Daniel Kahneman popularized this description of the mind (Kahneman 698–9).[2] System 1 is almost always on autopilot, accompanied by sensations of neither agency nor effort. The kinds of automatic actions attributed to System 1 include detection of the distance of objects in a visual field, spontaneous bodily orientation toward a loud noise, facial reactions in response to emotion-evoking stimuli, threat detection, and spontaneous memory retrieval (e.g., completing the phrase "2 + 2 = ?" or "The capital of the USA is . . ."). This list showcases the range of innate cognitive reflexes and distinctive cultural knowledge acquired through experience, practice, and stability of memory association. Essentially, the characteristic activities of System 1 are involuntary, automatic, and very fast in their delivery of information to the agent.

System 2 operations are diverse but unified by one feature—the activities are attention-intensive and thus are typically associated with voluntary activity. These are slower and more methodical than System 1 operations because they require uninterrupted effort that is easily disrupted by distractions. Some typical System 2 activities include, in order of ascending complexity: bracing for a starter pistol in a race, scanning a large crowd to locate a particular person wearing a blue hat, sifting through one's memory to match the song on the radio with its proper name, parallel parking on a crowded city block, self-monitoring one's social behavior at an office party to make sure no lines of propriety are crossed, and assessing the cogency of inferential relations in a complex argument. Each of these scenarios requires the agent to pay steady attention to the content of the mental operation in order to maximize chances of a beneficial outcome. These System 2 experiences of deliberation, conscious effort, and agency are typically identified with "the mind" or "the self" in the folk-psychological perspectives of many operating under the old, standard conception of the mind that we inherited from the early modern philosophical psychologies.

System 1 sorting mechanisms are deeply and intuitively involved in *social cognition*. System 1 delivers powerful, spontaneous behavior-guiding impressions that are often based on stereotypes and favoritism biases (e.g., favoring one's racial group, religious group, social group)—mostly beneath the conscious awareness of the agent feeling the impressions (Banaji and Greenwald 2013 54–61). A simple example of an unconscious favoritism behavior is selecting a seat on a bus away from a disfavored individual. This occurs instantly and unconsciously with no conscious deliberation. One simply sees a particular seat as desirable and another as undesirable. If one were to use System 2 to generate a self-report for the choice, one would *not* report a stereotype like: "I avoided person P because P is of racial group B, and B is associated in my memory with criminality and danger." However, it is possible that a behavior of seating choice indeed operates according to System 1 stereotypes and biases, despite a lack of awareness and claims to the contrary.

A general phrase for behaviors such as sitting on a bus is "implicit social cognition," and it occurs instantaneously to deliver action guidance about every range of human interaction in every social category imaginable. The distinction between System 1 and System 2 is a helpful way to show how social biases can affect behavior in a range of important social contexts that involve categories such as gender and race. Stereotypes and biases exist in System 1 processes, not typically in System 2 reflective judgments. Because the prevalent folk-psychological theories of mind identify the self and its agency with System 2, most do not acknowledge their ownership of stereotypes and biases, much less any actions that possibly flow from them.

III. THE IMPLICIT ASSOCIATION TEST (IAT) AS EXPERIENTIAL LEARNING

In the 1990s, social psychologists Banaji and Greenwald coined that phrase "implicit social cognition" and later generated a psychological test aimed at measuring the strength of implicit stereotypes and biases in System 1 and their variances from explicit beliefs and self-reports in System 2 (Banaji and Greenwald 1995 4–7, 2013 32–52). With respect to categories of race, gender, and sexuality, this new kind of test was designed to reveal whether a subject harbored an implicit preference or favoritism toward particular groups, a preference that was at odds with the subject's self-report about her egalitarianism. Their hypothesis, confirmed by research, was that self-reports cannot accurately measure the customary, implicit associations that are used by System 1, just as a self-report about bus-riding seat choices cannot accurately measure implicit social cognition, stereotyping, and biases.

Consider for example the way threat detection processes in System 1 can be affected by stereotypes and bias. In a famous case from 1999, New York police fired forty-one shots, killing unarmed West African immigrant Amadou Diallo when he reached for his wallet to show his identification. Events tragically similar to this are well-represented in the news in the years since. Researchers have suggested that there is a significant connection between implicit racial biases and heightened threat sensitivity (Correll et al. 1324–8). What is even more troubling is that behavior-implicating bias may be the default state unless extreme vigilance is applied (Payne 190–1).

How can we as philosophers address these issues? In my course, one of my aims is to use experiential learning (EL) to educate students about dual-process models of mind and the ways that stereotypes and implicit biases invisibly reside in System 1 processes. One of the biggest challenges is to convince students that this more complicated story of decision-making is *possibly* true. It is not that they are totally closed to the idea. It is rather that their skepticism comes from limited experience with their own biases and a consequential default allegiance to something like the standard Lockean perspective on the mind. This is understandable; after all, why should these twenty-year-olds endorse something they have never or only very rarely personally experienced, much less even heard of?

In order to open their minds to the more complicated story, I use a combination of three activities. First, they read a lot about dual process models of mind.[3] Second, they read a lot about Banaji and Greenwald's Implicit Association Test (IAT).[4] Third, I provide experiential learning opportunities at several different times through the course, in order for the students to recognize their own hidden biases. This particular combination is useful because it requires voluminous technical reading and critical thinking/discussion, plus readings in social science, and experiential learning opportunities.

The students in my course take the IAT. The IAT has many versions, but they all have in common the detection of System 1 implicit, attitudinal associations. Perhaps the most famous versions are ones that measure racialized bias, which I require my students to take. The task is essentially a combination of a sorting and pairing assessment. There are two sorting tasks. First, the test taker must sort a series of faces that flash on a screen as either "African-American" or "European-American"—basically, black versus white. Second, the test taker must also sort words flashed on the screen that are judged to be "good" versus ones that are "bad." These are words such as "joy," "happiness," "rage," "failure," etc. Category one is a racial description; category two is a simple valence evaluation.

The next task is one that involves pairing these two categories. The pairing task measures whether test takers are faster at pairing a racial categorization with a particular valence. For example, is a test taker faster at pairing a positive valence (e.g., "pleasant") with white faces or black faces? If so, then the possible implication is that such a test taker implicitly associates negative words or concepts with black faces more readily than white ones. There are four possible pairings: black-bad, black-good, white-bad, white-good. The measurement of bias is called a "D score," which measures how much faster test takers pair together black faces with negative valences than with positive ones or white faces with positive rather than negative valences.

Perhaps the best way to think of the IAT in the context of a philosophy classroom is that it is an experiential learning exercise that takes implicit and therefore invisible social biases and brings them into the daylight so that they can be addressed. The particular IAT I use explicitly polls the students' implicit System 1 processes of social cognition of racial identity. System 1 polls memorial connections between racialized categories like black and looks for weightier connections to valence categories that have been reinforced into their memory. The sources for memory reinforcement can come from anywhere in the agent's experience, including a whole lifetime of possibly biased news media, passive and active inculcation of one's regional values, a lifetime of exposure to entertainment media and American advertising, etc. This is all the more daunting in that these associations start to embed in children's social cognition as early as age three (McGlothlin and Killen 629–32).[5] System 1 looks for the weightier associations, and it does not care about careful analysis of the actual causal relationships between categories and valence; it cares mostly about a strong sense of memorial correlation.

Most students are shocked when they discover that there is a pervasive variance between their System 1 implicit associations that display negative implicit racial biases and their System 2 self-reports about their egalitarian values. This use of the IAT inevitably results in an uncomfortable phenomenological gap between the immediate judgment of System 1 and the conviction of System 2 that they are not the kinds of people who exhibit racist or prejudiced behaviors. This divided mind-set prior to full awareness is called dissociation (Devine 6–7, 15–6). It refers to the existence of mutually inconsistent ideas, attitudes, beliefs, associations, etc., that are isolated from one another yet in the same mind.

It is this pervasive variance that is difficult for students to accept, and merely reading about its possibility is not that convincing. However, when students take the IAT over and over again with the same result, they enter into a different cognitive phase. They move from their dissociations between System 1 and System 2 to a state of cognitive dissonance in which the students are consciously aware that there is a persistent conflict between System 1 and System 2.

A new awareness of the existence of these implicit associations is disturbing to students for three reasons. First, for many it is the first time that they are confronted with the possibility that they bear some prejudices that may be affecting their behavior. Second, this is shown to occur outside of the range of their traditional self-conceptions as autonomous agents. Third and most punishing, System 1 stereotypical attitudinal associations drawn from repetitive, past associations are slow-learning. Their output can change but only very slowly, with extreme effort, and sometimes never at all (DeCoster and Smith 119–22, McClelland, James L., Bruce L. McNaughton, and Randall C. O'Reilly 436–8). It can be overwhelming to experience the conflict between what one explicitly claims to believe versus one's actual implicit endorsements of racialized stereotypes. Cognitive dissonance is occurring, and precisely because it is so uncomfortable, it is also pedagogically promising. It is promising because students report that they would rather know than not. They testify to the power of the Socratic dictum—"Know thyself"—only now in the context of the more complicated story of the mind.

IV. EXPERIENTIAL LEARNING EXPEDITIONS

At this point in the course, class conversations about theories of race, gender, and sexuality typically turn to questions about whether it is even possible to recognize and change these largely implicit associations. The more forward-thinking students are especially interested in how to foster future environments and experiences to mitigate the pervasive enculturation and maintenance of these kinds of implicit, biased associations. One student of mine wrote to me just recently about her experience in the course, "I have learned that it is extremely hard to get rid of these implicit association biases. I've also learned that just being aware of them is a big step. Because I've become aware of these concepts, I've learned to notice when I have them and work against them."

This new awareness and openness can be secured through the relatively simple and repeated applications of the IAT. It is even more effective when combined with the creative use of experiential learning (EL) strategies. Providing an adequate overview of EL is not in the scope of this chapter,[6] but at its most general level, EL refers to a type of experience in which students apply knowledge and skills in a relevant setting. EL puts the student into a learning context that involves direct experience with the content of study more so than just reading about the content.

In my course, after my students spend a month taking IATs and discussing the psychologies of bias, they are ready for an EL expedition. The scale of an EL expedition will vary depending on institutional support. We have an off-campus office located in a local urban neighborhood with a full-time university community liaison whose job description is the creation of EL trips for university departments. These field expeditions vary each time I teach the course, but we have established a menu of community engagement options that range from relatively low-intensity to high-intensity. The distinction has to do with repetition, the time commitment of the event, and the kind of reflective assessment. For example, a low-intensity EL expedition would involve a one-time event such as a two-hour site visit to a K–6 afterschool homework tutoring site where students engage in conversations with K–6 students about their life circumstances. It is designed to be a fun, low-intensity, yet eye-opening time for students to appreciate the challenges that young, urban children in distressed areas face. The reflective assessment may consist of fairly simple journaling assignments. A high-intensity EL expedition would involve perhaps several eight-hour events with a more intense reflective assessment, such as a paper assignment that challenges students to apply their theoretical readings to the EL expedition or a group project presentation that aims at the same.

Here is an example of a mid-intensity seven-hour EL expedition. Our base of operations consists of the off-campus office of the university in the urban neighborhood with which longstanding community partnerships already exist. From that office, the liaison provides an orientation to the community, its demographics, and its history. The liaison explains the planned events for the day and will have already coordinated with community partners to group the students in small clusters with local urban families of all sorts of sociological types from the neighborhood (e.g., single parents juggling multiple responsibilities, immigrant families confronting culture shock, elderly residents of an assisted living facility). Clarity of mission is an important component. The community partners will have been carefully chosen by the liaison because of their interest in the education of college students.

Although an EL expedition can involve components of service learning that one finds in social work curricula, this particular menu is designed around the acquisition of new categories of social cognition for the students in this particular course. Other menus exist for other courses with different aims. In these clusters, they meet in the homes of these families to participate in various mundane activities. One popular EL expedition is to plan meals on very tight budgets and go grocery shopping, negotiating complex public transit needs without recourse to the luxury of personal automobiles. In this expedition, categories of race, gender, and class that these students have been formally studying for several weeks culminate in a generally familiar experience (i.e., grocery shopping) but refracted through a very unfamiliar set of social realities that up to this point have appeared mostly as inert pages of books and articles. The students are acquiring a store of personal experiences, depth of emotional tone, and vivid sensory memories of concepts such as "public transit," "socio-economic food desert," "welfare recipient," "social security," "senior citizen," "single parent," etc. (Hollenhorst, Mackenzie, and Son 78–9). These new experiences become new inputs for association in future System 1 processes that trade in the very categories that otherwise are ripe for stereotypes and implicit biases.

Several principles guide the student encounters with socio-economic and racial difference so that they are effective. First, the experiences are structured so that students must help make decisions that affect actual life outcomes. For instance, they are tasked to help families research things such as food prices, distance to stores that offer healthy foods, and commute times on public transit. They then travel with the families on the train or bus, do the shopping, do the meal planning, etc. This ensures a sense of responsibility and accountability to the concrete material experiences of real persons.[7] In another expedition, students ride public transit to a large urban high school that serves a socioeconomically distressed neighborhood. At this urban high school with a frighteningly high drop-out rate, students get to interact with high school students, talking with them about the various steps that must be taken to apply successfully to college. This is an eye-opening experience for my students, especially the ones who have little experience with underperforming urban high schools. They quickly discover that there are innumerable counter-instances to the stereotype of the lazy, inner-city high school student. They discover, instead, multiple, complex narratives about incredibly challenging home situations (including homelessness), malnutrition and its destructive effects on basic cognitive functioning, lack of easily available information about the most basic college-prep resources, lack of resources and even staffing of high school counselors (e.g., a ratio of two hundred to one), and lack of access to computers. This last one is particularly vivid, especially when I ask my students how their semester would be transformed if they themselves had little to no reliable access to a computer. The goal is again to create new experiences that become candidates for future System 1 processes.

Second, the experience is carefully chosen so that the experiences during the expedition recapitulate the theories and content they have been reading, discussing, and writing about for weeks. The dual reinforcement through lectures on the reading and the new sensory memories gained through the experience are reinforced through reflection assignments that invite students to revisit stereotypes and implicit associations. For example, students write brief reflective journals about the experiential difference between simply reading a description such as "forty-two-minute bus commute" and actually riding the bus for forty-two minutes just to get to a grocery store with affordable healthy food choices. They write journals in which they creatively reimagine their lives as these high-school students with no access to technology. The experience combined with the reflective writing encourages empathic humanization of individuals (Batson 11), merges cognitive and emotional engagement, and encourages critical reflection on stereotypes about urban families and youth.

Third, the EL expedition is tailored to become a data point in future System 1 processes and System 2 reflective assessments of generalizations from old associations. The new experiences prime students to perceive future experiences of human beings in these categories with an expanded consciousness of the more complex web of factors that go into the explanations of life circumstances and prospects.

The goal of the EL expeditions is to help disrupt old patterns of biased implicit associations. Recent social science research suggests that EL techniques can modify implicit biases by engaging students at the point of contact between System 1 and System 2. Several examples are available in research literature. For instance, a shift in social motives reinforced by the EL expedition is a crucial factor. When a student collaborates with a family to plan a week's meals, that experience reinforces different positive associations than, say, navigating to one's vehicle at dusk with the social motive of danger avoidance (Blair 242–9). These kinds of EL expeditions can provide vivid counter-instances to stereotypes that over time can dull the biased associations. Encountering a particular racialized group in the context of a community event, such as a religious or celebratory gathering, reinforces different associations than, say, encountering the same group in the context of law enforcement.[8] EL expeditions can also promote more complexity in the way that particular individuals are typed into categories. A person does not occupy just one social role or category, but simple stereotyping often obscures the multiple roles and categories into which one actually fits. The vivid experiences can encourage the salience of a positive category to overwhelm a negative stereotype. The experiences with families on the expedition can activate "father" or "mother" or additional experiences of commonality over distancing, racialized ones, or at any rate in addition to racialized ones, thereby tempering the negative associations (Banaji, Mitchell, and Nosek 467–8, MacNab and Worthley 80–2).

The pedagogical combination of using the IAT to initiate conceptual receptivity to the pervasive existence of biases and stereotypes, along with using various EL expeditions to provide new concrete experiences for the students, can encourage System 1 associations to parlay with System 2 correctives over time. The IAT and EL together create episodes of cognitive dissonance that hopefully move toward eventual reformation of implicit biases (Filipova and Peters 203–9). Even the cognitive dissonance alone is a great advance in a philosophy pedagogy, since a simple pause or disruption between the stereotypes about certain classes of humans (race, class, or gender) and interpretations of the new concrete experiences derived from the EL expedition can lead to revision over time.

It is too much to hope that one class or even many classes can rewrite System 1 scripts. However, even taking that which is at the level of mere dissociation and raising it to the level of conscious, cognitive dissonance is a great step toward the worthy goal of Socratic self-knowledge. Dismantling the structures that so deeply write the biased scripts for System 1 associations is a long-term project that requires collaboration between educators, activists, politicians, and families. The task is enormous, but the first step is the raising of consciousness. My modest claim is that philosophy can play a critical role in this process, and any hope of tutoring the scripts for System 1 social cognition resides in the inclusion of EL pedagogical tools such as the IAT and carefully designed field expeditions. It is the heart of traditional philosophy, the Socratic charge to "know thyself," and in doing so, the philosophy classroom can become the transformative, life-altering learning experience it is meant to be.

NOTES

1. For an excellent introduction to dual-process theories, see De Houwer and Moors 297–326; see also Carruthers 109–27.
2. See also Kahneman *Thinking* 89–96.
3. In this chapter, I have focused mainly on one brand of dual process model. There are many variants as well as many criticisms. I will not go into detail on the differences here.
4. "Project Implicit," Harvard University, https://implicit.harvard.edu/implicit/iatdetails.html
5. For additional perspectives on the relationships between implicit attitudes and developmental factors, see Banaji and Baron 53–8; see also Degner and Wentura 356–74.
6. For more information on EL, see Chapters 1, 3, and 4 in this book.
7. If this would be too intensive, a modification of the expedition into role play is a less intense substitute. Provide them with detailed "role identities" (e.g., student group A is a single parent household on a fixed income and has the following goals . . .) and task them with the same goals.
8. See the following for further examples and evidence: Bruder, Lenton, and Sedikides 183–96; Allen, Klauer, and Sherman 137–49; Judd, Park, and Wittenbrink 815–27; Bertolo and Kratzke 107–11; Donovan 161–77; Ozorak 97–104.

WORKS CITED

Allen, Thomas J., Karl Christoph Klauer, and Jeffrey W. Sherman. "Social Context and the Self-Regulation of Implicit Bias." *Group Processes and Intergroup Relations* 13.2 (2010): 137–49.

Banaji, Mahzarin R. and Andrew S. Baron. "The Development of Implicit Attitudes." *Psychological Science* 17.1 (2006): 53–8.

Banaji, Mahzarin R. and Anthony G. Greenwald. *Blindspot: Hidden Biases of Good People*. New York: Delacorte Press, 2013.

———. "Implicit Social Cognition: Attitudes, Self-Esteem, and Stereotypes." *Psychological Review* 102.1 (1995): 4–27.

Banaji, Mahzarin R., Jason P. Mitchell, and Brian A. Nosek. "Contextual Variations in Implicit Evaluation." *Journal of Experimental Psychology* 132.3 (2003): 455–69.

Batson, Charles Daniel. *Altruism in Humans*. New York: Oxford University Press, 2011.

Bertolo, Melissa and Cynthia Kratzke. "Enhancing Students' Cultural Competence Using Cross-Cultural Experiential Learning." *Journal of Cultural Diversity* 20.3 (2013): 107–11.

Blair, Irene. "The Malleability of Automatic Stereotypes and Prejudice." *Personality & Social Psychology Review* 6.3 (2002): 242–61.

Bruder, Martin, Alison P. Lenton, and Constantine Sedikides. "A Meta-Analysis on the Malleability of Automatic Gender Stereotypes." *Psychology of Women Quarterly* 33.2 (June 2009): 183–96.

Carruthers. Peter. "An Architecture for Dual Reasoning." *In Two Minds: Dual Processes and Beyond*. Ed. Jonathan Evans and Keith Frankish. New York: Oxford University Press, 2009. 109–27.

Correll, Joshua, et al. "The Police Officer's Dilemma: Using Ethnicity to Disambiguate Potentially Threatening Individuals." *Journal of Personality and Social Psychology* 83.6 (2002): 1314–29.

De Houwer, Jan and Agnes Moors. "Automaticity: a Conceptual and Theoretical Analysis." *Psychological Bulletin* 132.2 (2006): 297–326.

DeCoster, Jamie and Eliot R. Smith. "Dual-process Models in Social and Cognitive Psychology: Conceptual Integration and Links to Underlying Memory Systems." *Personality and Social Psychology Review* 4.2 (2000): 10–31.

Degner, Juliane and Dirk Wentura. "Automatic Prejudice in Childhood and Early Adolescence." *Journal of Personality and Social Psychology* 98.3 (2010): 356–74.

Devine, Patricia G. "Stereotypes and Prejudice: Their Automatic and Controlled Components." *Journal of Personality and Social Psychology* 56.1 (1989): 5–18.

Donovan, Sarah K. "Teaching Philosophy Outside of the Classroom: One Alternative to Service Learning." *Teaching Philosophy* 31.2 (2008): 161–77.

Filipova, Anna and Robert Peters. "Optimizing Cognitive-Dissonance Literacy in Ethics Education: An Instructional Model." *Public Integrity* 11.3 (2009): 201–19.

Hollenhorst, Steve, Susan Houge Mackenzie, and Julie S. Son. "Unifying Psychology and Experiential Education: Toward an Integrated Understanding of Why It Works." *Journal of Experiential Education* 37.1 (2014): 75–88.

Judd, Charles M., Bernadette Park, and Bernd Wittenbrink. "Spontaneous Prejudice in Context: Variability in Automatically Activated Attitudes." *Journal of Personality and Social Psychology* 81.5 (2001): 815–27.

Kahneman. Daniel. "A Perspective on Judgment and Choice: Mapping Bounded Rationality." *American Psychologist* 58.9 (2003): 697–720.

———. *Thinking, Fast and Slow*. New York: Farrar, Strauss, and Giroux, 2011.

MacNab, Brent R. and Reginald Worthley. "Stereotype Awareness, Development, and Effective Cross-Cultural Management: An Experiential Approach." *International Journal of Cross Cultural Management* 13.1 (2012): 65–87.

McClelland, James L., Bruce L. McNaughton, and Randall C. O'Reilly. "Why There are Complementary Learning Systems in the Hippocampus and Neocortex: Insights from the Successes and Failures of Connectionist Models of Learning and Memory." *Psychological Review* 102.3 (1995): 419–57.

McGlothlin, Heidi and Melanie Killen. "How Social Experience Is Related to Children's Intergroup Attitudes." *European Journal of Social Psychology* 40.4 (2010): 625–34.

Ozorak, Elizabeth Weiss. "We All Have to Eat: Experiential Learning in Courses on Food and Hunger." *Journal of Prevention & Intervention in the Community* 41.2 (2013): 97–104.

Payne, Keith B. "Prejudice and Perception: The Role of Automatic and Controlled Processes in Misperceiving a Weapon." *Journal of Personality and Social Psychology* 81.2 (2001): 181–92.

Project Implicit. Harvard University. Web. December 30. 2014.Stanovich, Keith E. and Richard F. West. "Individual Differences in Reasoning: Implications for the Rationality Debate?" *Behavioral and Brain Sciences* 23.5 (2000): 645–726.

8 Cultivating Citizenship

Assessing Student-Designed Civic Engagement Projects in Philosophy Classes

Susan C. C. Hawthorne, Monica Janzen, Ramona Ilea, Chad Wiener

In selected philosophy courses for more than five years, we have assigned a distinctive form of civic engagement project in which students choose, devise, and carry out their own activist or service projects. This paper assesses the project's effectiveness in achieving student learning outcomes in three courses on three campuses. Part I establishes the rationale for using student-designed civic engagement projects, as well as for the assessment project. Part II details the methods used to assess the projects, including pre- and post-course surveys, a qualitative analysis of students' final reflections, and standard course evaluations. Part III reports the results, and Part IV interprets the data. From the congruence of positive reports of student learning across data types, courses, and campuses, we conclude that the project and standard course content together increase student-perceived abilities in citizenship, communication, critical thinking, and practical skills.

I. STUDENT-DESIGNED CIVIC ENGAGEMENT PROJECTS: RATIONALE AND ASSESSMENT

Just as learning scientific experimentation requires doing experiments, many philosophical skills—particularly the philosophical skills and attitudes that will help students become engaged world citizens—are best developed through practice. Important among these are independent and critical thinking skills; the ability to participate in civil dialogue; and attitudes that include respect, empathy, motivated engagement, and recognizing one's own agency as a change-maker. Engaged citizens also need practical skills for follow-through. Traditional philosophy classes excel at teaching reasoning and communication skills, but they do not consistently shift students' attitudes toward reflective civic or interpersonal engagement or toward confidence in their own agency. They rarely help students develop practical skills for effective engagement.

Observing these limitations, the authors began including a student-designed civic engagement (CE) assignment, originally developed by Ramona Ilea, in some of our philosophy courses. Because agency, empathy, and motivation are among the skills and attitudes we wish to foster in our students, our CE assignment asks students to complete a project they identify and plan themselves—one through which they can make a positive difference for an issue or community they care about. The first key feature of this assignment is that we do not choose projects for our students, and we do not set up volunteer or other experiences for them. We encourage students to undertake activist projects—that is, projects that advocate social change rather than provide service—but not all choose this route. The fact that students choose their own projects differentiates our assignment from common forms of service learning. It also helps diminish a long-standing concern with *requiring* CE, which is that such requirements are coercive: they backfire both in terms of developing internal motivation and in terms of forcing particular ideas of the good on students. It's true that requiring CE at all does this to some extent—but then again, so does requiring reading or writing. By giving students a chance to craft their own projects, we embrace the idea that citizenship cannot be devoid of politics, but we do not require any particular political view or stance.

The second key feature of the assignment is its public component, which requires students to practice the philosophical skills of explaining and defending their reasoning and choices. The public component varies by project and institution. Some students advocate for causes on campus, organize a community event, or lobby legislators. Others create and advertise a blog or a video.

Given the differences between the institutions at which we do the project—a technical college in a Minneapolis suburb, a four-year women's college within a St. Paul university that focuses on professional degrees, and a four-year coed college within a regional university in a small town in Oregon—we adapt the key features to our varying courses and student bodies. Technical college students, who are required to work for fifteen hours on this project, have rebuilt and sold a car to benefit a charity, lobbied legislators for funding for people with brain injuries, and worked on international flood relief efforts. The students at the four-year colleges, who are required to spend up to forty hours on the project, have made and sold gifts crafted of recycled materials, donating the proceeds; established an on-campus bike-sharing program; and showed a middle school how to save $30,000 by completing an energy audit with its students. Students sum up their projects in an e-portfolio, where they present the process and results of their work, connect the project to assigned philosophical readings, and reflect on the project's overall effects.

Alongside their projects, students continue traditional reading, writing, and classroom activities. They thereby apply philosophical reasoning in various contexts, with synergistic effects documented by several researchers. For example, H.M. Giebel (2006) found that student volunteers could meaningfully connect their experience and classroom ethics readings. Judith Boss (1994) posited that real-life dilemmas steered service-learning students from preconceptions, helping them achieve greater gains in advanced moral reasoning, moral sensitivity, moral motivation, and follow-through than students studying the same curriculum with no service component. In addition,

Patrick Fitzgerald (1997) found that, relative to students who wrote papers, students who volunteered were more likely to report that their assignment helped them understand ethical issues and social responsibility. The volunteers were also much more likely to report preparedness for social responsibility. Scott Seider et al. (2012) concluded that the positive effects of service learning stem from the explicit content of course materials: in their case, philosophical and theological readings paired with service-learning aiding students to frame the experience as "serving" rather than "helping."[1]

We have used student-designed CE assignments at our various institutions in teaching introductory ethics, environmental ethics, critical thinking, and a course on socially engaged philosophy. Qualitative results have been consistently positive (Ilea and Hawthorne 2010). But because not all studies of service-learning efficacy are positive,[2] and because our CE projects differ significantly from traditional service-learning assignments, we wanted a more systematic assessment of how student-designed CE in philosophy courses affects student learning and development. For this pilot study, we evaluated outcomes in three courses that used our student-designed CE assignment in conjunction with philosophy course content. We developed the primary data sources—pre- and post-course surveys and a qualitative analysis of students' final reflections—and drew as well on standard course evaluations. We hypothesized that students would gain in four areas: (1) philosophical skills, such as ability to reflect critically on their own and others' actions and ideas; (2) communication skills, such as clearly stating their own and others' values and perspectives; (3) citizenship skills, such as motivation and agency for creating change; and (4) practical skills, such as problem solving and time management. All data sources showed strong student perceptions of learning. From the congruence of data across data types, courses, and campuses, we conclude that the project and regular course content jointly improve student-perceived achievement in citizenship, communication, critical thinking, and practical skills.

II. MATERIALS AND METHODS: ASSESSMENT PROTOCOL

We gathered data from an ethics course at Hennepin Technical College (HTC, thirty-seven students), an ethics course at Pacific University Oregon (PUO, twenty-five students), and a specialized course on socially engaged philosophy at St. Catherine University (SCU, seven students). Our primary data comes from: a) assessment pre- and post-course surveys we developed and b) a qualitative analysis of students' final reflections. Because of the relatively small number of students, we pooled the data rather than assessing intercampus differences, except as expressly noted under the Results and Discussion sections below. The protocols were approved by the Institutional Review Boards (IRBs) of SCU and PUO, and by an administrative body at HTC.

Pre- and post-course surveys. Figures 8.1 and 8.2 list the survey questions and allowed responses in the order presented. Pre- and post-course online surveys provided both quantitative and qualitative (narrative) data. Students took the pre-course survey the first or second week of class and the post-course survey during the last week of class. The central questions addressed students' assessment of their gains in critical thinking, communication, practical, and citizenship skills (see Figure 8.2).

No.	Survey questions	Response possibilities
	Pre-course	
1	How would you rank your involvement in community service or activism in the past?	1–6 point scale
	Central questions: See Figure 8.2	1–6 point scale
2	What do you hope to get out of this course?	Narrative
	Post-course	
3	Did you do your civic engagement project as an individual or with one or more students in the class?	Individual/With other students
4	Which of the following settings best describes your civic engagement project?	Volunteer work for an existing group Self-designed project for an existing group Independent self-designed project
5	Which of the following goals best describes your civic engagement project?	Provided a needed service Worked to change a system or institution Other [box for narrative answer]
6	Approximately how many hours did you spend on your project? Include planning the project, doing the project, and writing or creating the work included in your portfolio. Do not include reading, class time, or other assigned writing.	1–10 11–20 21–30 31–40 41–50 50+

Figure 8.1 Pre-course and post-course survey questions and allowed response possibilities, in order presented to students taking philosophy courses with a student-designed civic engagement component. For central questions and responses, see Figure 8.2.

No.	Survey questions	Response possibilities
7	Which of the following best describes the community your project was intended to reach?	Family/Campus/Religious group/ Political group/Nonprofit group not tied to a religion or political party/Local or city/ State/United States/Other nation, international, or global/Other [box for narrative answer]
8	Assess the impact of your project on the community your project was intended to reach.	Strong negative effect/Negative effect/No effect/Positive effect/ Strong positive effect
9	Assess the impact of your project on you.	Strong negative effect/Negative effect/No effect/Positive effect/ Strong positive effect
	Central questions: See Figure 8.2	1–6 point scale
10	Which aspect of the course contributed most to any improvement in your X [*critical thinking/communication/ practical/citizenship* (see Figure 8.2)] skills this semester?	No improvement in X skills Mostly the civic engagement project Mostly the other aspects of the course About equally the civic engagement project and other aspects of the course
11	When you compare your overall experience in this class to other classes you have taken, do you believe you have learned. . .	Learned less/Learned about the same/Learned more
12	Did you change your mind on any values or perspectives you held as a result of the course work or your project?	Yes/No
13	Will you continue work on your project in some way after the semester ends?	Yes/No/Maybe
14	After taking this class, is it more or less likely that you will do civic engagement in the future?	Much less likely/Less likely/No effect/More likely/Much more likely
15	Please describe the impact you think your project had on you.	Narrative
16	Please describe the impact you think your project had on others.	Narrative
17	Please add any other observations or comments you have about your learning in this course:	Narrative

Figure 8.1 (Continued)

Pre- and post-survey central questions: For each [critical thinking/communication/practical/citizenship] skill below, rank your abilities on a scale from 1–6, where 1 = I am uncertain or unable and 6 = I am very able. I AM ABLE TO . . .

	Mean PRE	Mean POST	p value*
Critical thinking skills			
Analyze arguments	4.11	4.87	.5
Understand philosophical theories discussed in class readings	4.00	4.82	.5
Argue for my own values or perspectives	4.50	4.95	.5
Understand other people's arguments for their values or perspectives	4.50	5.08	.5
Critically reflect on my own actions	4.39	5.05	.5
Communication skills			
Clearly state my own values or perspectives	4.47	4.97	.5
Clearly state other people's values or perspectives	3.79	4.84	.000006
Express myself in writing	4.18	4.79	.5
Express myself in speech	4.00	4.55	.5
Communicate with diverse people	4.55	4.92	.48
Practical skills			
Take a project from start to finish	5.24	5.39	.45
Overcome challenges or obstacles	5.03	5.13	.44
Manage time well	4.76	5.05	.49
Be a leader	4.68	5.00	.5
Work in a team	4.92	5.11	.45
Citizenship skills			
Recognize injustices and other social problems	4.49	4.95	.5
Initiate my own civic engagement projects	3.70	4.71	.5
Improve the community	3.76	4.87	.08
See myself as a person who can bring about change	3.84	4.97	.14

Figure 8.2 Central pre- and post-course survey questions presented to students taking philosophy courses with a student-designed civic engagement component, means of pre- and post-course responses, and the statistical significance (p value) of the PRE and POST difference.*

*The p value is calculated from individual students' paired pre- and post-test responses, not from the mean scores. The value should be .05 or lower for 95 percent confidence that students' gains did not occur by chance ("statistical significance"). The small number of paired values (37) makes it numerically difficult to achieve a statistically significant p value.

Qualitative analysis of final reflections. We also performed a qualitative analysis of students' final reflections on their projects. The final reflection assignment required students to evaluate their CE experience in writing. Briefly, students were asked to compare their actual experience with the stated objectives for the assignment. Two readers (Hawthorne and Janzen) independently read all the reflections, examining them to discover themes that illustrated students' own insights and explanations. After jointly determining which themes were significant, the readers separately coded the reflections for each theme, noting "positive" and "negative" instances of each. For example, if a student noted that a form of communication was useful, the readers coded the statement as a positive instance under the theme "Communication"; a report of trouble communicating was recorded as a negative instance under the Communication theme. In addition, the readers purposely sought out comments that evidenced students' relating the project to the philosophical content of their course and criticisms of the project or experience, thus imposing two themes we call "overtly philosophical comments" and "criticism of projects."

Additional data sources. As a crosscheck to our primary data, we gathered information from standard end-of-semester course evaluations at SCU and PUO (no evaluation was administered at HTC). In addition, we drew on results of an online survey administered by SCU's Community Work and Learning program to all students in SCU courses designated as service-learning courses.

III. ASSESSMENT RESULTS

Pre-and post-course survey. Fifty-six students completed the pre-course survey; 44 completed the post-course survey. See Figures 8.1 and 8.2 for questions. Thirty-eight responses were paired for pre- and post-survey analysis resulting in a paired response rate of 55 percent. The paired response rate was similar across schools.

Pre-course survey. Responses to Question 1 indicated that our students did not enter their courses with high levels of involvement in community service or activism. Sixty-eight percent of pre-course survey respondents rated their "involvement in community service or activism" 1 to 3 on a 6-point scale.

To Question 2, a few respondents expressed purely pragmatic goals for taking the course ("get my general ed credit"). But the great majority gave answers such as, ". . . get a better understanding or ethics and to realize different perspectives and a point of view other than my own."[3]

Post-course survey and pre/post comparison. On questions 3–7, students reported a diverse group of projects. Thirty-nine percent worked with other students, 61 percent alone. Most of the respondents volunteered for an existing group (40 percent) or did a self-designed project for an existing group

(37 percent). Only 9 percent reported doing an independent self-designed project. Similarly, 70 percent said that their project was service oriented, while 13 percent reported that their project targeted systemic change. Seventeen percent reported other goals, such as promoting healthy lifestyles. Intended beneficiaries of the projects varied. Family topped the list with fifteen projects.[4] Other common foci included campus and local schools (eight), nonprofits (eight), and local or city issues (seven). Sixty-three percent reported spending thirty-one or more hours on their project; none reported spending fewer than ten hours.

On all the central questions assessing student self-report of critical thinking, communication, practical, and citizenship skills, mean values increased from the pre-course to the post-course surveys (see Figure 8.2). However, only one skill increase—"Clearly state other people's values or perspectives"—was statistically significant at the 95 percent confidence level. Two other reported skill increases—"Improve the community" and "See myself as a person who can bring about change"—approached statistical significance. In addition, the difference between pre- and post-course means was large (>1 on the 6-point scale), although not statistically significant, for the citizenship skill "Initiate my own civic engagement projects." In the area of practical skills, the differences in means of the pre- and post-groups were small (<.33 on the 6-point scale).

Question 10 asked students to indicate the source of any skill improvement. Fifty-two percent of those who reported improvement in critical thinking skills said that the CE project and the other aspects of the course contributed about equally. For communication skills, that number was 57 percent. For practical skills, the number was equally divided between "mostly the civic engagement project" and "about equally the civic engagement project and other aspects of the course," with the two totaling 93 percent of respondents who felt they had improved. For citizenship skills, the totals in those categories were the same (93 percent), though more answered that improvement stemmed from the combination of the CE project and the traditional course features.

We also gauged students' overall course experience. On Question 9, 46 percent of respondents reported that doing the project had a strong positive effect on them personally, and an additional 50 percent reported a positive effect. On Question 12, 74 percent reported that they had, as a result of the course work or their project, changed their mind on a value or perspective they had held. Ninety-eight percent also said that the projects had positive or strong positive effects on the communities they were intended to reach (Question 8). In narrative descriptions of the personal impact of the project (Question 15), most students gave examples of positive effects on their degree of civic engagement or their thinking, listening, or planning skills. For example, students wrote, "This project impacted the way I think about people and the needs f the people. . ."; "i learned to listen to all ideas before making judgement hence avoiding dogmatism. . ."; and

"I think I learned how to prepare further into the future and plan a project from beginning to end."

Looking to the future, 57 percent said that they would continue their project in some way at semester's end, 28 percent indicated "maybe," and 15 percent of respondents said they would not do so (Question 13). On the more general Question 14, 46 percent and 35 percent, respectively, reported that it was more likely or much more likely that they would do CE in the future, while 13 percent reported that the class had no effect and 6 percent that the class made it less likely that they would do CE.

When asked, at Question 11, to compare their learning in their CE course with that in other courses, 74 percent of students reported they had learned more; 9 percent said they learned less. Narrative "observations or comments" were almost all positive. For example, "I really dig the class, what is taught, how it helps younger people start taking an actual look at the world and gets people to start thinking about and visualizing the world they want to live in." Of those with less-positive responses, two observed that they had learned nothing. One said, "Almost everyone i talked to waited until the last minute to do their project."

Additional data sources: Standard course evaluations. The SCU response rate on standard course evaluations was 100 percent; PUO's was 80 percent. Narrative comments echoed those on the surveys and final evaluations. All SCU students took the course to fulfill a distribution requirement; PUO's rate was 57 percent.

Additional data sources: St. Catherine University Community Work and Learning Survey (CWL). Six of the seven SCU students responded to the CWL evaluation. Five of the six agreed or strongly agreed that their CE projects enriched their educational experience. The five also reported examining beliefs, reflecting on leadership, better understanding social justice, and developing time-management skills.

Qualitative analysis of final reflections. We analyzed the final reflections of all SCU and HTC students and 80 percent of PUO students.[5] In these reflections, we identified eight themes and purposely sought out ("imposed") instances of two others themes. See Figure 8.3 for the themes and the number of instances of each.

Many instances of the "Motivation" theme were project-specific, such as ". . . encourage students to consider and hopefully attend college post-graduation." Others rooted motivations in their own experience: "The reason why I chose to help out in a elementary school was partly due to my own early education experience. During my elementary school education I really struggled with reading, writing, and math. . .." Other students professed more general goals, such as getting more involved in community, or drawing connections from philosophic thought to the proposed project.

The "Awakenings" category includes expressions of insight and personal growth. Several students shared a newfound gratitude: "From this project

Theme	Positive instances	Negative instances
Motivation	14	0
Awakenings/insights	43	1
Values in action	9	0
Relationship/community/connection	19	5
Communication	17	5
Work skills	7	2
Disappointments, frustrations	12	0
Overlapping category (Disappointment + Work, negative)	18	0
Imposed themes		
Overtly philosophical comments (e.g., naming a philosopher or school of philosophy)	16	0
Criticism of projects (negative instance = praise of project)	5	3

Figure 8.3 Themes identified in students' final reflections on their civic engagement assignment, and the number of times that theme occurred in the final reflections. "Positive" occurrences indicate that the student reported an instance of the experience, value, or skill named by the theme. "Negative" occurrences indicate that the student reported experiencing the converse. The two imposed themes are those the analyzing readers sought, as opposed to discovering them on reading.

I kind of realized how lucky I am to even be going to college." Some said they became aware of their own capabilities: "I grew as a leader and began feeling more comfortable in an authoritative position. . ." Many became more aware of social or human conditions: ". . . I didn't know that there were that much people that came to the Salvation Army to eat." Others noted benefits of volunteering or taking action: "Neither of us had ever volunteered before or done anything like this, but it was a great new experience." A few expressed change or enrichment of their own values as a result of the projects: ". . . I found that I really enjoyed spend the quality time with [my daughter] every night. . ."

The "Values in action" theme consisted of statements that a student had acted on a value s/he already held. For example, a student doing volunteer lacrosse coaching tied her project to the role of sports in ". . . teaching fundamental abilities and characteristics such as teamwork, hard work, integrity, commitment, reliability and so on," and a student who chose to spend time with a boy with an absent father observed, "By spending time with [A], I hope to touch base on a few of my own ethical values. Kindness, Understanding, Life, and happiness are just some that come to mind."

Many students commented on ways they formed or deepened relationships, interpersonal connections, or community. The comments we labeled "negative" in the "Relationship/connection/community" category uniformly expressed students' regrets that they had not done more to establish connections, whether getting more people involved in their project or restructuring the project to work more directly with beneficiaries. Among the positive comments, the importance of developing personal relationships stood out. One student observed, "By eating with [the homeless people], you were able to gain connect and that is something a lot of people miss out on." Several others observed more generally that forming connections was important: ". . . volunteerism is something that is necessary. . . to keep people engaged in their communities, and to build relationships with others. . . ."

As with the "Relationship" theme, the negative comments in the "Communication" theme pointed toward missed opportunities—in this case, lost chances to ask questions or to reach out to others about the students' projects and their goals. Several students, however, commented that communication was easy: spreading word of their project via fellow football players, for example. Others noted, in various ways, that communication is an important responsibility: one student acknowledged that he had miscommunicated with teachers he worked with and described how he sorted out the resulting difficulties.

Only a few students commented on work-oriented or practical skills. Most of the commenters claimed that they had gained organizational skills. Other skills mentioned by at least one student included speaking, social, leadership, delegation, and teaching.

What one reader coded as "Disappointments, frustrations," the other coded as "negative" instances of work or practical skills gained. Because of the consistency of this coding difference, we report an overlapping theme with eighteen instances. A few "disappointed" students wished they had taken on a more ambitious project. Wrote one, "With this being my first semester of college I didn't know if I would have been able to give everything I had to the make the [project] happen. Now I do think I could have done it." A second type of disappointment was to wish that they had structured the project differently. One wrote, "I would have also liked to do more legislative work. I think that this is key in helping get more resources for people who are homeless." The most common disappointment was students' recognizing that their project would have been better if they had started earlier, planned more carefully, or better anticipated roadblocks.

We purposely sought criticisms of the projects. However, few students criticized the assignment itself, and three of the five retracted the concern. One said, "The Civic Engagement Project was kind of a bummer at first, but once you get your idea and get rolling on it, it isn't so bad. Would I like to do one in all of my classes? No, But it was not a Terrible experience." The three with general praise all expressed the same basic point: In the words of one, "I think it is much easier to learn when you apply the concepts you learn in class to real life."

The imposed "Philosophy" theme was defined by specific reference to philosophy, ethics, a specific philosopher, or school of philosophy. Many comments under this theme tied theory to the project: "My project also relates to Utilitarian ethics. . . I am doing the greatest good because I am working to solve the problem of pollution and global warming. . ." Others found challenges in the philosophy. "The question is why do some people have all [Nussbaum's ten] capabilities and other's don't?"

IV. DISCUSSION: RESULTS INTERPRETATION

Prior to this pilot study, we hypothesized that completing courses that combined the study of philosophy and student-designed CE projects would help students develop some of the cornerstone skills of citizenship: critical thinking, communication, practical, and citizenship skills. The data supported our hypothesis; means increased on post-test paired data in all areas assessed, although most of the changes were not statistically significant. The gains in "citizenship skills" were particularly strong, especially student-rated ability to "Improve the community" and "See myself as a person who can bring about change." Many students expressed increased awareness of ethical and justice issues, and nearly three-quarters stated that they had changed their mind on an issue—a strong indication that they are engaging with issues and thinking critically about them.

In addition, a strong majority of students expressed satisfaction and a positive outcome of the courses and the CE projects on the course evaluations at SCU and PUO and the Community Work and Learning program evaluation at SCU. While these findings do not demonstrate any educational effects with certainty, the trends in the data and the coherence among the data sources suggest that the courses had positive results for a strong majority of students. Given that the results of any single course should not be expected to be strong, these trends are encouraging.

Strengthening the broad applicability of these results, students were not highly self-selected. The students were not particularly predisposed to activism or volunteer efforts, as suggested by their reported low levels of involvement in these activities. Nor did they choose the courses as an elective: at all schools, the courses were required for distribution credits, and most students chose the courses for that reason.[6]

Our most complete data set comes from the final reflections of 93 percent of students. Given that our qualitative analysis identified only instances on which the two coders agreed, we more likely underestimated than overestimated the instantiations of any theme. Thus, another trend supporting positive results of our CE assignment is the large number of clearly expressed newly gained insights into personal and community-oriented values, actions, or responsibilities relative to the small number of disappointments and criticisms. One interpretation of this result is that it's an artifact of the assignment: students recognize that expressing insights is part of the job of writing and that expressing disappointments and criticisms might not be strategic at grading time; they attend pragmatically to these norms. But the relative lack of criticism correlates with the positive assessments in other sources. In addition, the disappointments express a rich set of lessons learned. Finally, the insights appear to be genuine and are appropriate to the students' projects: we are able to tie the reflections to individual students and to note consistency with their other work and with their interactions with us and with classmates. Given this background, it seems reasonable to trust the students' words.[7]

Several points suggest that it is the *combination* of studying philosophy and doing a student-designed CE project that provides the educational benefits: first, 74 percent of post-test takers said they had learned more in this course than in their other courses. Second, when asked what contributed to improvements in their critical thinking, communication, and citizenship skills, students tended to attribute gains to the combination of classroom and project work. Third, many students expressed insights that drew on both their CE experience and the vocabulary and philosophical frameworks covered in class. It remains possible, however, that the focus on CE detracts in some ways from a pure academic focus, given that the less positive quantitative results relate to academic and practical skills. Surprising to us was that the least overall change from pre-test to post-test was in practical skills. One reason might have been that the students ranked themselves high on these skills on the pre-test.

Ilea and Hawthorne argued in earlier work (2010) that students' engagement in activism, as opposed to service work or volunteering, has unique benefits for inspiring civic engagement and agency. This may be the case. However, most of the projects our study students undertook were not activist. The projects were, however, self-chosen. Even most of those who volunteered with an existing organization had a significant role in planning and implementing their activities. This feature of the project likely contributes to the marked change in students' assessments of their citizenship skills.

Several aspects of our data require us to interpret our results cautiously. These include lack of a control group; small initial sample size; the smaller paired pre- and post- samples; the possible selection bias of students completing both pre- and post-surveys; and the diversity of projects, courses, and student bodies, which leads to the question of whether we were observing relevantly similar courses on the three campuses. In addition, no tests corroborate the students' reports of skills gained, and we have no way to judge whether the reported changes and commitments to engage in their communities will last. However, the consistency and breadth of alternate sources of data likely mitigates the possibility of selection bias in the paired surveys. To mitigate the small sample size, we continue to survey courses and will report our findings in a future publication. The grouping of the diverse courses would presumably tend to mask trends by variation in responses; the fact that trends survived consistently across the data types suggests that the CE/philosophy study combination had robust positive effects on student learning.[8]

We conclude that pairing student-designed CE projects with classroom study of philosophy helps students gain important philosophical and citizenship skills. In agreement with earlier researchers, we find that the combination helps students achieve more in these areas than does philosophy study alone.

V. CONCLUSION: APPLICATION

Very few of our students will be philosophy majors. Even fewer will go on to graduate study in philosophy. For the great majority of students, recognizing the importance of philosophy means recognizing the ways it can deepen their engagement with their own thoughts, attitudes, and actions and with the thoughts, attitudes, and actions of others. Our results suggest that doing student-designed CE projects helps spark this recognition, often beyond what academic study alone achieves. Our students' reports of newfound insights into values and actions, the importance of community and communication, changes of perspective on issues, experience of personal agency, and satisfaction with their achievements—as well as their reports of the concrete results of their various projects—amply demonstrate that their CE projects helped them recognize the importance of being both thoughtful and engaged. For the few students who choose a philosophical career, the skills gained through CE assignments are similarly well worth cultivating. Finally, our conclusions also contribute to supporting the role of philosophy in a liberal arts curriculum, as growth in citizenship skills is among the primary goals and strengths of liberal arts study. In our complex and crowded world, these skills are greatly needed.[9]

NOTES

1. Scholars across a wide range of fields and courses also report positive results from experiential learning: achieving agency (Rose 1989); improving students' self-efficacy (Giles 1994); increasing positive attitudes toward dementia patients (Yamashita et al. 2013); prosocial reasoning and decision making (Batchelder and Root 1994); increased awareness of issues, commitments to philanthropy and social change, and interest in socially responsible careers (Keen and Kelly 2009). The changes may persist (Youniss 1997) and may shift students' career goals (Jones and Abes 2004).
2. Not all studies of service learning or civic engagement demonstrate learning or changed behavior. For example, Hunter and Brisbin (2000) found volunteering did not consistently change political science students' cognitive skills, attitudes, or political values. Seider et al (2011) found that the link between service learning in college and increased civic engagement after college is tenuous.

3. Throughout, we quote student comments verbatim without noting errors and only edit them to protect the identity of the student.
4. Family-focused projects were allowed only at HTC.
5. Some PUO students who submitted their final evaluations in hard copy did not also submit an electronic version.
6. We do not have data for this section of the HTC ethics course, but historically HTC students report that they take Introduction to Ethics because it is a distribution requirement.
7. In addition to the data presented, we have two additional sources that help us regard the reflections as genuine. First, we get to know much about CE students personally and academically because CE is so labor-intensive in regard to contact hours. Second, Pacific University of Oregon student Max Seiler conducted an excellent study of the civic engagement projects in Ramona Ilea's earlier classes at Pacific University Oregon. His analysis included in-depth interviews with students in addition to surveys.
8. Of course, it is also important to be aware of students for whom the course structure and format do not work. It might be possible to help such students alter their approach to their project or their other course work to improve the experience.
9. We would like to thank the American Philosophical Association for an American Philosophical Association Grant Fund and Pacific University Oregon for a Faculty Development Grant. These grants enabled us conduct the assessment studies we discuss in this chapter and to set up Engaged Philosophy, http://www.engagedphilosophy.com/. We would also like to thank St. Catherine University student Cody Flaherty for help with developing questions for our assessment questionnaires and for improving our website, www.Engaged Philosophy.com. Finally, thank you to Max Seiler (see Footnote 7).

WORKS CITED

Batchelder, Thomas H., and Susan Root. "Effects of an Undergraduate Program to Integrate Academic Learning and Service: Cognitive, Prosocial Cognitive, and Identity Outcomes." *Journal of Adolescence* 17.4 (1994): 341–55.

Boss, Judith A. "The Effect of Community Service Work on the Moral Development of College Ethics Students." *Journal of Moral Education* 23.2 (1994): 183–98.

Engaged Philosophy: Civic Engagement in Philosophy Classes. http://www.engaged-philosophy.com/.

Fitzgerald, Patrick. "Service Learning and the Socially Responsible Ethics Class." *Teaching Philosophy* 20.3 (1997): 252–67.

Giebel, H. M. "In Defense of Service Learning." *Teaching Philosophy* 29.2 (2006): 93–109.

Giles, Dwight E., Jr., and Janet Eyler. "The Impact of a College Community-Service Laboratory on Students' Personal, Social, and Cognitive Outcomes." *Journal of Adolescence* 17.4 (1994): 327–39.

Hunter, Susan and Richard A. Brisbin, Jr. "The Impact of Service Learning on Democratic and Civil Values." *PS: Political Science & Politics* 33.3 (2000): 623–26.

Ilea, Ramona and Susan Hawthorne. "Beyond Service Learning: Civic Engagement in Ethics Classes." *Teaching Philosophy* 34.3 (2011): 219–40.

Jones, S.R. and E. S. Abes. "Enduring Influences of Service-Learning on College Students' Identity Development." *Journal of College Student Development* 45.2 (2004): 149–65.

Keen, Chery and Kelly Hall. "Engaging With Difference Matters: Longitudinal Student Outcomes of Co-Curricular Service-Learning Programs." *Journal of Higher Education* 80.1 (2009): 59–79.

Seider, Scott C., Samantha A. Rabinowicz, and Susan C. Gillmor. "The Impact of Philosophy and Theology Service-Learning Experiences upon the Public Service Motivation of Participating College Students." *The Journal of Higher Education* 82.5 (2011): 597–628.

Seider, Scott C., Susan Gillmor, and Samantha Rabinowicz. "The Impact of Community Service Learning upon the Expected Political Voice of Participating College Students." *Journal of Adolescent Research* 27.1 (2012): 44–77.

Rose, Suzanna. "The Protest as a Teaching Technique for Promoting Feminist Activism." *NWSA Journal* 1.3 (1989): 487–88.

Yamashita, Takashi, Jennifer M. Kinney, and Elizabeth J. Lokon. "The Impact of a Gerontology Course and a Service-Learning Program on College Students' Attitudes toward People with Dementia." *Journal of Applied Gerontology* 32.2 (2013): 139–63.

Youniss, James, Jeffrey A. McLellan, and Miranda Yates. "What We Know About Engendering Civic Identity." *American Behavioral Scientist* 40.5 (1997): 620–31.

Part II

Examples: Experiential Learning Courses

A. Social Change through Philosophy

9 Emergent Learning in Independent Studies

The Story of the Accessible Icon Project

Brian Glenney

> Don't learn to do, but learn in doing. Let your falls not be on a prepared ground, but let them be bona fide falls in the rough and tumble of the world; only, of course, let them be on a small scale in the first instance till you feel your feet safe under you.
>
> —Samuel Butler (104–5)

I. INTRODUCTION

Experiential learning requires that students experience learning for themselves. Learning experiences require risky conditions, where "falls," to use Samuel Butler's metaphor, or forms of conflict and failure, are intrinsic to learning. The "small scale" of the classroom environment mitigates this conflict and failure through a multitude of small risk strategies: "discussion, group work, hands-on participation, and applying information outside the classroom" (Wurdinger and Carlson 2010). By contrast, the "publish or perish" environment of professional academia is viewed as high-risk. This paper describes two independent study courses that simulate aspects of this high-risk academic environment, requiring each student to submit a paper to a conference or journal to pass the course.

My goal in this essay is to show that high-risk learning environments, such as courses with high-risk course requirements, are a form of experiential learning. In this chapter, I argue that this high-risk strategy cultivates more authentic and engaged forms of experiential learning, including elevated discussions in and outside of the class, more collaborative group work with authentic hands-on participation by each student, and life-enriching integration of this learning with one's lived life.

I argue for this claim in Section II by framing this high-risk pedagogy in Thomas Kuhn's theory of conflict and discovery, which I articulate as a theory of emergent learning. In Sections III and IV, I describe the two independent studies, the first one on sensory substitution devices (SSDs), devices that translate the input of one sense, like vision, into another sense, like audition, and the second course on the language and representation of disability. Along the way, I describe how each course opened up avenues of discovery that initiated the origin and promotion of the Accessible Icon Project (AIP), a movement to change the "disability" symbol (the International Symbol of Access, or ISA) from a static, machine-like image to one that is active and embodied to stimulate a public conversation about disability stigma.[1] I conclude in Section V with a brief description of how to implement this high-risk strategy in larger courses.

II. CHAOS, CONFLICT, AND COLLABORATION: THE STRUCTURE OF EMERGENT LEARNING

Thomas Kuhn's widely cited book *The Structure of Scientific Revolutions* (SSR) is a pedagogy treasure trove for high-risk strategies for experiential learning.[2] Kuhn diagnoses the structure of scientific discovery in chaos and conflict and thus provides the basis for its potential re-creation in the classroom:

> The process [of discovery] is the selection by conflict within the scientific community of the fittest way to practice future science. The net result of a sequence of such revolutionary selections, separated by periods of normal research, is the wonderfully adapted set of instruments we call modern scientific knowledge. . . And the entire process may have occurred . . . without the benefit of a set goal. (172–3)

Kuhn maintains that discovery is not goal-oriented; discovery, like evolution, requires certain conditions: a crisis of survival; conflict; random mutation; and finally, adaptation by way of trait selection.

High-risk strategies of experiential learning course design simulate features of a natural evolutionary environment: the learning is not goal-directed but rather emerges as a product of survival in hostile conditions, or at least *perceived* hostile conditions, through evolutionary phases.[3] I found several pedagogical stages mirroring these evolutionary phases in the two courses described below:

> **Crisis of Survival:** The student's grade is totally or largely dependent on a binary determiner: submission of a presentation at a professional conference and/or publication to a professional journal. Without a presentation/publication submission, the student does not "survive," failing the class.
>
> **Conflict:** The student finds professional research sources to include terse and largely inaccessible specialized research papers, awkward academic interactions with experts, experiences of raw critical feedback, and general discomfort of feeling displaced, "in over one's head."

Randomness Mutation: The student discovers new ideas and tries to articulate and defend them, but this is unpredictable and very often untimely, particularly when up against deadlines.

Adaptation: Overcoming these hostile conditions requires "thick skin" for accepting criticism, developing self-confidence in one's ideas, clearly articulating one's ideas, and developing professional authority when presenting one's ideas.

Integrative Learning: Taking the often-abstract ideas that have purchase in philosophical discourse found application in the student's way of life and thought, bringing about a felt revision in the student's overall view of reality.

The first phase of conflict deserves special attention. The student's perception of the crisis of survival is important for discovery of original ideas. Yet, real crisis cannot be a part of the class environment, as protection from such realities is what makes the classroom environment distinct. So crisis conditions are simulated. Behind the scenes, instructors will likely do a significant amount of the professional research work themselves, from finding an appropriate conference/journal for the student to submit their work, locating and integrating relevant literature with the ideas of the student, to helping to prepare the manuscript for submission. The job of the instructor is to take the raw ideas and research of the student and refine it while integrating it with the specialized literature. In addition, instructors should strive to interact with their students as research collaborators, deferring to the students' own interests and abilities, but refrain from controlling the student's research or ideas. Allowing students to follow their rabbit trails and dead ends provides the conditions needed for them to experience the failure and defeat intrinsic to the process of real discovery.

The learning that takes place in these contexts is best described as "emergent," a natural phenomenon of orderly patterns forming under chaotic conditions. The products of emergence are non-teleological and unpredictable but can produce large-scale or exponential change. Emergent learning is the best term to describe the process and product of the following independent study courses.

III. CLASS STUDY 1: INDEPENDENT STUDY ON SENSORY SUBSTITUTION DEVICES

In the summer of 2009, two students enrolled in a monthlong summer independent study course that focused on a technology known as a sensory substitution device (SSD). Invented in the 1970s by Bach-y-Rita, these devices take input from one sense, like vision, and use a computer to process the information so it can be received by another sense, like audition. The vOICe (with letters capitalized that sound out "oh-I-see"), created by Meijer, is a particularly successful example: it receives input from a head-mounted camera and translates luminance contrasts of objects in the world into "soundscapes" or sonified screen shots that a subject hears through headphones and learns to correlate with external objects. Hearing sounds that are correlated with concrete paths (a whoosh-whoosh-like sound) or stair sets (a click-click-like sound) allows those with visual deficits to better navigate their lived environment.

The course provided an opportunity for students to develop their own SSD projects based on their interests and experience. Each student succeeded in producing and presenting a professional paper on the subject of SSDs leading to publications in the conference's *Proceedings*, though there were no textbooks, assigned papers, or lectures beyond the submission requirement.

Crisis and Resolution

A week into the class, both students were acquainted with SSDs and had created a sketch of their initial research projects. Both agreed on the goal of submitting a paper for an Asian-Pacific Computing and Philosophy (APCAP) conference in Tokyo, where the submission date was close to the date on which this class would end. This made the paper submission requirement a felt reality, increasing the anxiety in the students as the realization of the difficulty of their projects and a desire to reach their goal set in.

In response to this anxiety, a meeting was arranged with an SSD researcher at a nearby university with hopes of finding a collaborator to share the burden of programming and/or creating a way to test and measure the effectiveness of an SSD-training technique. However, this researcher had discontinued his work and reported that in four years of research he had not found any significant SSD projects that merited further attention. This produced a deeper sense of panic in the students and myself as the instructor.

To mitigate this panic, I invited students not enrolled in the course to participate as volunteer subjects for ongoing experimental testing of both projects. This put pressure on my students to create small-scale experiments that anticipated the arrival of student volunteers. Having these readily available test subjects stopping by on a regular basis reduced the feeling of the overwhelming scale of the projects and maintained motivation, and because the students were peers, the experiments became more playful and eloquent.

One student project involved creating software for an SSD that sonified color instead of luminance contrast, and it benefitted significantly from this peer interaction. Student subjects provided daily friendly feedback about their experiences, and modifications were routinely made. For instance, the beta version of the color sonification SSD, which we called the "Kromophone," correlated sounds with the hue, saturation, and luminance of colors. But subjects without musical training could not easily distinguish between the different tones. In other words, it was difficult to tell the difference between the unique tone that matched with the color "red" and the one that matched with the sound for the color "blue." In response, the students modified the Kromophone so that more variegated sounds matched with specific colors: red sounded like a trumpet, blue like an oboe, etc. This differentiated the sounds significantly, increasing the ease of users' identification of colors, and hence objects, through sound (Capalbo & Glenney 2009).

The other student project involved developing a more effective training technique for SSDs, which are notoriously difficult to use. The default SSD-training program on the vOICe software familiarized subjects through playing tic-tac-toe on a computer, where the "X" and "O" each have a unique sound that correlates with their location on the screen. We began by finding a way to test how long one might have to play SSD tic-tac-toe before one could be considered to have learned its use. We developed a testing paradigm where subjects trained on SSD tic-tac-toe were then asked to turn off several "touch" lights in a closet as quickly as possible—the quicker the subject completed the task, the more effective the training (Reynolds & Glenney 2009).

Adapting to the Environment

By week three, panic had subsided as the students made noticeable progress on their projects. At this point I felt it was time to enrich the environment by inviting another researcher, local design artist Sara Hendren, to join us in the final stages of testing the devices. Sara has an interest in disability studies but is not an expert in SSDs. Her goal in participating was to document her own experiences with the devices for an art installation on technology and disability studies on which we were collaborating. Her comments helped the students make significant discoveries on their projects and in their own thinking about disabilities and technology. This interaction also provided a framework for thinking about disabilities that eventually led to redesigning the "disability" symbol (ISA).

Sara's comments immediately began to reshape the students' thinking about SSDs. Like other student volunteers, Sara often described her experience of the SSDs, but her descriptions were within the context of disability studies. This new context began to revolutionize the design of both projects and their output as the use of SSDs shifted from a kind of curiosity to a hope to actually improve lives of people with visual deficits. In this regard, the ethos the students worked in evolved from experimental play to a kind of naïve advocacy.

Specific practical changes occurred as well. For one, Sara noted how the SSD tic-tac-toe training, which involved sitting and clicking, did not encourage the active use of the SSD in the touch-light test, which involved

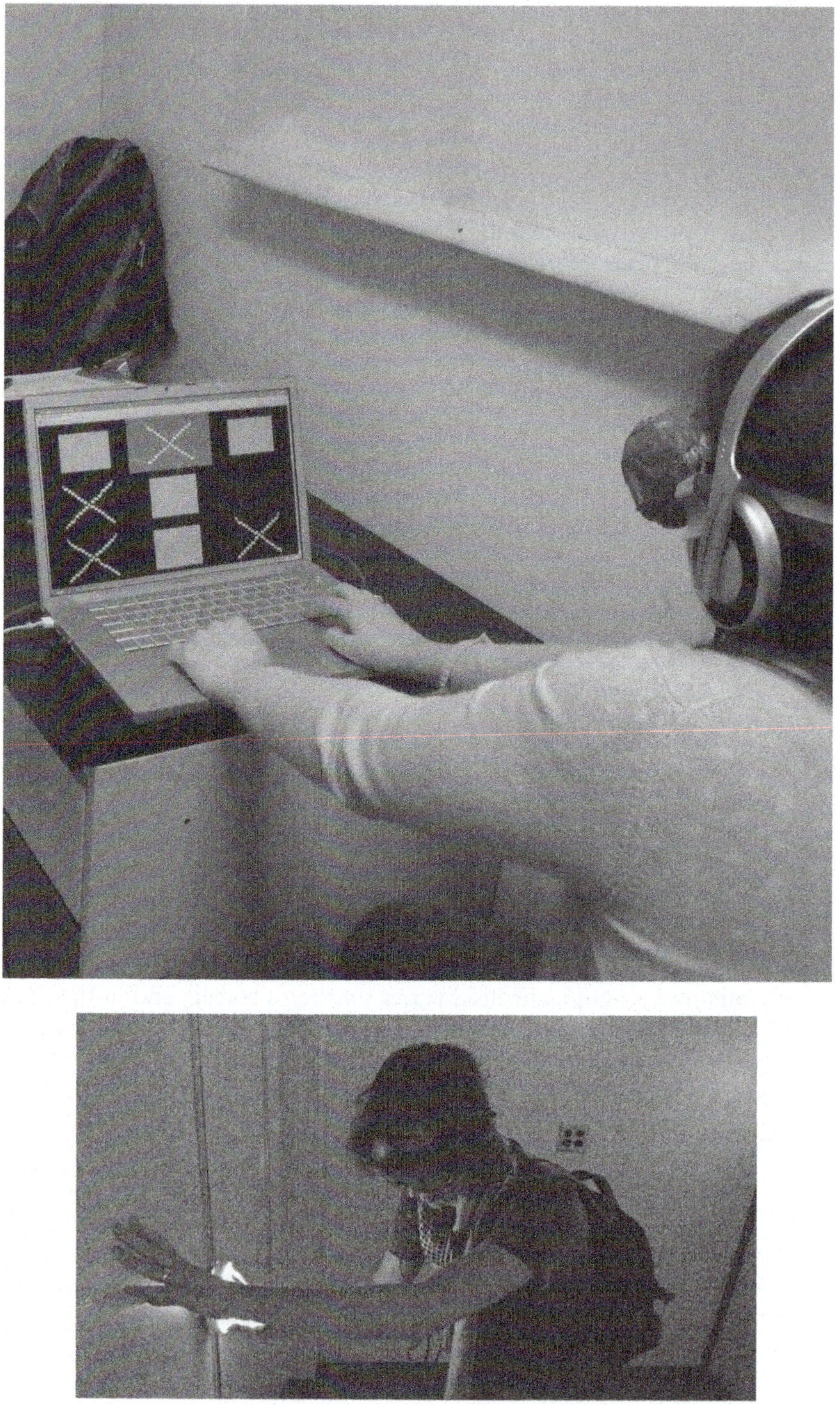

Figure 9.1 A test subject wearing a blindfold and headphones trains using the vOICe's default tic-tac-toe technique. After a specified time, the effectiveness of the training is tested in a timed trial of turning off three touch lights in a dark room.

movement of her entire body. Sara's criticism, along with some original thinking of the students, eventually led to a novel interactive training technique called SSD tag. Two subjects outfitted with SSDs on their heads and touch-lights in the shape of hearts on their chests compete to touch the heart shaped touch-light of the other subject before their own touch-light is turned off by touch. Initial experimental trials suggested that this training technique was twice as effective as the passive tic-tac-toe technique in teaching a subject how to use the SSD program.

In these SSD tag trials, Sara made a further interpretive discovery; as Sara's sight was occluded by the SSD device, her hearing discrimination increased, as did her appreciation for this sense to find her way in a hostile environment. In other words, the SSD helped Sara locate herself within the perspective of people with visual deficits and experience a feature, albeit temporarily and at a very small scale, of their lived world of having a kind of "supersense," a claim supported by the experimental research of Fang, Stecker, and Fine. The students shared these supersense experiences when using the SSD once they were encouraged to attend to this possibility and gained a deeper appreciation of this more positive aspect of living with a visual deficit. This novel positive perspective of people with disabilities led to a further unexpected realization by the students, to which I now turn.

Integrative Learning: Some Conceptions of Disability Are Invalid

In the fourth week, as students finalized their individual projects, Sara documented her experiences using the color sonification SSD and the training

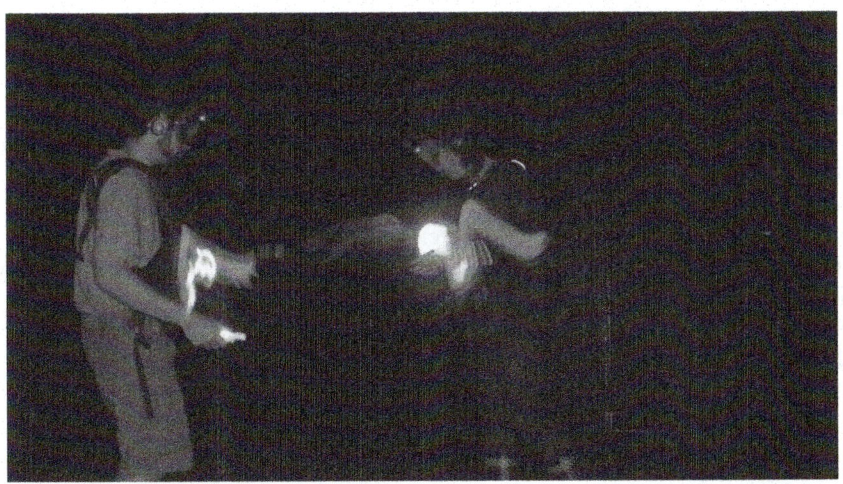

Figure 9.2 A student volunteer (left) and Sara Hendren (right) play SSD tag, an interactive SSD training technique, where subjects race to be the first to turn off the heart shaped touch-lite of their opponent, relying exclusively on the sounds of the SSD to locate their opponent.

technique with drawings of the device, robotic appendages, and clever sensory-based Rube-Goldberg devices. I worked as a behind-the-scenes instructor integrating the student research with specialist literature, helping to write up their projects as professional papers that could be submitted for presentation to the target conference. Also, both students and another student volunteer worked with Sara and me on a video project for our art installation that showed a subject wearing the device navigating his world of color by sound.

As we worked together, the students began articulating a general view about the relationship between technology and disabilities: that technological progress will solve or cure disabilities. This initiated a wonderful discussion on the nature of disability. Sara noted that while most people view disabilities as something to be cured or solved, this conception is invalid. The students, who soon came to agree with Sara, began asking themselves a set of questions without answer: how did we arrive at this "cure"-based view of disability? How is the stigma of disabilities perpetuated? Why is "able-bodied" the paradigm of normal health?

The students' questions and their projects significantly influenced an art installation project Sara and I were working on, which we titled "We Never Asked to Be Made Human." This title captures the implicit bias that to be fully human is to be fully able-bodied and able-minded and also conveys that we did not ask to be heirs to this "ableist" construct. The goal of our art installation was to disrupt this construct, at least in the limited locale and context of the art museum.

The Origin of the Accessible Icon Project

About a month after our installation's premier at the Barrington Center for the Arts in November 2009, the issue of disrupting ableist conceptions of humanity was receiving attention elsewhere. Sara discovered accessibility signage at the Museum of Modern Art in New York City and at a local Marshals store, which portrayed people with disabilities as active and embodied. She posted pictures of that signage, which was created by Brendan Murphy in 1994, on her blog, www.ablersite.org. This symbol signaled a different strategy to disrupt ableist categories, one that reached a broader, more public locality than the college campus or museum.

The next day, I suggested that Sara create a new disability symbol and that we do a kind of street art campaign, whereby we would "replace" old signs in the parking lots with new ones. Soon, Sara and I began placing Sara's first symbol design on accessibility signage in various locations on my college campus, a design that emphasized the person over the disability by only using a figure of a sitting person leaning forward over the old symbol. We then began the long process of creating and implementing a revised symbol that included a wheelchair in motion, which we then placed over the old symbols around Boston in 2010. The progress of this campaign is well documented in various media outlets.

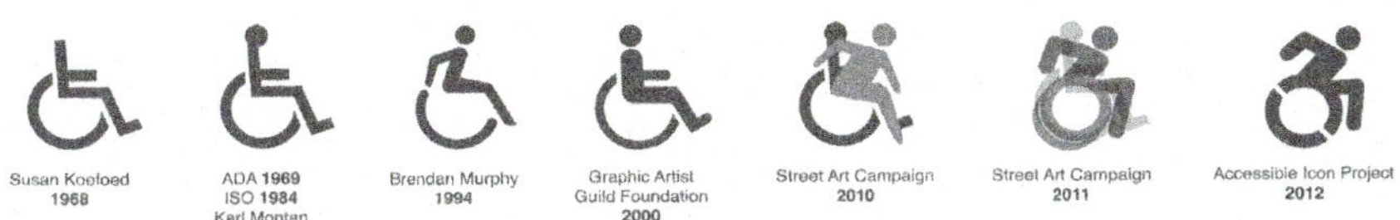

Figure 9.3 This is a timeline of the evolution of the International Symbol of Access. The symbol by Brendan Murphy that is used by Marshall's and other stores became the catalyst for our Accessible Icon Project. Note that the street art campaign began by Sara and myself placing an orange sticker of a seated person over the old symbol; our 2011 campaign used a transparent figure that included orange wheels. In 2012, our colleague Tim Ferguson Sauder standardized our symbol under the guidelines of ISO and we returned to a "safety blue" color (Basken 2013).

IV. CLASS STUDY 2: INDEPENDENT STUDY ON SEMIOTICS

By fall 2012, two local journalists, Billy Baker and Jon Phelps, had covered the street art project for the *Boston Globe* and the *Salem News*. Another article, written by Leah Serao, a student at my college, mentioned data that I had been collecting that suggested there were social effects of the new disability symbol on disability stigma. As the new icon became more prevalent around campus, surveys of students suggested an increase in anxiety about having close relationships with people with disabilities—sharing a dorm room with someone who had a physical disability was viewed with more discomfort. I met with Leah about her article, and after some discussion we decided to do an independent study course with the sole requirement being submitting a paper to a conference on disability.

Crisis and Resolution

Leah felt pressure to pursue my research data on the symbol for her coursework. But her goal was to make an original contribution, and she decided to set out on her own independent project. Leah's own independent research in semiotics uncovered the idea that words are a kind of symbol. This led Leah to a discovery: symbols evolve just as words evolve. She applied this idea to disabilities with an insightful result: just as society has moved beyond words like *cripple* to describe people with physical disabilities, so too must society move beyond passive and machine-like symbols to represent people with disabilities. This insight became significant to the public acceptance of our project to change the symbol, as I describe below.

Leah then sought an explanation for why the "disability" ISA symbol had not evolved when words to describe people with disabilities had. Leah's research on symbols turned up an intriguing explanation from a paper on the ethics of symbols and advertising by Katherine Sullivan. Sullivan argues there that, "Through societal norms, we have grown accustomed to accept images as truth without using the same analytical process to pick apart images in the way we do text" (24). For Leah, this point suggested that society had not changed the symbol because it had not been educated on their interpretation. Thus, in order to gain public acceptance of the new disability symbol, the public needed a brief primer on analyzing symbols.

Adapting to the Environment

Leah began her own survey campaign to both collect information and educate the public about symbols. The basis of the study was to document descriptions from the public of the old symbol (e.g. "static," "passive," "stick figure") in contrast to the new ("forward moving," "active," "person"). Leah presented the results of this survey in her presentation, "Moving Forward: Activating and Evolving the International Symbol of Access," at the University of Tennessee's Disability Issues and Advocacy.

She began her presentation by simulating her survey, collecting descriptions of the two symbols from the audience, and helping them to recognize for themselves (a strategy of experiential learning) the significant meanings that symbols convey. She concluded that the new active-looking ISA should be adopted as it is an expression of a change in attitude—from viewing people with disabilities as passive and needing help toward viewing them as active contributors to society who need extra access because of their activity.

Integrative Learning: Our Symbols Need to Evolve As Our Words Have

From this discovery Leah constructed a way to publicly describe the efforts of the Accessible Icon Project (AIP) beyond the conference itself: just as society adapts to different ways of talking about disability, so too should society adopt different symbols of disability. With this, Leah took a formative role in moving the AIP from a street art campaign to an advocacy project. After the course ended, she participated in a range of interviews with news outlets, using her own ideas to frame the project in a way that reflected AIP's philosophical commitments. As newspapers and magazines continued their stories about our project, the slogan "evolve the symbol as we evolve our words" became a common message. For instance, in my interview by CNN reporter Holly Firfer, the editors chose to have my piece conclude with me stating, "Our symbols need to evolve in the same way that our words need to evolve."

By spring 2014, state legislators in New York were discussing the project in a manner that mirrored this slogan. The parallel between words and symbols was expressed in Bill #A.8193/S.6846 in the State Senate of New York, which endeavored to change *both the language and symbol* of people with disabilities; the word "handicapped" would be replaced with "accessible" and the old, passive symbol would be replaced with our active symbol. On July 25, 2014, New York Governor Andrew Cuomo signed the bill into law.[4]

V. CONCLUSION: RISKY EXPERIENTIAL LEARNING BEYOND INDEPENDENT STUDY COURSES

Since having success with this model of learning in two independent studies, I have implemented similar strategies of emergent learning in larger courses on a student-by-student basis. When I observe a student engaging in extra independent research, I further encourage these explorations with the challenge to submit their work to a target conference or journal. In many cases, the realization that their work may have significance beyond the classroom environment changes their overall attitude toward learning, and they approach their "classwork" with more seriousness. Though the extra effort of submitting an article is not explicitly rewarded with a grade, the effort generally translates into an excellent final grade on the writing assignment. I have implemented this strategy about a dozen times in my regular courses. About half of the papers submitted to conferences and journals were coauthored by me, as the topics were more technical, in order to increase the chance of their acceptance, while the other half were individually written by the students themselves and accepted.

To conclude, I have argued here that the "rough and tumble of the world" mentioned by Butler at the beginning of this essay can be created in the generally stable world of the classroom by creating opportunities for genuine failure for students; nevertheless, the students' "falls" while conducting their scholarship can be mitigated by the instructor's care and attention. This process of emergent learning requires a high-risk environment but has increased potential for significant learning, preparing students for fully independent work, "till you feel your feet safe under you."

NOTES

1. The Accessible Icon is now the legally required symbol for indicating accessible parking and way-finding in the state of New York. A similar requirement is in litigation in New Jersey, with similar efforts beginning in Massachusetts and North Carolina. The icon is also in use by private schools, hospitals, places of worship, and businesses throughout the world.
2. This may be intentional to some extent, as Kuhn himself was inspired by Piaget's own experiments on learning patterns in adolescent children. "A footnote encountered by chance led me to the experiments by which Jean Piaget has illuminated both the various worlds of the growing child and the process of transition from one to the next" (Preface).
3. By "evolutionary phases" I mean something like the story of evolution from land to sea, which involves fleeing predators, then finding food sources in a novel water environment, then mutating a variety of traits, and last, adapting through trait selection—webbed feet and the like.
4. At the time of this writing, legislation to change the symbol is up for debate in the New Jersey assembly, a campaign that began with a letter sent by Leah to her local state senator, and follows the lead of the New York state legislation: "where the word 'handicapped' would be used . . . the word 'accessible' shall be used instead" (New Jersey Bill A3743).

WORKS CITED

Baker, Billy. "Enabling a New Icon." *The Boston Globe*. 12 February. 2011.

Basken, Paul. "A Team of Academics Redesigns an Icon." *Chronicle of Higher Education* (9.37 (2013): A15.

Butler, Samuel. *The Note-Books of Samuel Butler*. New York: E.P. Dutton & Co., 1917.

Capalbo, Zach, and Brian Glenney. "Hearing Color: Radical Pluralistic Realism and SSDs." In AP-CAP 2009: The Fifth Asia-Pacific Computing and Philosophy Conference, October 1st-2nd, University of Tokyo, Japan, Proceedings, edited by Carson Reynolds and Alvaro Cassinelli, 2009: 135-141.

Fang, Jiang, G. Christopher Stecker, and Ione Fine. "Auditory Motion Processing after Early Blindness." *Journal of Vision* 14.13 (2014): 1–13. DOI: 10.1167/14.13.4.

Firfer, Holly. "Iconic Symbol Gets Moving in Makeover." *CNN*.com, 3 December. 2013.

Glenney, Brian and Sara Hendren. "We Never Asked to Be Made Human." *Barrington Center for the Arts* (November–January 2009). https://vimeo.com/11064419/

Kuhn, Thomas S. *The Structure of Scientific Revolutions: 50th Anniversary Edition*. 4th ed. Chicago: University of Chicago Press, 2012.

Meijer, Peter B. L. "An Experimental System for Auditory Image Representations." *IEEE Transactions on Biomedical Engineering* 39.2 (1992): 112–21.

Phelps, Jonathan. "Gordon College Adds New 'Accessibility Icon' to Parking Lots." *The Salem News*. 20 Nov. 2012.

Reynolds, Zachary, and Brian Glenney. "Interactive Training for Sensory Substitution Devices." In AP-CAP 2009: The Fifth Asia-Pacific Computing and Philosophy Conference, October 1st-2nd, University of Tokyo, Japan, Proceedings, edited by Carson Reynolds and Alvaro Cassinelli, 2009: 131-134.

Sullivan, Katherine. *At the Edge of Information: Changing Ethical Dilemas*. N.p.: Ethica, 2007: 24–39.

Vanhemert, Kyle. "How a Guerrilla Art Project Gave Birth to NYC's New Wheelchair Symbol." *Fast Company*. 6 June. 2013. www.fastcodesign.com/.

Wurdinger, S.D., and J. A. Carlson. *Teaching for Experiential Learning: Five Approaches That Work*. Lanham, MD: Rowman & Littlefield Education, 2010.

10 Taking Animals Seriously
Ethics in Action

Kathie Jenni

Philosophy is widely regarded as divorced from the practical, but in ethics, nothing could be further from the truth. Not only do philosophical assumptions shape public policy and individual practice, but arriving at responsible moral judgments requires robust awareness of current practices and their experienced consequences. Animal ethics exemplifies these truths especially well. Many people care about animals, but their compassion remains inconsistent, free-floating, and inert—unanchored by knowledge of animals' lives and the effects of common practice on their welfare. My course, Taking Animals Seriously,[1] aims to ground compassion and action for animals in careful moral reasoning and empathic understanding gained through experience of animal lives.

The course objectives are simultaneously philosophical and practical. I aim to (1) introduce students to philosophical thought about animal ethics; (2) train them in skills of unearthing and questioning assumptions, making conceptual distinctions, identifying and evaluating arguments, and arriving at well-reasoned judgments; (3) enhance their understanding of animals through direct experience of them; and (4) provide training and practice in caring for abandoned, abused, and rescued animals. A separate hope goes unstated on the syllabus but is often fulfilled: to (5) equip animal activists with the knowledge, practical wisdom, and motivation to carry on sustainably and effectively.

I. THE COURSE

Taking Animals Seriously is an introductory seminar in animal ethics combined with volunteering and field trips to a variety of rescues. I teach it in a four-week short term that frees students to take a single, immersive course. Two three-hour class sessions per week are devoted to discussions of readings, documentaries, and experiences with animals explicitly tied to philosophical arguments. A typical class involves sharing reflections on volunteering or films for half an hour, examining readings for roughly two hours, and screening a documentary. Because of our intense schedule, I keep the readings short (roughly twenty pages per class), using selections from

Tom Regan and Peter Singer's *Animal Rights and Human Obligations* and Susan J. Armstrong and Richard G. Botzler's *The Animal Ethics Reader*.

Two four-hour sessions per week, alternating with class days, are devoted to hands-on work (and play) with animals: feeding, socializing, exercising, and grooming dogs and cats; cleaning kennels and pens and pastures; facilitating adoptions.

I've taught the course in two different formats; at least one should be available to most philosophy teachers. For twelve years I traveled with students each May to Best Friends Animal Sanctuary in Kanab, Utah, one of the largest no-kill sanctuaries in the nation, and taught for four weeks on site. Thus we had workers at this superbly managed sanctuary and the resources of Best Friends Animal Society (the nonprofit organization responsible for it) available to us throughout the month.

It's hard to overstate the profound effects of working full-time in this setting, with roughly 375 employees providing care to more than 1,500 animals. We were immersed in a culture of consistent and thoughtful care for animals of all species: the dogs, cats, rabbits, pigs, horses, goats, and birds who had lost their human companions to death, prison, or moves; disabled wild animals who were given sanctuary and featured in educational tours: corvids, owls, minks, ducks, and pigeons; and the wild and free residents of the beautiful red-rock canyon in which Best Friends makes its home: snakes, lizards, wild turkeys, rabbits, and squirrels. Care and respect for *all* animals, tailored to individual needs and preferences, was manifest in everything we witnessed. Meals on site were vegetarian and vegan—a daily reminder of the ethic of respectful care that permeates the sanctuary.

We often felt we had entered another world—certainly a different culture. In this community, students learned that they were not aberrant or foolish for empathizing with all sentient beings or for thinking there must be better ways to treat them. Upon returning to the "real world" outside the sanctuary's borders (including the tiny town of Kanab just five miles away), where consistent respect for animals is regarded as borderline crazy, we treasured the solidarity of a community that accorded every animal care and respect as a matter of course. We felt that silent army of fellow spirits with us as we returned to the relatively callous world "outside." And we learned to carry the spirit of Best Friends with us as a state of mind and practice wherever we might go.

I recently changed the course to a format more practicable for faculty who do not have a world-class animal sanctuary nearby. In this version we stay local, meeting for class two half-days per week and working for two half-days at local animal shelters. On weekends we visit regional sanctuaries: a horse rescue, a farm sanctuary, a wolf refuge, a sanctuary for exotic animals surrendered or retired from Vegas entertainments, and a wildlife rehabilitation center. My discussion below refers mainly to this all-local version of the course, although the philosophical topics and readings are the same in both.

Beginning the first week, students work in two types of shelter: an animal control center in a low-income city and a private sanctuary in a more affluent town. I ensure that students experience each setting over several days, splitting the group in two and dividing my time working alongside them; each cohort switches to the other shelter midway through the course.

In this case we experience not one but two sub-cultures, and the contrast is heartbreakingly instructive. The animal control facility is loud, overcrowded, and stressful for both humans and resident animals; the kill rate is high (roughly 70 percent); an inordinate number of pit bulls are relinquished, most unneutered and most of them put down; there's an obvious shortage of staff; and "owner surrenders" constitute a large number of animals brought in. We arrive in the morning to see a long line of residents waiting to relinquish family pets or newborn litters of kittens. We depart for the weekend and return to find that many cats and dogs we had encountered earlier are gone—most, we know, having been killed. We talk with employees who are caring but overwhelmed by massive workloads, dispirited by understaffing, frustrated with an uninformed public, and longing for retirement.

The no-kill sanctuary is another world. Privately owned and funded by donors, this adoption center has as its mission keeping animals *out* of city and county shelters when they lose their human guardians. The director has the luxury of choosing which animals to accept (no pit bulls are taken), although they do pull dogs from high-kill shelters (including the one we work for), thus saving the lives of a significant number every year. Care for resident animals is top-notch; the atmosphere is peaceful and relaxed; potential adopters are a frequent sight; and animals will stay for as long as they need to. One student's perceptive reflection described the stark contrast in tone of the barking at the two shelters: at this one it is joyful, anticipatory, and playful, while at the city pound it's fearful, aggressive, and desperate.

In daily written reflections and a final essay (completed outside of class) I ask students to tie philosophical ideas to their experiences, enabling me to assess their integrative learning. I focus the assignments in such a way as to engage philosophical questions and arguments—intellectual content—although we also embrace the appropriateness of moral emotions as we confront the flourishing of some animals and the suffering and deaths of others. We discuss "Descartes' error" of dualism (Damasio 1994), and class conversations engage passions openly embraced but expressed in terms of moral reasoning. In fact a central conclusion of the course is that students should trust their moral emotions, so long as they are grounded in understanding of animals' experience and supported by moral reasoning, and hold strong in the face of societal indifference, self-deception, and avoidance. For the final reflection I leave the focus open-ended, asking students to select two or three ideas from the course that they have found compelling and to connect their experiential learning with them. The course is offered on a credit/no credit basis, which frees me from assigning grades to reflections that are at times quite personal and frees the students from worries about making the "right" points and connections. (This seems imperative in a course so physically, intellectually, and emotionally demanding.)

Philosophical readings bear directly on our activities. Our communal examinations of texts alternate with and (as experience in the field accumulates) are intermingled with observations from our work with animals. We begin with the ethics of caring for animal companions; essays by Bernard Rollins, Clare Palmer, and others illuminate the neglect and suffering of pets caused by uninformed guardians and anthropocentric social attitudes. Arguments about individual and communal responsibilities to domesticated and feral animals are powerfully brought home as students confront multitudes of homeless animals, "owner surrenders," and the continuous killing of healthy dogs and cats in city shelters.

We turn next to the lives of farmed animals, with readings by Peter Singer, James Rachels, and others, conjoining study of the ethics of meat production and consumption with a visit to Farm Sanctuary. This workday brings revelations about the mental and emotional capacities of chickens (who call to one another as we work among them), turkeys (who love being rubbed under their wings), cows (who lick our legs with sandpapery tongues and follow us like dogs), and pigs (who sleep peacefully together and revel in chin-rubs). The formal tour highlights the animals' cognitive, emotional, and social capacities and their horrendous lives and deaths in factory farms.

Next we turn to wildlife, focusing on the problem of balancing humane values with respect for the natural lives of wild animals. Readings by Baird Callicott enliven this inquiry, while Dale Jamieson's "Against Zoos" clarifies the moral dimensions of keeping wild animals captive. The issue's urgency emerges as we tour a refuge for wolves formerly kept as pets and two other wildlife centers: one with concrete pens housing solitary, bored, and pacing animals, the other an excellent wildlife rehabilitation center. At the former we witness a common outcome of humans keeping wild animals as pets or entertainers. At the latter we encounter an approach that restores animals to their natural lives through rehabilitation and ultimate release, where (only) animals disabled and unequipped to survive in the wild are kept in enriched captivity and respectfully used in educational tours.

We end by examining the legal status of animals in our society, followed by theories of animal ethics. Through readings by Gary Francione, we see that the legal status of animals in our nation—they are *property*, pure and simple—makes almost any neglect or abuse allowable under certain conditions. The Animal Welfare Act explicitly excludes farmed animals and allows what amounts to torture of cows, pigs, chickens, and turkeys in U.S. agribusiness. "Common farming exemptions" make legal any practice that is routine in industry; thus acts that would bring charges of felony animal abuse, were the perpetrators individual citizens and the victims family pets, are standard procedure in factory farms. The absence of laws (in many states) that would prohibit keeping as pets wild animals such as tigers, lions, and wolves make animal suffering (when the animals are eventually relinquished) and harm to humans (when they escape confinement) virtually inevitable. The best lives such animals can hope for is the one of bored confinement we witnessed at the exotic wildlife sanctuary. Finally, the status of animal companions as property entails that one may abandon a family pet to life and death in a city pound for the sake of mere convenience.

We contrast this state of affairs with theories of animals' moral status by Peter Singer, Tom Regan, and their opponents. Here students are empowered to integrate thoughts, feelings, and judgments they've experienced throughout the course and to ground them in broader foundations. This is a pivotal moment for many, as they determine whether to embrace a full-on theory of animal *rights* (to life, liberty, natural ways of life) or a less-radical approach of caring for animal *welfare*. Typically the groups are mixed in this respect; but they unanimously and (to all appearances) autonomously come to the conviction that many current practices are unequivocally wrong—and must be changed.

II. CHALLENGES, ADVICE, AND TRANSFERABILITY

It's helpful (when possible) to *select students* for a class like this who will be reliable workers, committed to animals or authentically interested in them, prepared for dirty and unglamorous work, and companionable "mates." I try to ensure a good cohort by interviewing students and selecting those who seem most promising. I ask about academic and personal interests, previous or desired experience with animals, and what they hope to gain from the course. Above all, I try to get a sense of the student as a person. Will she be a dependable worker and amiable company (for animals; for her peers; for me)? Will she be resilient in the face of inevitable disappointments and heartbreaks (not being able to work with favorite animals or species; having an animal friend put down; animals' sickness and deaths)? Is she simply looking to fill a graduation requirement or really interested in experiencing animals?

Having particular viewpoints is *not* a criterion for selection. I would not want to teach only students with a commitment to animal rights. In fact, one powerful aspect of the course is that many students share a deep love and commitment to animal companions but have given little thought to farmed animals, wild animals, or animals used in research—and have never encountered philosophy's care and rigor in considering moral questions. One can "leverage" students' commitment to animal companions to invite them to think about and empathize with animals less visible in our society and to consider practices that harm them. A preexisting affinity with dogs or cats or horses often comes with openness to considering other animals' fates that is less hindered by defensiveness about accustomed practices than one finds in the general population.

A class size of ten to fifteen is ideal in light of the need to supervise students' work, and I'm fortunate to teach in a setting where such practical restrictions are respected by my dean. I give preference to those who are pursuing our human-animal studies minor[2] (if they seem responsible) and to juniors and seniors. I turn away some students each year after conducting the interviews (sometimes a handful, once as many as twenty). Usually I advise them to wait for next year and apply again, but in some cases I guarantee a future spot to an especially promising candidate. When I'm worried about a student's reliability, my hope is that in another year they will have matured and can demonstrate that in the next interview. Fortunately (and not surprisingly), those who do not seem sufficiently committed almost never return the next year.

Certainly one can be fooled in an interview, but screening students increases the probability of having a conscientious, thoughtful group. This is important in at least three ways: it improves the chances of a good class, enhances the animals' experience, and helps to solidify the university's reputation as a dependable source of excellent volunteers.

It's important to cultivate *community partners* in an experiential course like this. Doing so can open up opportunities and avenues of learning that wouldn't normally be open to us. Mutual trust between shelter employees and my student cohorts has grown strong over the years. This is so even for the high-kill shelter workers, who are often reluctant to introduce volunteers to the grimmer side of operations for fear of bad publicity and dropouts. Given the desperate need for help, and experience with university students, rescues that would not ordinarily accept volunteers without a long-term commitment have welcomed our monthlong help and have waived the background checks ordinarily required at city shelters. The hard work my students have put in has endeared them to the leadership of various rescues, so that (for example) Best Friends welcomed us joyfully when we returned each spring. Once they witness students' conscientious work, shelters have also been willing to entrust them with special tasks: bathing kittens, working one-on-one with fearful cats or rambunctious dogs to make them more adoptable, and even training new volunteers.

It's enormously helpful if students have the chance to *get to know each other* ahead of time, as well. Toward that end, we meet several times in the semester before class begins to discuss common interests, previous experience, special affinities for animals, scheduling for class and volunteering, and which rescues to visit—and get to know each other a little. Students work better once class begins if they have a pal or two, and they then have someone with whom to compare notes and share the triumphs (adoptions! a shy dog coming out of her shell!) and tragedies (wonderful animals put down; a litter of kittens dying overnight) of routine shelter life. We don't discuss philosophical viewpoints yet but keep things casual, because I want to minimize potential tension and wait until class begins to introduce students (many of them new to the discipline) to philosophy proper. I do take the opportunity to stress that no particular viewpoint is assumed, expected, or (of course) required; that I expect our group to be typical in including a variety of diets (carnivorous, vegetarian, and vegan); and in other ways put students at their ease.

I'm lucky to be at a university with a short term, a strong service ethic, and a commitment to innovative teaching. Still, the "all-local" model of this course can be adapted to semester-long courses and other topics in philosophy. One could combine work in philosophy of law (especially theories of punishment) with getting to know juvenile offenders. A feminist philosophy course could be combined with appropriate service to shelters for battered or homeless women, or with transgender people. A medical ethics course could incorporate volunteering with local hospitals, advocacy organizations, or patient groups. A course on social justice and poverty could be conjoined with service to homeless shelters or tutoring in underfunded schools.

The difficulties involve, above all, coordination of student schedules and arranging for transportation to off-campus sites. One way to meet the challenge of transportation is to charge a course fee to cover the costs of van rentals, fuel, and other needs. At my university this is accepted practice: travel courses are self-supporting through course fees calculated by the instructor to cover envisaged expenses and advertised before student selection begins. Coordinating student schedules is tough in a regular semester but could be handled by organizing sub-groups of students who can volunteer at the same time each week, or by including as a prerequisite availability on Saturdays or other times.

III. TRANSITIONS TO ACTIVISM

I do not endorse specific moral positions in class (although I note the strengths and weaknesses of arguments)—but neither do I need to, to witness profound shifts in judgment about common practices and an altered stance toward activism in my students. In animal ethics, as in other social and moral arenas, forming *personal relationships* (in this case, with non-human animals) and *experiencing the undisputed facts themselves* (about animal killing in shelters, about the mental and emotional capacities of animals) conspire to effect personal transformations, changes in worldview, and commitments to long-term activism.

As we reflect on causes of dog and cat overpopulation—thoughtless breeding by pet owners, profit-driven puppy mills, poverty and lack of education, the irresponsibility of many guardians—we witness the devastating consequences of the problem: healthy and adoptable animals killed by the millions in "shelters"; litters of kittens killed with their mothers; dogs experiencing days of fear and loneliness, followed by anxious and lonely deaths. It's virtually impossible for a thoughtful person to spend time with these animals, and the shelter workers tasked with killing them, without concluding that fundamental social change is called for. It's nearly impossible to spend a day with cows, pigs, chickens, and other "food animals" without seeing that they are sentient, social animals not much different from our pets at home. It's difficult to come to such realizations without grasping the profound injustice of how animals are treated in our culture. And for many of my students, it's practically impossible to arrive at such conclusions without setting out to *combat this injustice in action.*

Not all of them become activists or professionals in animal care. But many do, and the ones who don't often begin supporting organizations such as Best Friends Animal Society, the Humane Farming Association, the Animal Legal Defense Fund, the Performing Animal Welfare Society, and local nonprofits that rescue animals. I know this because I serve as advisor for the student animal club on campus, and I've followed the group's self-initiated and wide-ranging activities for the past five years. Their efforts include talking with elementary school kids about factory farming; volunteering at horse, dog, cat, and wildlife rescues; hosting screenings and discussions of documentaries such as *Earthlings*; and leafleting about product testing. One has become director of a regional Humane Society; others have gone on to study animal law; some are pursuing degrees in veterinary science; and others have completed internships at rescues as a stepping stone to permanent work in animal protection. Many more have changed their lives (especially their diets) to lessen their complicity in animal abuse.

IV. CONCLUSION

The experiential outcomes of Taking Animals Seriously are dramatic—often life-changing. Students gain knowledge of acquaintance of animal minds and animal suffering at human hands. They move beyond stereotypes and dogma to intimate familiarity with the mental and behavioral capacities of animals, engaging issues in philosophy of mind in a context highlighting their urgent importance. They experience and reflect on the consequences of unexamined philosophies such as anthropocentrism and moral psychological phenomena such as self-deception and willful ignorance.

Perhaps the most eloquent testimony to the power of experiential ethics comes from a former student who is director of operations at the Central Vermont Humane Society and chair of the Vermont State Euthanasia Board for Animals (which supervises euthanasia in Vermont shelters), who also teaches courses on compassion fatigue and humane communication at New England animal shelters. Recently she wrote this to me:

> So many things brought me to today and your class was a big part of it. I'm grateful to have had the opportunity to experience BFAS [Best Friends Animal Society] and the . . . City Animal Control in the safety of an educational course. I watch new staff and volunteers struggle with

> the issues of animal welfare without the support of classmates and a mentor and I know their emotional needs are not being met. So many questions go unasked and unanswered and without that support those who struggle rarely are able to stay in the field and create the change they believe in. I really struggled for a long time with what I learned while at Redlands and thereafter and I hope to be able to help others find health in such a challenging field . . . .

Doing animal ethics in a communal and practical setting enables students to develop the resilience needed to manage the emotional demands of animal advocacy: "to stay in the field and create the change they believe in." They attain a vivid sense of what it is like to work for animals full-time and acquire a pragmatic repertoire of ways to care for animals—and as they do so, for themselves. They learn to *take animals seriously*: intellectually, emotionally, and practically.[3]

NOTES

1. I borrowed the title from David DeGrazia's 1996 volume *Taking Animals Seriously: Mental Life and Moral Status.*
2. The minor requires five courses selected from biology, environmental studies, philosophy, psychology, and English literature, plus a practicum consisting in substantial experience working with animals and a cross-disciplinary report on the experience.
3. I'm grateful to Julinna Oxley and Ramona Ilea for helpful suggestions on earlier versions of this essay.

WORKS CITED

Armstrong, Susan J. and Richard G. Botzler, ed. *The Animal Ethics Reader*. 2nd ed. New York: Routledge, 2008.

Damasio, Antonio. *Descartes' Error: Emotion, Reason, and the Human Brain*. New York: HarperCollins, 1994.

DeGrazia, David. *Taking Animals Seriously: Mental Life and Moral Status*. Cambridge: Cambridge University Press, 1996.

Regan, Tom and Peter Singer, ed. *Animal Rights and Human Obligations*. 2nd ed. Englewood Cliffs, NJ: Prentice Hall, 1989.

11 Experiential Learning in a Social Justice Course

Philosophy as Transformative Experience

Megan Halteman Zwart

I. INTRODUCTION

On the first day of my introductory philosophy classes, I always ask, "In all honesty, how many of you would be seated here if philosophy weren't a general education requirement?" Without fail, perhaps one or two hands go up, but the vast majority keep their hands at their sides, shift in their chairs, and try to avoid eye contact with me. "So this is the elephant in the room," I say. "Now that it's out in the open, I get to spend the semester showing you just how important philosophy is, no matter what you go on to do in life." My argument for the relevance of philosophy unfolds over the whole semester, but when forced to give a pithy explanation in a sentence or two, there is one answer that I always turn to first: philosophy as a discipline is uniquely well-positioned to help students pursue harmony between their beliefs and actions, and the pursuit of this sort of harmony may be nothing short of transformative.

Admittedly, that is a high bar for an introductory class—one that is surely not cleared in the case of every student—but my bold claim introduces students early on to the ideal that philosophy can and should provide them with a transformative experience. Though it is my hope that all my philosophy classes can be transformative for students, there is one class in particular that students most frequently report has this effect on them—Philosophy 254: Social Justice. My impressions and the responses of students suggest to me that adding experiential learning[1] to this course—in the form of site visits and service learning—has helped facilitate the transformative experience for students that is my goal. Having taught the class both with and without experiential learning, I am optimistic that this addition to the course has been significant, though further data collection will be necessary to evaluate just how significant.

In this chapter, I describe the course aims and requirements. I then identify two ways in which experiential learning in this class can help facilitate transformative experiences for students: first, by connecting students to a broad vision of philosophy as a way of life that challenges their beliefs and provokes the integration of the theoretical and practical. Second, by facilitating service learning opportunities to help counteract the powerlessness students can experience while passively studying systemic social injustice. Though this process may initially cause distress as students confront challenges to their beliefs, ultimately, it can promote harmony between belief and action.

II. PHILOSOPHY 254: SOCIAL JUSTICE

This class on distributive justice and our consumption habits at Saint Mary's College—a Catholic, women's, liberal arts college in Notre Dame, Indiana—fills consistently with students from a range of majors and class levels, most of whom take the class as an elective. In this course, students investigate various classical and contemporary theories and principles of distributive justice. Theoretical investigations are woven together throughout the course with experiential learning exercises that require students to interrogate and evaluate their own consumption habits, paying attention to how these habits might exacerbate injustices that disadvantage those on the margins of society. We use food as an organizing principle for the course; our inquiries about what we should eat (or shouldn't) prompt further investigations into local and global poverty, environmental degradation, gender injustice, treatment of non-human animals, worldwide health disparities, and a host of other bleak social conditions.

We begin from an understanding of "social justice" as the fair distribution of benefits, privileges and burdens among groups. We spend the first three weeks of the semester engaging theories of justice by reading and discussing primary and secondary sources on Mill, Hayek, Nozick, Kant, and Rawls.[2] Having developed a common theoretical vocabulary, we move to applied issues in food ethics. We gather information about food production from the accounts of those who grow, pick, process, and serve our food, investigative journalists, documentary film makers, and media sources like commercials and newscasts. We read arguments on food ethics by contemporary thinkers, including Peter Singer, Tom Regan, Carol J. Adams, and others. I encourage students to draw their own conclusions about which theories do the best job of promoting just distribution or remedying existing injustice. Students endorse a diverse range of responses to injustices based on evidence from arguments, data, and their own experiences. However, I try to show that by any account, be it a Rawlsian theory of justice, utilitarianism, libertarianism, or Catholic social teaching, many elements of our food system promote exploitation, oppression, and injustice, unfairly burdening the most vulnerable.

The experiential learning component of the course enables students to engage with local organizations working to ameliorate these injustices in our community. These community partners are as diverse as they are inspiring: an urban co-op in a food desert in the poorest part of our city; a sustainable farm with wind power, its own eco-friendly water-treatment process, small-scale animal agriculture, and a CSA; a community gardening organization empowering the community to grow nutritious food in abandoned lots; and an aquaponic urban farm providing jobs for adults with autism. The experiential learning component of the course includes two parts: first, we take group field trips to each of these community partners during class time; second, each student completes eight hours of service learning outside of class time with one of the community partners we've visited.[3] The field trips are interspersed throughout the course: we visit the low-cost co-op and the urban gardening organization early in the semester as we read about issues of access and affordability in urban communities; we trek to the sustainable farm as the weather warms and our focus shifts to the environmental costs of industrial food production.

To ensure that connections are being made between their experiences outside and inside the classroom, students write journal entries connecting their experiences off campus with the course material and our large and small group discussions. Students are assessed by ten formal journaling assignments in response to prompts, several of which explicitly require connections between the student's placement and other course work (30 percent of course grade).[4] Students receive 50 points (5 percent of course grade) for completing their service learning hours satisfactorily.[5] The remainder of the course grade is comprised of participation (15 percent), several brief analysis papers (30 percent), and a final research project that requires students to investigate a food justice issue that has captured their interest and to propose a plausible action plan they might personally adopt for responding to their chosen issue (20 percent).

III. PHILOSOPHY AS A WAY OF LIFE

Since revising the course to include the experiential learning component, I find that students are more likely to report that this class has a significant—even transformative—effect on both what they *believe* and how they *act* in the world.[6] I aim to augment this transformative effect by framing the course with a broad vision of philosophy as a way of life that encourages students to integrate the theoretical and the practical. This view of philosophy as the transformative pursuit of harmony between word and deed is well-precedented in the history of philosophy, though often downplayed or outright ignored in contemporary philosophy. As French historian of philosophy Pierre Hadot alerts us, if we consider ancient philosophical practices, we will note that "philosophy then appears in its original aspect: not as a theoretical construct, but as a method for training people to live and to look at the world in a new way. It is an attempt to transform mankind [sic]" (107). Many of our philosophy classes today, it seems to me, focus on the theoretical aspects but not so much on the transforming piece.

Hadot addresses this divide between the merely theoretical and the more broadly transformative by highlighting a distinction between *philosophical discourse* (theoretical discussions about philosophy) and *lived philosophy*.[7]

He argues that it is an important distinction to observe if we are to understand the transformative role of philosophy. For Hadot, "philosophical theories are in the service of the philosophical life"; he cites an Epicurean saying: "Vain is the word of the philosopher which does not heal any suffering of man" (267). On this view, philosophical discourse is an important tool but must be understood as propaedeutic to living the philosophical life rather than as sufficient in itself.

From the beginning I invoke this expanded vision of what philosophy is and emphasize the importance of integrating the theoretical and practical in the pursuit of transformation. We read some Hadot, interspersed among the more common canonical figures mentioned above. Our readings and discussions require students to put a mirror up to their own habits, dispositions, and beliefs and confront the unseen consequences of many aspects of our lifestyles. These engagements with philosophical discourse are important, particularly for the way in which they are able to issue challenges to students' beliefs.

But we intentionally do not stop at this theoretical discourse, important though it may be. If living philosophically requires the pursuit of harmony between the theoretical and practical, then a class that aims to provide transformative experience must help students connect the theoretical exercises that take place in class with the practical dimensions of lived philosophy. According to Hadot, "concern for living in the service of the human community, and for acting in accordance with justice, is an essential element of every philosophical life. . . the philosophical life normally entails community engagement" (274). By taking students beyond the classroom and into the community, students can cultivate community engagement that is important for the integrated philosophical life. They can experience for themselves that the problems we read about and discuss are real, meet individuals whose lives are affected by unjust systems, and engage with those whose lives are devoted to genuine community engagement. Students often report that the class affects not only what they believe but also how they act in the world. Consider the following comments taken from anonymous course evaluations and journaling assignments:

> This class really challenged my thinking in the best way possible and motivated me to do something about it in a proactive way. (evaluation)
>
> As a whole, this course has challenged my thinking about the issues of animal justice, environmental concerns, and human justice. I have noticed that the material we have discussed within each of these sections has affected my choices and lifestyle. . . Visiting [the urban gardens], the food bank, and [the low cost co-op] helped me understand that many people cannot afford food let alone healthy food. . . This opportunity has taught me a lot, and I enjoyed getting to know individuals that I would not have met otherwise. (journal)
>
> Not only is the class interesting and enriching, but it provides an intellectual challenge unlike any other class I have taken. . . The class

> itself took philosophical principles and connected them with pressing, real world issues that we do not often think about past the stories on the news. It forces one to evaluate their own life and how their actions compare to their beliefs. . .[This class] has truly changed my life and that is not an exaggeration in the slightest. (evaluation)

In each of these accounts, students comment on the connection between philosophical discourse and lived philosophy and identify the importance of integrating theory and practice. In my experience, community engagement through experiential learning is a valuable tool for enabling students to pursue the kind of harmony between belief and action that philosophical living demands.

However, pursuit of this sort of harmony is an ongoing process,[8] not something easily achieved simply by reading some relevant material and then depositing students into the community. In fact, after learning about injustices students often report a kind of paralysis: if the problems are so widespread, and the structures are so broken, students worry that nothing they can do will matter. This feeling of futility can have an anesthetizing effect on students, rendering them pessimistic about the possibility of change.[9] In this case, though philosophy can perform the valuable role of raising awareness of injustice, and unsettling students who may realize they are unwittingly complicit in these injustices, it also runs the risk of causing moral paralysis. Thus, in deciding exactly what kind of experiential learning to integrate into the course, my goal was to choose specific exercises that would counteract this threat of moral paralysis.

IV. WHY SERVICE LEARNING

I used to notice this paralysis frequently in students when I began teaching social justice. In its initial version, we investigated many of the same issues through readings, video clips, documentaries, and class discussion; there was some experiential learning in the form of a culminating farm visit and a celebratory end-of-semester shared meal, but the course did not include the additional service learning component, and there was limited formal reflection about our off-campus experiences built into the syllabus. After studying a semester's worth of social injustices, even the uplifting elements of the course—articles and videos about activists and promising incremental change, our enjoyable field trips—could be drowned out by the anxiety and pessimism of students about seemingly intractable problems. I remember many class sessions ending with the defeatist, rhetorical (rather than the practical) question: "What can we do?"

Concerned that I was doing students a disservice by leaving them with this basic question unanswered, I decided to amplify the experiential learning component of the class. I added more class field trips to food justice organizations, the eight-hour service learning component, and several formal assignments that require reflection on our community engagement. When students would throw up their arms and ask, "What can we do?" I wanted to take them to a number of concrete organizations, staffed by passionate, realistic-but-optimistic individuals addressing injustices in one tiny corner of the world. I wanted students to hear the stories of how these individuals remained energized in the face of staggering injustice. I wanted them to see how communities can creatively meet challenges and how individuals with motivation can plug into existing organizations or dream about developing their own, and I wanted them to reflect on how they might participate in remedying injustice in their communities.

I have been very pleased by the way these additions to the course have furthered my ultimate goal of promoting philosophy as a transformative experience. Consistent with the body of literature extolling the benefits of service learning in philosophy courses,[10] I have found that expecting students to perform service at a community organization not only amplifies their integration of the theoretical and the practical but also provides them with the tools to respond to social injustice, rather than feel paralyzed by the scope of such injustice. Consider the following students' reflections that service can provide a corrective to the inaction of purely theoretical inquiry:

> Learning about theories in a classroom is different than seeing them in action in the world. . . . Every week, I read so many things that influence the way I want to act. However, more often than not, the things I read influence thoughts I have about my actions, but not my actual actions. Considering this, I think that the experiential learning component is necessary in order to see thoughts translated into actions.[11] (journal)
>
> I've been reminded in this course of the importance of service. There are many different kinds of service and ways to volunteer, but volunteering at [the co-op] was associating with very vulnerable members of our community. This, I think, is vital to the transformation of communities and to bettering the world. We must get our hands dirty where help is needed. It is entirely too easy to sit back and learn and discuss, when actually we are sitting on the resources needed for action. (journal)

I have adopted several strategies aimed at facilitating a productive service learning experience for students. First, we visit most of the community learning partners together early in the semester, so students can pick an organization for their service placement that is a good fit with their skills and interests. This enables them to meet site supervisors, know how to get where they are going, and know what to expect when they arrive to volunteer.[12] Students report that this decreases their anxiety about volunteering off campus and decreases the likelihood that they will put off beginning their service-learning placement until late in the semester.

Second, I have tried to ensure that formal course assignments as well as class discussions allow students ample opportunity to reflect on their placements and share their experiences with others.[13] The culminating assignment of the course asks students to choose an injustice that matters to them, argue for why this should be addressed, and develop a modest, personal action plan for how one might respond. The addition of service learning to the course has helped many students develop action plans that are genuinely plausible because they are informed by the students' own volunteer work. For example, one student's action plan, which was "directly inspired by the volunteer work I did with [the co-op] here in South Bend," argues that local co-ops can help communities meets the needs of vulnerable individuals and can achieve success if they "work from within communities at risk not outside them." Another student draws on her experience visiting the food bank, the community garden, and the co-op to argue that improving access and affordability of nutritious food must be accompanied by community partnerships that ensure that co-ops are providing foods that members of their community enjoy and know how to prepare. She suggests that co-ops might offer "classes to educate various member of the community how to cook the food the co-ops sell." A student who served at the sustainable farm argues for purchasing from small-scale, organic farms to improve animal welfare. Though similar arguments could have been made in prior years by students who didn't engage in service learning, in this case, each of the students draws on her own practical experiences, integrates these with the theoretical exercises of class readings and discussions, and envisions concrete, practical approaches to social injustices that she has not only witnessed in action but also participated in herself.

V. CONCLUSION

Based on my impressions and students comments, I am optimistic that supplementing the traditional course work with site visits and service learning can help students engage with a broad vision of philosophy as a way of life and move beyond the paralysis that may result from challenges philosophy issues to their beliefs and behaviors. Though further data will be important to determine just how significant the impact of experiential learning is on students in the course, my experience so far suggests that the integration of experiential learning into the philosophy classroom can provide the tools to pursue harmony between belief and action, and the pursuit of this harmony can be transformational.[14]

NOTES

1. Here I use the term *experiential learning* to apply to any learning activities that take place off-campus. I use *service learning* to refer specifically to the subset of experiential learning activities that require students to perform service at a community organization.

2. We read primary source excerpts from Mill, Kant, and Rawls, but use Michael Sandel's *Justice* (Farrar, Straus and Giroux: 2009) as a secondary source guide to the various theories of justice.
3. My course includes a hybrid of experiential learning—some during class time and some outside of class time. For a discussion of the benefits and pitfalls of each, see Giebel 96–98.
4. For example, one journaling assignment requires students to reflect on a way in which some element of their experiential learning has modified or enriched their reflection on a particular reading. We discuss these journal entries in class.
5. Students are considered to have completed the service learning hours satisfactorily if they finish and document all eight hours, and if their site supervisor confirms that they have met the organization's expectations. Though all students who meet these expectations receive the fifty points, students who make particularly good connections between their service learning placement and class discussions and readings will receive strong grades on the relevant journal entries. Thus, students are rewarded not only for doing the hours but also for reflection on them and integrating their experiences with the course themes and readings.
6. This claim is based on my impressions of student comments in class and on anonymous evaluations and in journal entries. I have taught this class six times but am currently in the midst of teaching it with the experiential component for the second time, and thus I need further data to confirm these impressions statistically.
7. For Hadot, "It is perhaps necessary to have recourse to the distinction. . . between *discourse about* philosophy and *philosophy itself*. . . Philosophy itself is no longer a theory divided into parts but a unitary act. . . We no longer theorize about moral action, but we act in a correct and just way" (267).
8. For Hadot, the philosopher is always a moral progressive—one who is trying to move in the right direction—rather than a sage who has arrive at moral perfection. Thus exercises that bring one's theoretical and practical commitments into harmony must "be taken up again and again, in an ever-renewed effort" (103).
9. Fitzgerald addresses this concern, see 254. Ilea and Hawthorne also worry that "the classroom mode of questioning all sides of a moral argument" might produce "moral skeptics rather than critical thinkers" (220); their paper describes a civic engagement project that can help avoid this pitfall.
10. For further discussion of the benefits of service learning in philosophy classes, see Geibel. Here she reviews the literature showing the effectiveness of service learning and responds to several common objections that deter faculty from adopting service learning. See also Fitzgerald for a discussion of how ethics classes in particular can benefit from the addition of service learning. Seider and Taylor argue that students who participated in service learning in a philosophy class exhibit "a significant increase in their interest in philosophy" (197), suggesting that service learning increases student engagement in not only the course but also the subject matter more broadly.
11. This excerpt is taken from a student's journal at the outset of the class, describing why she was drawn to a class with experiential learning.
12. Ideally, this will help reduce the likelihood that a student will end up with a service placement that is not enjoyable or personally beneficial, though this remains an ongoing concern of mine, as a small minority of my students have reported that they are bored by their experience or feel that their skills are underutilized. Fitzgerald addresses this concern and offers some responses (263–64).

13. Fitzgerald mentions the use of hourlong reflection seminars to encourage this sort of reflection (257); I integrate this reflection into class discussion and journal prompts on a regular basis.
14. I am grateful to all my students who have participated in this "experiment" with me for their patience, insightfulness, and enthusiasm. We have all learned together along the way. Thanks also to Matt Halteman for reading a draft of this paper.

WORKS CITED

Fitzgerald, Patrick. "Service-Learning and the Socially Responsible Ethics Class." *Teaching Philosophy* 20.3 (1997): 251–67.

Giebel, H. M. "In Defense of Service Learning." *Teaching Philosophy* 29.2 (2006): 93–109.

Hadot, Pierre. *Philosophy as a Way of Life*. Oxford: Blackwell Publishing, 1995.

Ilea, Ramona and Susan Hawthorne. "Beyond Service Learning: Civic Engagement in Ethics Classes." *Teaching Philosophy* 34.3 (2011): 219–40.

Sandel, Michael J. *Justice: What's the Right Thing to Do?* New York: Farrar, Straus and Giroux, 2009.

Seider, Scott and Jason Taylor. "Broadening College Student Interest in Philosophical Education through Community Service Learning." *Teaching Philosophy* 34.3 (2011): 197–217.

12 Feminist Philosophy and Civic Engagement

The Educational Fair

Sharon M. Meagher

Experiential learning can take many more forms other than traditional service learning. In this chapter I discuss an experiential learning model that I used effectively in philosophy courses I taught at the University of Scranton, namely, the educational fair or teach-in. While this pedagogy is particularly apt for feminist philosophy courses, it can be adapted to a wide variety of other philosophy courses and works very well in all courses that address social justice issues.

In my feminist philosophy class, we created a teach-in that we called the "feminist fair." Students who organize the fair learn by teaching as they share their newly acquired knowledge of key feminist principles and practices with the rest of the university community. In addition to the goal of introducing others to feminist ideas, the fair also puts feminist pedagogy into practice. While the central goal of the feminist fair is to help both students who organize the fair and those who attend it to better understand key feminist concepts, students also develop an understanding of feminist pedagogy and praxis.

In this chapter, I first outline the feminist theoretical and pedagogical motivations for this experiential learning method. I then explain the logistics entailed in doing an educational fair in conjunction with a foundational feminist theory course, followed by a discussion of some particularly creative projects that students developed for the fair, including the creation of a life-sized board game used to organize the fair. Then I outline guidelines and criteria for student evaluation and assessment, including how and why students are expected to document their work. I conclude with a brief discussion of how this model of experiential learning can be adopted in other philosophy courses.

I. FEMINIST THEORY AND PRAXIS

Feminist philosophy is predicated on a concept of praxis—that is, on recognizing the complex interrelationship between theory and practice. Feminist pedagogies therefore demand that instructors find ways to integrate both theoretical and practical experiences into feminist courses in ways that help students understand feminist praxis. Praxis is defined as "the synthesis of theory and practice seen as the basis for political and economic change" (*OED online*, def. 1). As bell hooks discusses in her chapter "Feminism: A Movement to End Sexist Oppression" there is no feminist movement without praxis. The aim of the introductory feminist philosophy course that I teach, Philosophy 218: Feminism: Theory and Practice, is to help students understand the richness and diversity of feminist theories and their complex relationship to various feminist practices. Working from the assumption that feminism is often misunderstood, the goal is to start with students' conceptions and misconceptions, building on the former and debunking the latter.

A popular misunderstanding of feminism is that it entails personal attacks on individual men, when in fact feminists of all stripes actually engage in critiques of institutional and structural problems. Naïve perceptions of how power circulates between individuals and social institutions are the source of much of the problem. The pedagogical challenge is to help students move beyond popular misunderstandings of feminism to a more nuanced view. The concepts of sexism and oppression play a central role in most feminist philosophical analyses, but these are difficult for students to grasp given that we live in a culture that emphasizes individuality and solipsistic understandings of subjectivity and selfhood that ignore or efface social and political structures.

Feminist pedagogy aids in this challenge, as it calls on instructors to engage students in ways that counter individualist as well as authoritarian teaching methodologies; it demands that students be colearners and take responsibility for their learning. Course assignments utilize feminist pedagogy and are keyed to the two primary learning outcomes for the course. Students are expected to: 1) develop a sophisticated understanding of feminism, including knowledge of how to identify and critically analyze resources and references to feminism in academic literature, politics, and popular culture; 2) develop leadership qualities and teamwork skills that are necessary for the creation and maintenance of an equitable and just world.

II. LOGISTICS OF THE TEACH-IN

A major course assignment that addresses both course objectives is the feminist fair, an interactive teach-in where the students introduce key concepts of feminism to students on campus, with a particular emphasis placed on overcoming the misconceptions of feminism caused by naively individualistic worldviews.

This model was developed in response to a university community need. When developing the feminist theory course as a foundational core course for the women's studies program, I chose to focus on an experiential learning component that served university rather than wider community needs for several reasons. Although service-learning courses can be of great value to both students and the community members they serve, students in lower-level philosophy courses often lack both the knowledge and skills necessary to do meaningful service for the external community that has value for those constituents. I therefore designed the foundational course in a way that would incorporate an experiential learning component while at the same time aid students in developing both the knowledge and skills necessary for more demanding external community-based service learning or internships they might take in the future. I learned from the University of Scranton Jane Kopas Women's Center director at the time that there was an urgent and ongoing campus need; many students, faculty, and staff lacked a basic understanding of feminism and did not understand the rationale for a women's center on campus. Since students usually only remain on campus for four years and then are replaced by a new cohort, the need to do campus-wide education around feminism remains steady. And it can be met by integrating the feminist fair into the course, which is offered every fall.

Planning for the fair begins four weeks into the course when the students have completed foundational readings that introduce students to various feminist theoretical frameworks as well as key feminist concepts, such as gender, oppression, and sexism. Since philosophy courses rarely prepare students well for group work, preparation for the planning day includes students reading about group dynamics and asking students to reflect on their own patterns of group work. They are also given a handout that outlines the key questions they will need to answer for themselves if they are to contribute well to both the group planning process and the implementation of the fair. The handout summarizes stereotypes of group contributors (e.g., "Do It All Dottie," and "Seldom Seen Steve") created by Linda Lerne (1995) and provides an excellent prompt for students to honestly assess their typical roles in group work and to think about how they can change group dynamics.

In addition, the planning document includes questions that ask them to think about the learning objectives for the fair (what do they hope the people who attend will gain from the fair?), whether they want a theme, what visuals or other effects they might use to create a unified fair theme, as well as basic logistical questions such as how they will divide their work and how we will generate publicity for the event. Students are encouraged to share initial ideas via an online discussion board in advance of the class meeting. When they arrive at the class planning meeting, the instructor does not attend; instead, the students have to organize themselves. Based on student reports, the students struggle at first, but every class has developed a coherent plan. They are responsible for sending the instructor minutes immediately following the class so that the instructor can help if needed, and then the students are responsible for writing a short paper in which they summarize the group project and explain their particular roles/contributions.

To best prepare, students are provided with a frequently asked questions (FAQ) sheet. It includes a list of qualities of excellent feminist fair displays/ presentations, namely, that it is *educational*—it has a clear focus that aims to inform the university community about some women's and/or feminist issue; it is *interactive*—the table/ booth draws fairgoers to it and involves them in some way; it is *creative*—students are encouraged to draw on multimedia, handouts, colorful poster presentations; it is *well-researched*—the table/booth is developed on the basis of informed research and presents further resources to fair-goers interested in the topic; and it deals with a *substantive topic or issue* that merits further investigation.

Students are asked to both envision what the overall fair will look like and to think about their own group projects. As a group, they are asked to select a fair theme, to figure out an overarching visual theme or other way to connect group projects, to decide on how the labor and topics will be divided so that they can form small work groups, and to think about how they will promote the fair and how they will evaluate it. That said, I do provide students with examples from prior fairs so that they do not have to reinvent the wheel. In some years, I have picked the fair theme in advance so that I could better organize the readings or because I felt the class could not handle it. But generally I have found that allowing the students as much decision-making power as possible allows them to take ownership of the project as well as develop organizational and communication skills.

Once students have made most preliminary decisions, I then work with them to ensure that they have covered everything. Small groups then need to meet to decide what they will actually present and how they will divide the labor. Students are expected to do most of the work outside of class, with only one or two class meetings assigned to follow up on fair organization and preparation. I meet with groups outside of class as necessary.

III. VISUAL REPRESENTATION AND PARTICIPANT INTERACTION

While fairs and poster displays are fairly common in the social sciences, making them work in philosophy is more of a challenge. The greatest challenge for both students and the instructor is helping the students figure out how to communicate complex philosophical ideas rather than just reporting facts. The students who have been most successful have often created visuals that illuminate metaphors that philosophers and other feminist theorists use to explain concepts. Given that philosophers make frequent use of metaphors in many subfields of philosophy, the educational fair model can be used effectively in a wide range of philosophy courses, particularly those that focus on social justice or ethics issues that are taught utilizing feminist or other democratic and participatory pedagogies.

For example, one year students created a life-sized interactive board game modeled on *Monopoly* that they called "Manopoly." Students were inspired by reading Allan G. Johnson's essay on patriarchy in which he explains how we are complicit in perpetuating patriarchy when we play within a system's rules that privileges male status and experience. Just as well-meaning people can become greedy players when playing the game *Monopoly* because they are "just following the rules," so we are often complicit in systems of oppression when we fail to question the rules of the system that oppresses. At the feminist fair, students constructed educational booths with alternative feminist visions of the world and tried to coax fair attendees into breaking the rules of patriarchy and leaving the game of "Manopoly." For example, the game was constructed so that the players were given different amounts of money to start the game, based on factors such as gender and race. Students in the class then asked participants whether that was fair and suggested that they might not play the game of patriarchy and might want instead to visit their educational booth on pay equity.

Each year, students are responsible for repurposing the game or developing a similar interactive learning tool that utilizes one or more metaphors from the assigned readings. Some years students have created a giant bird cage, the metaphor that Marilyn Frye uses in her analysis of oppression to help us understand that while any one barrier (cage bar) might seem easily overcome, oppression is formed by a network of barriers (the cage) (1–15). Another year students were inspired by the game *Chutes and Ladders* and built a life-sized game board to illustrate how different types of oppression cause members of some groups to fall behind while members of other groups climb quickly to the top.

Since I incorporated pedagogies that focus on collaborative group projects to imagine and create visual representations of oppression and sexism, the students in the class have a much stronger understanding of the concepts compared to those who attend the fair. Metaphors play important roles in philosophical theorizing; when we ask students to make those metaphors come alive, the learning is greater and more rewarding. But it is not just a matter of making the metaphors come alive but of making philosophy come alive. There are many metaphors that we use to describe the role of the philosopher in public life (e.g., Socrates's midwife and gadfly, Arendt's pearl diver, John Dewey's metaphor of the philosopher as public liaison officer). Thus metaphors play a critical role not only in our comprehension of philosophical concepts but our understanding of the task of philosophy itself, and it is important pedagogically to invite students to explore those metaphors.

Utilizing feminist pedagogies that emphasize the dialectic between theory and practice can be valuable in all philosophy classes, and I have utilized the methodology of the educational fair in other courses; in fact, I have even repurposed the "Manopoly" game board in other courses. Games are particularly useful in helping illustrate complex social structures and individuals' interactions with/in them.

IV. STUDENT EVALUATION AND ASSESSMENT

Students are evaluated on the strength of their projects (including their impact on those who attended the fair), the documentation of their work, and their contributions to their team. Students create an assessment tool that measures feminist fair attendees' understanding of feminism when they enter and when they exit the fair. Student self and group evaluations are factored in during grading. An important part of the pedagogy includes teaching students how to document their work. Emphasis is placed on the documentation of both students' individual substantive contributions to the group project and their group learning process.

While project documentation permits better evaluation of student work for grading purposes, it is a critically important part of the students' formative process. We often view and discuss the documentary *Women Organize!* as preparation for documentation. The purpose of documentation is threefold: first, it demands that we give value and credit to our work; second, it helps others learn more about what we did so that they might replicate the work; and third, it presents us with an opportunity to reflect critically on our work. Students need to learn the importance of valuing their work and documenting it sufficiently well so that it can be carried out or on by others. The failure of people to document their work causes leadership transition problems in all organizations, from student groups to nonprofit and for-profit businesses.

I require four sets of documentation: 1) documentation of the students' work on the feminist fair display itself; these may include notes, journal entries, a narrative summary, and/or links to Internet-based discussion with group members (to explain what they did and how they did it); 2) reflections on the students' role in the group and how well the group functioned; 3) reflect on the content of the fair display and how people responded to it; and 4) research notes and bibliography. I provide a list of prompt reflection questions that include: what were your goals/objectives in creating/designing your booth? Did you accomplish those goals? What pedagogies did you use in your booth? Were they feminist pedagogies? Why or why not? What concepts were most important to understand in order to create your booth? Why? Which authors/resources most informed your work? Why? How? Which feminist controversies/issues were most at stake in your booth project? Why? How? How might you have revised/improved your booth?

Students earn individual grades based on their documentation and my notes from the fair presentations themselves. Criteria used to evaluate the fair presentation include: clarity of display; level and quality of interactive pedagogies used; choice of focus; and how issues were communicated/handled. Fair documentation is graded based on individuals' contribution to the group (based on their own self-assessment and other group members' feedback), the quality of the research, the quality of the reflection, and the quality of the documentation itself.

Students are responsible for developing an assessment tool by which we can measure the learning of those who attend the fair; in that way, they are held accountable for their work by the community (in this case, the university community) that they serve. Over the years the students and I have developed a measure in which fair attendees rank their knowledge and attitudes on feminist knowledge before and after they attend the fair. The tool is not objectively reliable, as we rely on participants' self-ratings, but the results consistently show the participants perceive a shift in their attitudes and knowledge about feminism as a result of their fair attendance. Participants also rank the content of the fair with traditional letter grades, and on average over the years, more than 87 percent rate the fair quality as a B or better.

Students are also accountable to one another. Given the feminist pedagogical precept to share the power, students engage in both self-evaluation and in the evaluation of their peers. I developed an evaluation form that first encourages students to identify their group's dynamics and to take responsibility for their contributions (for good or ill) to those dynamics. They are then asked to reflect on the roles of other group members. Since I implemented both the group dynamic discussion prior to fair planning and the group evaluation tool, I found that students became excellent at monitoring their own group dynamics and no longer relied on me to adjudicate difficult situations.

The pedagogy and course are assessed in two ways: first, at the end of the course, students respond to both Likert-scale and open-ended questions, including additional questions that directly assess the feminist fair assignment in light of the student learning outcomes. Open-ended responses to a general course question frequently include comments similar to this one: "This is the first class where I enjoyed group work and learned a lot from it." I lack pre-feminist fair class data by which I can compare answers to the Likert scale questions, but students generally rate their learning on outcomes very highly, and the quality course work supports their claims. Second, all women's studies students (majors or concentrators) enrolled in the course participate in the women's studies portfolio program and document their learning in a portfolio that extends across their four-year career. We have found that students frequently document work conducted for the fair project in their portfolios.

V. UTILIZING TEACH-IN AND EDUCATIONAL FAIRS IN OTHER PHILOSOPHY COURSES

I have utilized the pedagogy of the educational fair in other courses. In my course on philosophy and the city, for example, students have developed presentations on environmental justice in cities for Earth Day. In one case, students repurposed the life-sized "Manopoly" board, given that the original *Monopoly* game references neighborhoods in Atlantic City and includes high- and low-rent districts. So rather than visualizing a metaphor, they were helping Earth Day participants visualize and participate in decisions that cause low-income neighborhoods to carry a disproportionate environmental burden in cities. Another way to think of game use, then, is to think of games as visually compelling and interactive ways to help students think about power and how power works. Indeed, as I discussed at the outset of this chapter, Allan Johnson's use of the metaphor of the *Monopoly* game was intended to illustrate how power works by helping us better think about how individuals interact with systems. Just as individuals rarely question the rules of the game when they play games, individuals usually fail to question the rules of the system when they engage in it. People thus perpetuate existing power dynamics because they fail to question existing structures and rules. Bringing a game to life can help students reflect on how power is perpetuated and how it can be transformed.

I am now exploring the possibility of integrating such pedagogies into courses with my colleagues at Widener University. Engaged pedagogies such as those described here can be classified as a type of collaborative project that George D. Kuh (2008) has identified as a "high impact practice," that is, one that has a greater effect on student learning outcomes. Furthermore, the research of Finley and McNair (2013) provides evidence that these high-impact practices have a disproportionately positive impact on students from historically underserved groups. Furthermore, they ensure that diverse perspectives are included and that each student finds his or her voice. The educational fair or teach-in provides an opportunity for students to develop teamwork and communication skills necessary for more meaningful community-based service and work while at the same time encouraging students to learn by teaching. The stakes are high for students and they know it; they want to impress their peers with their knowledge, and most develop a passion for issues of justice that helps them recognize the importance of educating others in the campus community about social justice. And by playing the role of the philosopher who facilitates thinking about justice, the students better understand why and how philosophy might matter in their lives as citizens and as persons.

WORKS CITED

Finley, Ashley and Tia McNair. *Assessing Underserved Students' Engagement in High Impact Practices*. Washington, DC: American Association of American Colleges and Universities (AAC&U), 2013.

Frye, Marilyn. *Politics of Reality: Essays in Feminist Theory*. New York: Crossing Press, 1983: 1–15.

hooks, bell. "Feminism: A Movement to End Sexist Oppression." *Feminist Theory: From Margin to Center*. 2nd ed. Boston: South End Press, 2000. 18–33.

Johnson, Allan G. "Patriarchy, the System: An It, Not a He, a Them or an Us." *The Gender Knot: Unravelling Our Patriarchal Legacy*. Philadelphia: Temple University Press, 2005.

Kuh, George D. *High-Impact Educational Practices: What They Are, Who Has Access to Them, and Why They Matter*. Washington, DC: American Association of Colleges and Universities (AAC&U), 2008.

Lerne, Linda D. "Making Student Groups Work." *Journal of Management Education* 19.1 (February 1995): 123–25.

"praxis." OED Online. June 2000. Oxford University Press. 15 December 2014. http://dictionary.oed.com/.

Shrewsbury, Carolyn M. "What Is Feminist Pedagogy?" *Women's Studies Quarterly* 25.1/2 (spring–summer 1997): 166–73.

The Union Institute Ctr. for Women & Women and Organizing Documentation Project. *Women Organize!* Director Joan E. Biren, 2000.

B. Service-Learning and Community Engagement through Philosophy

13 Engaging with Global Justice through Internships

Ericka Tucker

Global justice, on its face, seems like an impossible task. As citizens of wealthy and powerful countries, the task of economic, social, and political justice seems to outstrip our intellectual, practical, and emotional abilities. Considering the scope of "global" justice, it would appear that a massive coordinated effort would be necessary to overcome the problems of global injustice, yet it would seem that such coordination it impossible. The difficulties of seeking justice between nations led John Rawls (2001) to suggest that we can only hope for a kind of humanitarian goodwill between states, which in his view was a less-than-robust requirement for international justice. Amartya Sen, in *the Idea of Justice*, recently argued that it is not justice that we seek, since seeking justice in a global sense is impossible.

Given the capitulation of such philosophical luminaries, it is no wonder that philosophy students often find the problems of global justice and injustice to be intractable and indeed, overwhelming. However, when students engage with those whose everyday work involves chipping away a specific problem of global justice, they learn not despair, but hope, and more importantly, they learn how issues of global justice are addressed in practical terms. Those who work on these local issues not only have an understanding of the connection between local, national, and global aspects of these issues, but they also solve these problems and can show students how everyday decisions on a local level affect issues of justice on a larger scale. Working with such individuals and organizations helps students understand the work of justice and its local, national, and global faces.

I. EXPERIENTIAL ENGAGED LEARNING IN PHILOSOPHY TO THE RESCUE!

In my course Global Justice, I use internships with social justice organizations to give students a look at the everyday, often difficult, but essentially manageable work that goes into solving issues of injustice at the local, national, and global levels. I call this work engaged learning. Engaged learning is a variety of experiential learning that seeks to integrate theory and practice through project-based internships that foster strong university-community partnerships. Each student is assigned a semester-long internship with a local organization working on issues of global justice. Through these internships, students work through larger theoretical questions while engaging in the everyday work of global justice practitioners. In what follows, I describe how I organized this class and what elements of the course work to both create good experiences for my students and build community relationships that persist beyond the semester.

Like issues of global justice, the practical details of organizing a successful engaged learning course could seem overwhelming to many philosophy instructors. While such courses are not easy to organize, they are not impossible. In this chapter, I outline the practical details of creating courses where sometimes abstruse theorizing can join with active community engagement and learning to provide the kind of educational experience that can lead students to read the course materials differently and to ask more informed questions about theories of global justice.

In section II, I will set out the details of the course I taught, starting in 2009. I will go through the different elements of the syllabus, paying special attention to the "internship" and "final project" components of the course, which is what makes this an engaged-learning course. In Section III, I will address the practical details and requirements for organizing and teaching an engaged-learning course.

II. THE ENGAGED-LEARNING GLOBAL JUSTICE COURSE

Thematically, I organize the course into five areas: 1) War and Violence as Issues of Global Justice, 2) Human Rights, Development, and Global Institutions, 3) Immigration and Refugees, 4) Gender and Justice in Global Perspective, and finally, 5) Democracy and Communication. These five themes organize our readings and the internship projects. Each student chooses an area of interest from these five and chooses an internship project with an organization that works primarily on one of these areas.

The first assignment of the course is a short essay, described below, in which students choose their internship project from a list of organizations and internships and answer a set of questions about it. I post the organizations, along with a short description of possible projects that the students could work on, which are provided by the organization. These projects are related to the ongoing work of the organizations but are shaped through conversations with the person who will manage the student intern several weeks before the beginning of the term. There are three major requirements for each project. It must be: 1) a project that can be completed or on which major work can be done in the space of a semester, 2) a project that is meaningful to the organization, and 3) a project that is related to social or global justice, such that it will enhance the student's experience in the course.

Students choose an internship from a list of organizations and internships, which I organized in the previous term. Most of the organizations are local nonprofits working in some area of global justice. Having worked as a volunteer for WRFG Community Radio, Sagal Radio, and with the refugee organizations it served, including the Refugee Women's Network and the International Rescue Center, I had a strong connection to these community organizations. As I will discuss below, these personal connections are essential for developing substantial projects for my students. I worked with organizations to define project requirements as specifically as possible, so that students have a clear set of responsibilities and a tangible result for their final project.

Internship projects included:

- Interns with the *Radio Diaspora* program produced by the Latin American and Caribbean Community Center (LACCC) develop a radio program on issues of immigration in greater Atlanta.
- Intern with the Georgia Coalition for the People's Agenda assists in their Citizen Education Program and develops literature about voting rights.
- International Rescue Committee interns work with high-school student asylees to produce radio programs about their experience in the United States.
- Interns with the Georgia Alliance for Children research and write grants while shadowing those working for the GAC.
- Interns with the American Friends Service Committee Truth in Recruitment campaign and educate about the issues of military recruitment in U.S. schools. The intern develops a pamphlet for high school students and travels to schools around Atlanta while working with other student interns and veterans.
- Interns with the Sutherland Law Firm, which supports the Advocates for Human Rights and the Truth and Reconciliation Commission of Liberia through the Carter Center, organize educational materials for public outreach.
- The American Friends Service Committee Peace Building Program intern helps organize a Youth Convergence Project, bringing together one hundred youth for a conference on peace and justice.
- Interns with WRFG Community Radio have the option of working with station volunteers to organize a fund drive or working with the radio program *Class Chronicles* to help research and produce a radio program on issues of poverty and justice.
- Interns with Sagal Radio HEARMe project work with volunteers to research and produce health-related radio programs. Interns with web experience are also needed to support volunteers with local news bite section of Sagal Radio website.

Students were directed to research their organization and to write a short proposal answering the following questions:

1. How would this project and working with this organization support and enhance your personal, educational, and career goals?
2. What skills do you bring to this internship, and what would you like to learn?
3. What interests you most about the organization and the problems it addresses?

Students submit this proposal and their resume, which are then sent to the internship organization of their choice. Students then meet with their intern coordinator, and design a project that can be completed in the time allotted. Students and write up a final proposal describing this project.

After this initial development of their internship project, the class operates for the most part just like a traditional philosophy class. Students read articles and books on global justice. Students write short papers on theoretical issues of global justice. However, some class time is reserved for discussing internship projects and addressing any worries or problems that came up with the individual internship projects.

To regularly check in with student progress, I ask the students to prepare "project blogs." Each student maintains a blog about his or her internship project. Each week we go through these blogs as a class and discuss the relevance of their experience in the field with the issues we are discussing in class. Students are encouraged to reflect on their experience both personally and philosophically. This is also a time when students can express any problems or frustrations they are experiencing and where they can receive advice from their fellow students.

For their final projects, students are expected to bring together theory and practice by bringing insights from their internship project to bear on a theoretical problem of global justice. In their final projects, students choose one philosophical problem from our readings and a practical issue provided by their internship experience to write a final paper, which they then present for the entire class and invited community partners. Working with students one-on-one is essential for helping students find the right balance of practical explanation and philosophical analysis. This is time intensive, but this is where the real work of engaged learning happens. Engaged learning means that the students are bringing together the theoretical frameworks we have discussed in class while analyzing their own internship experience. To a certain extent, we practice this as a class during each internship reflection session and I try to bring in examples from the students' projects during lectures. Ultimately, this is a difficult task, but it is the kind of task where students can produce exciting and original work.

For the final class meeting of Global Justice, each student prepares a presentation of his or her final paper. Each presentation begins with a discussion of the student's internship project and an abstract of the philosophical problem the student engaged in his or her final paper. We invite community partners for the presentations afterward and have a banquet for the final day of class. These presentations allow the students to present their philosophical-practical work for a more general audience than for their paper. This experience offers students another way to think about their ideas and their internship experience as an exercise in public philosophy. Students' final papers tend to focus more on the philosophical aspects of their experience; however, since they are intended for a public audience, the presentations focus more on the internship experience, allowing the students the opportunity to talk about the philosophical concepts that guided their practice. I highly recommend such a paper-presentation final project and inviting community partners, as these presentation meetings provide unique opportunities both for students and for community partners to see the results of their cooperation. These kinds of engagements with community partners also help sustain the partnerships for future courses.

III. ENGAGED PHILOSOPHY COURSES—A HOW-TO GUIDE

Global Justice is just one of many philosophy courses that lends itself to an engaged-learning experience. I have developed courses in Social and Political Philosophy and Ethics and Human Nature (a staple of the Jesuit institution where I currently teach) with engaged-learning components. I have worked with others designing engaged-learning courses in Environmental Ethics, Religious Ethics, Feminist Philosophy, and Philosophy of Race. The key element for the success of these courses is, I will propose, the engagement of the instructor with his or her community. This engagement allows the instructors to work with their community contacts to develop good projects for their students. Such engagement not only models the kinds of engagement we wish our students to have with their community partner, and more broadly with their community, but also is the building block of university-community trust upon which the best engaged learning courses are built. However, as instructors, we are not alone. In what follows I will outline the variety of resources available to instructors to develop engaged learning courses and explain how the capacity for such courses can be built while teaching.

The course described above was supported and funded by the Office of University-Community Partnerships at Emory University in Atlanta, Georgia (OUCP), as part of a graduate fellowship in engaged teaching. The OUCP is an innovative organization that seeks to build long-term relationships in the greater Atlanta metro area through program-based projects and through collaborative community research. Before teaching through OUCP, I had been a community-partners fellow working at a refugee community radio station in nearby Clarkston, Georgia, and had been a long-term volunteer at a community radio station, WRFG, in Atlanta. With the support of the OUCP and my own network of nonprofit contacts, setting up internships for my students was relatively easy. Not every university has such an institution, and not every faculty member has been a long-term volunteer in the community in which his or her academic institution resides. However, both institutional support and individual engagement in the community are essential for successful engaged-experiential learning courses. In what follows, I will present ways to build capacity for such courses by offering preliminary steps for instructors and some proposals for identifying institutional support. There are many productive ways to build up to a full engaged-learning course with internships and the kinds of final projects discussed above. The main element of building capacity for such courses is identifying community partners—nonprofits, etc.—that can offer good internship experiences for your students.

IV. INSTITUTIONAL SUPPORT

While not all academic institutions have a full center of community-engaged research and partnerships, most have some elements of such programs (e.g. service-learning programs, ethics centers, prison teaching programs, partnerships with local K–12 schools, affiliation with religious organizations). These groups on campus can be excellent sources for identifying community partners. Colleagues, perhaps in other departments and perhaps in neighboring institutions, are also a rich source of information for what organizations are open to student internship projects. Colleagues are also essential sources of information about logistics, funding, and ideas. Funding for innovative, engaged learning, service learning, and experiential learning is available at most academic institutions. Applying for this funding is often a first step to finding colleagues who work on such courses and identifying the key staff members who facilitate community interaction on campus. Whether one can obtain a mini-grant or a course release, such funding begins the process of building capacity through finding partners and understanding how your campus works with faculty engaged in these projects. Depending on your institution, there may be legal issues with working with community partners, sending students off-campus, etc.

V. BUILDING (UP TO) AN ENGAGED-LEARNING COURSE

Given the often-itinerant nature of academic culture, instructors at all levels often find themselves in new communities and new colleges and universities. The engagement of the instructor in the community is the single most important element of successful engaged-learning courses with internships.

However, instructors in new positions need not despair. Getting to know one's community can be integrated into one's pedagogy.

While you are building up to a full engaged-learning course, your students can help identify organizations that work on a specific issue. When I first moved to my current institution, my global justice students worked together on a project to identify local social and global justice organizations. Their projects included interviewing the director of an organization, profiling the organization, and analyzing the organization's contributions to the issues in our class (e.g., gender, violence, refugees and immigration). A student volunteer, funded through an internal grant for student research, created a database of these projects. This student also followed up with these organizations to determine what kinds of projects the organizations might have for future student interns. This database then became the source of future community partners and also for identifying good in-class speakers.

Identifying good community partners is essential for fostering strong internship programs. Having students involved from the beginning gives them valuable experience engaging in community work. Often students will already be involved with local organizations or campus-based activism and volunteer organizations. They can serve as local experts and lead groups of students through the process. Those students who are from the area can also serve as local experts, which can build ties between commuter students and those living on-campus.

Engaged learning courses are some of the most rewarding courses to teach. They challenge students to bring their theoretical knowledge to bear on practical problems while working with local organizations that do the work of justice at local, national, and global levels. These courses take time to plan and to build. Building the instructor's capacity to do engaged learning is the first step. Learning how one's institution works, applying for grants to support such projects, engaging with community organizations, and getting to know the leaders of these organizations is essential for knowing where the students will have a good experience.

A good engaged-learning experience is not necessarily one that is problem or conflict-free. Instructors need to be able to communicate honestly with the local coordinator of the students' internships so that if a problem comes up, it can be handled effectively. Problems will arise. These problems, while often minor, are to be expected given that students will be in new situations and are being asked to extend their intellectual skills into a new practical realm. Community partners, whether a nonprofit organization or a local grade school, are hectic places where your student may feel ignored or out of place. These sorts of issues are to be expected and are why I reserve regular class time for discussing internship projects and project blogs. If one is lucky enough to work at an institution with dedicated staff to handle student-community partnerships, then these issues should generally be handled through these staff members. For the rest of us, knowing those in charge of the internship project is the best way to make sure that problems with the student or the organization are handled earlier rather than later.

VI. CONCLUSION

Engaged experiential learning experiences in philosophy courses offer the possibility of integrating theoretical and practical studies, which, for many of us, is the holy grail of the college experience. They are never without complications and often bring up social, political, economic, and emotional issues that are often unseen in traditional classrooms. However, these interactions and complications genuinely prepare our students to be thoughtful and engaged world citizens. Further, and this is the topic, no doubt, of another volume, these experiences allow our students to see the kind of engaged, thoughtful professions and careers that their work in philosophy prepares them to pursue. The experiential nature of this course shows philosophy students that a philosophical future may include but is not limited to graduate studies in philosophy. Our students are thoughtful and passionate. In courses like Global Justice, students want to know "what they can do" about the problems and issues global justice theorists raise. Their internship projects allow them to "do something" and to reflect on the kind of work done by organizations working for justice at the local and global levels. These courses allow them to use these qualities to engage in the world in a constructive way. Witnessing the activity of the organizations in which they are interns gives students a practical introduction to the work of justice. As such, engaged learning courses allow us to model engaged citizenship in the often far-removed context of the philosophy classroom.

WORKS CITED

Rawls, John. *The Law of Peoples*. Cambridge, MA: Harvard University Press, 2001.
Sen, Amartya. *The Idea of Justice*. Cambridge, MA: Belknap Press, 2011.

14 Cultivating Responsible Global Citizenship

Philosophical Exploration & Service Learning in Guyana

Katherine E. Kirby

I. INTRODUCTION: INTERNATIONAL SERVICE LEARNING & LEVINAS'S CONCEPTION OF ETHICS

According to Emmanuel Levinas, the ethical relation is not determined through reason but rather through the revelation that occurs in ethical discourse—in the face-to-face relation with another person who transcends rational conceptualization. The self is called into question by the Other[1] and is commanded to suspend its rational intentions, goals, projects, and self-interest and return to a more original relation of peace. The radical self-examination that philosophy requires and the discovery of the meaning of the good or the true that philosophy seeks are only possible through the ethical relation of face-to-face discourse.

Given the interconnectedness of our lives in this era of globalization, I am compelled to challenge my students to extend their ethical considerations beyond their local communities and recognize themselves as global citizens. Peter Singer suggests the following in *One World: The Ethics of Globalization*: ". . . how well we come through the era of globalization (perhaps whether we come through it at all) will depend on how we respond ethically to the idea that we live in one world. For rich nations not to take a global ethical viewpoint has long been seriously morally wrong" (13). In my endeavor to guide students in cultivating a robust sense of responsible global citizenship, I have found international service learning, grounded in Levinas's ideas, to be invaluable, as it opens the face-to-face relation across borders, calling students to suspend their own ideas and judgments, listen wholeheartedly to Others, and philosophically examine the transformative power of ethical encounter.

This chapter will describe the upper-division undergraduate course I teach, "A Study in Service," which engages students in service learning encounters with individuals living in vulnerable communities in Guyana. I will first provide an overview of my course, offering recommendations for how to organize such experiences. I will then articulate the philosophical theory that grounds the course and explain how I integrate it with service engagements and assignments, with suggestions for how to create meaningful course content. Finally, I will discuss potential dangers inherent in international service in developing countries, and I will argue that careful philosophical and ethical grounding, coupled with a commitment to prioritize local organizations' wisdom, will not only avoid these dangers but will also prove to be transformative for both students and community partners in a way that is not possible without face-to-face engagement.

II. COURSE OVERVIEW & PREPARATION

"A Study in Service" is a two-credit service learning course during which we spend two weeks in Guyana, in Georgetown and in an Arawak village in the jungle interior. The course integrates service engagement at a variety of volunteer sites with nightly class sessions, texts and written assignments, and opportunities for cultural immersion and learning about Guyana. I have taught the course three times, always with another faculty member as co-leader.

The first stage in preparing an international service learning course is finding hosts and appropriate service opportunities. There are many organizations that pair volunteer groups with local hosts in countries around the world.[2] In addition, many colleges and universities have extracurricular programs offering service trips abroad. I met the Guyanese man who hosts my groups, Anthony Archer, when I first traveled to Guyana in 2003 as a graduate student chaperone for just such an extracurricular service trip through Fordham University. After acting as an unofficial host for many years, Anthony created his service-based travel-hosting business, *Allan's Travel and Hospitality Services*, in 2010.

The most desirable arrangement is one in which the international hosts handle all of the practical in-country preparations, such as lodging, meals, transportation, excursions, and emergency and security protocols.[3] It is crucial to be in dialogue with hosts about your group's expectations and needs, but in-country hosts will be the experts in making the necessary arrangements.

It is also essential to select hosts who have intimate knowledge of the needs and desires of the organizations and individuals with whom your group will volunteer. For my course, Anthony and I collaboratively select the kinds of volunteer opportunities students will have, and then he makes the arrangements, having cultivated open and responsive long-term relationships with those who operate and staff our sites to ensure that volunteer groups are meeting the real needs of those they serve. The volunteer sites I have chosen engage students with individuals experiencing the realities of poverty, illness, and/or abandonment.

In our work with children, we spend time playing, tutoring, and assisting the caregivers in five orphanages for children from infancy to young adulthood. Some of the children have experienced very serious abuse, while some come from families who simply cannot afford to care for them. Students witness the difference between orphanages that are privately funded through the Red Cross or religious organizations versus the facilities that are publicly funded. Anthony arranges a private meeting for us with the Child Care and Protection Agency, during which we learn about the challenges their office faces in providing care, establishing a foster care system, managing adoptions, and securing sufficient funding.

In our work with adults, we visit two sites. Mahaica Leprosy Hospital is a dilapidated government-run residence for individuals living with the effects of Hansen's disease (leprosy). Because there is great misunderstanding and stigma surrounding this disease, individuals who experience debilitating effects often choose to live at Mahaica. Given that there are fewer than ten residents, the government designates very modest funding for its upkeep. We also visit the Palms Geriatric Institution, a government-run facility that houses approximately two hundred seniors and persons with disabilities, who have very few personal resources or possessions. At these two sites, we simply engage in conversation—sharing life stories, enjoying a good song or a laugh, or simply chatting.

Anthony also arranges for us to travel via speedboat to an Arawak village, where we enjoy the hospitality of his wife's family and community for three days. Students learn about their history, environment, culture, governing structures, lumber industry, agricultural practices, and education and health systems.

Once hosts and service sites have been selected, I recommend using an application and interview process to select student participants. The main criterion should be that the students take seriously the service dimension of the course. I have found that the ideal number of students is between eight and fifteen. Fewer than eight increases many of the costs, and more than fifteen would be difficult to manage in terms of transportation, accommodation, and safety in Guyana.

Preparing students for the course requires meeting regularly during the spring semester in order to accomplish four main goals.[4] First, we make all necessary practical preparations, such as booking flights, getting passports, receiving vaccinations, collecting money, and completing health and liability forms for the college. For these tasks, I work closely with our Study Abroad Director, Finance Office, Campus Health Services, and local travel clinics. Second, students read about Guyana's history, politics, economics, culture, and environment, using history books and newspapers. We also discuss how their majors and prior coursework might inform their upcoming experience and learning. Third, we get to know each other through team-building activities. This creates the beginning of a structure of support that will be invaluable during the trip. Fourth, at the conclusion of this preparation semester, students are assigned five articles that will be the core texts for our class sessions in Guyana.

III. COURSE CONTENT: THEORETICAL GROUNDING & EXPERIENTIAL INTEGRATION

International service learning is differentiated from simple volunteer work abroad by course content and structure. Philosophy professors are perhaps uniquely positioned to guide students in the kind of critically reflective intellectual contemplation and personal self-examination that can be ethically transformative. Grounding service learning in ethical theory enables students to better understand what the theory means when applied, and it helps students process and understand the experiences and powerful emotional responses they are having.

I can easily imagine how a course with service activities like mine could be grounded upon a number of ethical theories, such as virtue theory, Kantian deontology, rights theory, or utilitarianism. To ensure a clear, consistently reinforced focus, I recommend choosing just one or two core ideas—or one central theory—to act as the organizing intellectual framework throughout the course. International service learning courses ought to be structured with clear objectives, not only for students but also for community partners.

In my own course, our first objective is to engage in ways that genuinely serve the individuals with whom we volunteer. This begins with simply being present and attentive, engaging in discourse, and listening and welcoming what they reveal to us. We then strive to do whatever we can to meet the needs that are expressed, to provide companionship and care, and to support them and the organizations tasked with providing care. This first objective is inextricably bound to the second objective, which is student learning and development. Here, I guide them in: (1) engaging in self-examination and questioning their assumptions, judgments, and beliefs; (2) philosophically exploring the role and limits of reason and the role of emotion in ethics; (3) developing an understanding of need, as *revealed by Others* rather than determined by interior reasoning; (4) discursively exploring the call to responsibility, the nature of obligation, the reality of suffering (and of suffering *with another*), the difficulty of enacting justice, and the challenge of balancing self-interest with self-donative care, in a global world; and (5) putting their talents, skills, and education to use for the benefit of Others. The core assignments are: participation in service activities, participation in class discussion, reading assignments, journal-writing assignments, and group projects.[5]

Our class sessions in Guyana take three forms, and each journal prompt aligns with the upcoming session. One-third of our class sessions are purely reflective, offering students an opportunity to talk with one another (and often our Guyanese hosts) about the experiences they're having, how they're feeling, and what they're thinking. Open-ended journal prompts prior to these class sessions help students process difficult reactions they are having, prior to being asked to share them. It is important that they have class time to discuss these responses because it helps them to hear that others are having similar reactions, it pushes them to think differently than they might on their own, and it makes them better able to keep an eye on each other when they are on-site.

Another one-third of our class sessions integrate our texts on Levinas's theory with our service engagements. These sessions take place during the first week so that the core ideas can guide us throughout our stay. I use both primary texts and secondary literature that explicitly applies the theory to the kind of service we are doing.

For example, in an article entitled "Uniqueness," Levinas critiques Western philosophy's individualistic rights-based ethical theories, arguing that they fail to adequately explain the urgency of being concerned for the Other who suffers even when all of her rights are fulfilled. He describes an "anxiety of responsibility," wherein "[t]he fear of each for himself, in his own mortality, does not succeed in absorbing the scandal of indifference toward the suffering of the other" (Levinas 192). What he then seeks to explain is "peace as a relation with the other in his absolute otherness, a recognition in the individual of the uniqueness of the person" (Levinas 195). This challenge that calls into question the priority of self-interest is not possible through reason alone, according to Levinas, but rather occurs in the face-to-face relation with the unique Other, who calls the self to non-indifference—a "not-being-able-to-stand-apart" (194).

After we visit Mahaica for the first time, in preparation for our class discussion of this article, I post a journal prompt asking the following questions: do you feel any *responsibility* to return to Mahaica to visit the residents? If not, what *do you feel* about returning? Why? If you *do* feel a responsibility to return, why? Are their rights being violated? If yes, why is it *your* responsibility to return, rather than someone else's? Does your return somehow change that rights violation? If you think their rights are not being violated, then what is it that makes you feel responsible to return? During class discussion that evening, many students say things like, "I feel like we *need* to go back," and "It was really hard to leave, because I know she didn't want to stop talking with me." On the basis of such answers, we then discuss this feeling of being compelled, or obligated, and we consider Levinas's idea of the "*anxiety* of responsibility." We discuss whether companionship is a right or perhaps there are human desires and goods *beyond rights* that equally compel us to ethical action. We also consider whether we are *responsible* to return or rather whether our return would be a kind of *optional* act—kind and beneficial (to both them and us) but not ethically required.

Secondary literature helps students work through this kind of application further. For example, in "Relational Care: Learning to Look Beyond Intentionality to the 'Non-Intentional' in a Caring Relationship," Dennis Greenwood argues for prioritizing the initial, non-intentional moment of relationality in senior nursing care, when the caregiver is called out of his/her judgments and is *surprised* by the Other who speaks and reveals him/

herself. He discusses a resident, saying, "he had the label 'dementia'. . . and [this] inevitably coloured my response to Rodney. . ..The 'there is,' as perceived by me, that existed between Rodney and me in our meetings was swamped by my intentionality and consequently allowed very little possibility for Rodney to exist as an 'other,' separate from my view of who he could be" (Greenwood 229).

This Levinasian application to nursing care *radically* directs our engagement at our volunteer sites. In journal writing and class discussion, we consider what it would mean to enter our service sites with the intentions and judgments of reason and what it would mean to suspend reason and be open to being surprised and challenged by another person who overturns our ideas and expectations. We discuss how our prejudgments, even when well-intentioned: (1) *miss* the Other instead of welcoming his/her revelation, and thus fail to be accurate; (2) perpetrate a kind of injustice against the Other, reducing him/her to less than who he/she is; and (3) are grounded in a fear of discomfort and a desire to protect ourselves from uncertainty.

This is a moment of real self-examination, wherein students start to see how important it is—and how difficult it is—to let go of their desire to control and direct their interactions with Others. We wrestle with Levinas's idea that the only way to engage ethically—to do *justice* to the Other—is to *allow the meaning of the ethical relation to be shaped and determined by that Other*, not by one's own preconceptions or aims. This means that, when we visit our volunteer sites, we are not conducting interviews or aiming to gather data or seeking to find answers to questions we have. We are not planning out ahead of time what activities we will do. We are listening. We are looking to see who wants to speak with us. We are making ourselves available to hear whatever it is that each unique Other—patient, resident, staff member, etc.—wishes to express to us. This, for Levinas, *is the ethical relation.* We then strive to base any response, and any action we might take, upon what is revealed.

The final one-third of our class sessions, taking place during the second week, are devoted to creating long-term benefit through our collaborative projects with Anthony to support his business. Though he is a master at hosting groups, Anthony has no formal educational training in business or writing. In the most recent iteration of the course, students: (1) created photo slideshows, a promotional video, and a website; (2) identified potential volunteer groups and created outreach marketing materials; and (3) identified sources of funding and wrote grant applications.

Consistent with Levinas's ethics, we begin in discourse, listening to Anthony and allowing our own prejudgments regarding what his business should be to be called into question. Students donate their skills, knowledge, time, and labor to support *his dream*, as revealed by him. Very quickly, students realize how difficult it is to truly capture Anthony's vision in their work. They learn that, just like at our service sites, we must always return to the prior ethical openness that simply listens—to the proximity of discourse, in which the Other is honored and given priority.

IV. AVOIDING PITFALLS: EXPLOITATION & DISRUPTION VS. SERVICE & TRANSFORMATION

International service work in developing countries has been met with significant critique. One common criticism is that the money spent for travel would create greater benefit if volunteers stayed home and made donations to organizations abroad. Another set of criticisms begins with the concern that short-term encounters can be exploitative, in that they might reduce the individuals with whom students engage to merely passive recipients of students' supposed beneficence and/or they subject already-vulnerable communities to *use* as mere educational tools to benefit wealthy Westerners. Further, the presence of volunteers can be disruptive or counterproductive for local organizations, and it can be painful for individuals with whom students engage when the short-term experience ends and the students disappear. Finally, such experiences might reinforce a dangerous "savior complex," wherein students see themselves as swooping in to provide assistance and care that they arrogantly assume local communities are not able to provide.

Indeed, when international service falls into such egregious failure—that is, when it is exploitative, disruptive, painful, or naïvely arrogant—the money spent *is* wasted and the activity itself is undoubtedly unethical. However, this certainly need not be the case. Many writers have considered the potential failures of international service projects, as well as potential solutions and benefits. Useful recent articles include: Bamber (2015); Bamber and Pike (2013); Sharpe and Dear (2013); and Crabtree (2013).

It should be noted that this kind of exploitation and/or disruption could just as easily occur in *domestic* service learning. In either case, this is a real danger. However, when service learning fails in these ways, the problem, I would argue, is not the engagement in service, but rather the arrogance, ignorance, and disregard that *might characterize* service engagement.

Such failure can be overcome if two key elements are present. First, by grounding international service learning in philosophical ethical theory, we can challenge students to recognize that encounters with Others call us to suspend self-interest and attend to Others with sincerity and authenticity, and it commands philosophical self-examination and contemplation of what is good, right, and just. Such rigorous philosophical grounding opens the possibility for a revolutionary unsettling of the self as we give *priority to the Other* in determining the ethical relation. This precisely forbids the arrogance, exploitation, self-interested *use* of other persons, and disregard for possible harm that might otherwise occur, as it *calls into question* students' motives, assumptions, and conceptions of themselves as beneficent "saviors."

Second, we must always work closely with local hosts and organizations abroad, recognizing them as authorities in terms of understanding what their community needs.[6] We must open a discursive space that prioritizes their voices and *their understanding* of what is beneficial and what is not, both short-term and long-term. This is a way of honoring them and recognizing that we must learn from them. We can model for our students the understanding that we are servants, not "saviors."

The criticism regarding the cost of travel remains.[7] The central questions for me, in responding to this criticism, are the following: would people in Guyana receive the same benefits if we stayed in the United States and simply sent money? Would the transformations that I witness in students be possible without engaging face-to-face with people in Guyana?

Surely, material resources could be donated without traveling to Guyana. But is this as meaningful as engaging with a person? The conversation, companionship, and care that occur at our sites are not possible from afar. There would be no discourse, no revelation, no compassionate opening to one another. There would be no proximity, which, for Levinas, opens up the ethical relation itself. I have learned through interviews with individuals and staff in Guyana that engagement with students is tremendously valued. As one gentleman at the Palms told me repeatedly, when someone wants to hear his story, and might remember him or "tell someone in America," it brings "a breath of life" to him that does not quickly fade. This means more to him than an anonymous clothing donation would.

Anthony has confirmed this benefit over the years. He was raised in orphanages from infancy, and he remembers vividly that visits from volunteers made him feel like there were people out in the wider world who cared about him and his future. Though he found it difficult when visitors left, he felt hopefulness, knowing others would come. He visited the residents of Mahaica with the two Sisters of Mercy who raised him, and this further revealed to him the value of giving one's attention to Others. Anthony's business is his way of prioritizing, and donating to, individuals living in vulnerable communities and to volunteer visitors.[8]

I strongly recommend both valuing the short-term benefits of study abroad and finding a way to contribute long-term benefits to community partners. Our group projects seek a long-term benefit for Anthony and the communities his business serves. There is no way students could adequately support Anthony's business without engaging with Anthony, listening to him, and experiencing what he offers. How could they understand why their generalized notion of what a business "should be" must be challenged when applied to a different country and culture? How could they possibly describe *his dream* from afar, never having met him or experienced the Levinasian welcome that he provides? Surely, without the ethical reorientation of the self that makes room for *Anthony* to create meaning, their projects would only be reflections of themselves. Every student course evaluation reveals this. As one student says, "If we tried to help support Anthony's business and had never done any of the site volunteering, we wouldn't understand the essence of his business. . ..Without hearing from Anthony what he has lived through, how he was impacted as a child by groups just like the ones he hosts, we cannot understand the importance of his business. . .." Students come to feel responsibility for Anthony, and this drives them to support his work, creating benefit well beyond their stay in Guyana.

In regard to the potential transformations for students, while I cannot say for certain that this trip was *the sole cause*, many of the students from this course have gone on to lives of service and global engagement. Of those with whom I still have contact, three are in law school, one taught in South America, one has worked as a case worker for three child welfare organizations, one is pursuing medical school to work in global health, one has worked for the Egyptian embassy in DC, one is in AmeriCorps in Alabama, and three are applying to teach abroad next year. Some students return to Guyana.

Even if their future careers will not take them abroad or into service fields, students consistently express that their worldviews have shifted significantly. Journal entries and evaluations reveal the beginning of a reorientation toward greater global awareness and/or service. One student said the following in a final journal entry, when describing the effect that a young boy, Calvin,[9] had on her:

> It is easier to avoid situations where you have to question yourself and everything you think you know. When the Other shakes the very foundation you stand on, there is always (at least for me) a desire for the ground that was solid, only a moment ago, to return. But that moment passes, and the truth of the interaction is healing; at the very same time that it rips you apart, it rebuilds you to be stronger, more compassionate, and more alive.

This student eloquently, yet simply, captures the potential for transformation in the face-to-face encounters of service learning. Reading about children living in orphanages in Guyana, or reading about Calvin specifically, or even seeing a video of Calvin, could never create the impact that being in his presence created. At seven years old, Calvin doesn't speak. And yet, he has the power to call into question a person's conceptions and judgments, to awaken someone to global responsibility, and to call a person to compassion and care and service.

NOTES

1. The "Other" means the other person. I capitalize the O in line with Levinas' emphasis on the dimension of the other person that transcends understanding and commands ethical response.
2. Two organizations with which I have previously worked are the Sisters of Mercy and *Community Links International*.
3. In-country hosts may also be able to facilitate other unique experiences. For example, Anthony arranged for me to meet the former president of Guyana,

Bharrat Jagdeo (while he was still in office), as well as various government ministers.

4. I recommend creating a pre-trip prerequisite course, as this ensures attendance and completion of required preparation assignments.
5. I also require that students "unplug" from their technologies. This encourages them to be present and attentive to our hosts and each other.
6. See Crabtree's idea of "attend[ing] deeply to partnerships," 55.
7. I recommend discussing this matter very directly with students.
8. Each group's budget includes a sizable donation to each volunteer site as well.
9. Name changed to protect anonymity.

WORKS CITED

Bamber, Philip M. "Becoming Other-wise: Transforming International Service-Learning Through Nurturing Cosmopolitanism." *Journal of Transformative Education* 13:1 (2015): 26–45.

Bamber, Philip M. and Mark A. Pike. "Toward an Ethical Ecology of International Service-Learning." *Journal of Curriculum Studies* 45.4 (2013): 535–59.

Crabtree, Robbin D. "The Intended and Unintended Consequences of International Service-Learning." *Journal of Higher Education Outreach & Engagement* 17.2 (2013): 43–66.

Greenwood, Dennis. "Relational Care: Learning to Look Beyond Intentionality to the 'Non-Intentional' in a Caring Relationship." *Nursing Philosophy* 8 (2007): 223–32.

Levinas, Emmanuel. "Uniqueness." *Entre Nous: Thinking of the Other*. Trans. Michael B. Smith and Barbara Harshav. New York: Columbia University Press, 1998.

Sharpe, Erin K. and Samantha Dear. "Points of Discomfort: Reflections on Power and Partnerships in International Service-Learning." *Michigan Journal of Community Service-Learning* 19.2 (2013): 49–57.

Singer, Peter. *One World: The Ethics of Globalization*. 2nd ed. New Haven: Yale University Press, 2004.

15 Studying War and Contributing to the Community

Joe Cole

How can students develop a better understanding of ethics, war, and institutional change using the tools of philosophy and experiential learning? This paper will discuss my course on Pacifism and Just War Theory, where we practiced a variety of experiential learning activities inside and outside the classroom to prepare students for designing and implementing a final community engagement project. I will draw from two recent iterations of the course to describe how the course treats philosophy as a domain of experiential knowing for the purposes of philosophical reflection, personal growth, and community engagement. I describe how my college supports student engagement in the community, my own approach to pedagogy and experiential learning, the classroom resources and activities, the parameters and outcomes of the final project, and how the students engaged with the community to gain a deeper understanding of just war theory and practice.

I. COLLEGE PRINCIPLES AND EXPERIENTIAL LEARNING IN PHILOSOPHY

The Pacifism and Just War Theory course fulfills the Guilford Social Justice requirement, whose purpose is to prepare students to be more effective agents of change. The course is cross-listed between philosophy and peace and conflict studies. The goal of the course is to enable students to evaluate different meanings of justice and responsibility in society and explore methods of pursuing change at the personal, social, and/or institutional levels. Guilford College upholds five academic principles, three of which are relevant to the course: innovative student-centered learning; ethical dimension of knowledge; and practical application and service to the larger community. Both the academic principles and the social justice learning outcomes encourage students and teachers to reach beyond the classroom and engage in the community while exploring personal and social change, both of which provide a structure for experiential learning.

Experiential learning is a pedagogical framework that highlights the centrality of experience and practice for gaining knowledge and guiding personal development. Experiential learning can include projects, community service, collaborative learning, and social action (McDonald, Spence, and Sheehan 67). David and Alice Kolb view learning as a holistic process where conflict and difference drive learning and where participants create knowledge (Kolb and Kolb 194). The Kolbs also emphasize respect for learners and their experience; building on what the students already know; creating a hospitable space for learning; making space for conversational learning, for acting and reflecting, and for feeling and thinking; and making space for students to take charge of their own learning (Kolb and Kolb 207–09).

I apply these principles in several ways. For research papers, I encourage students to choose topics that are meaningful to them; students create and give their own quizzes on reading material; group projects and small-group activities encourage conversation and collaborative thinking; and sharing circles that invite students to discuss their feelings on issues that concern them. I also rely on facilitation and group process techniques to better engage students in the classroom. Early in the semester we begin with small group activities that students study later in a book on facilitation and community transformation. Students reflect on their experiences and discuss how the techniques might be applied to issues of war and peace. Throughout the semester, as we move deeper into our theoretical studies, the classroom is a small-scale version of conflict management and resolution in a community. By creating a situation where the students must work together, students use what they are learning about war, conflict, and peace to resolve conflict and manage their classroom relationships.[1]

In planning and designing course assignments and lesson plans, I implement Kolb's four-step model of experiential education: experience, reflection, generalization, and application. These four stages constitute a cycle of learning that can keep building on itself: the application/testing stage is a new experience that continues the cycle. For example, early in the semester, I have students journal about their personal experiences with conflict; then they share their experiences aloud and reflect on their meaning. Next we look for patterns or concepts we can use to understand and categorize types of conflict and responses (here I might introduce a new framework for thinking about and/or responding to conflict), and then we apply the concepts to their personal experience, current events, or in role plays and have a new, shared experience to re-engage the learning cycle.

II. PHILOSOPHY FOR THE WHOLE PERSON AND DIRECT EDUCATION

For me, the tradition of philosophy is a craft for enhancing our lives and engaging the whole person—body, emotions, spirit, and intellect. The practice of philosophy originates from our experiences of wonder, doubt, or distress and leads to deep questioning about who we are and how we might live good lives together. To engage the whole person, I use group process techniques in the classroom to increase vitality and connection. Professor and facilitator George Lakey proposes a version of experiential learning called "direct education" that is effective for learners in a variety of group contexts to open new possibilities for growth and understanding (Lakey 7). The teacher/facilitator must engage multiple forms of intelligence; direct education values kinesthetic and emotional learning channels often overlooked in a traditional academic setting that privileges auditory and visual learning.

Direct education also welcomes conflict as a way of promoting learning and integrates anti-oppression concepts as integral to experiential education.[2] It raises issues of power, diversity, and justice and strives for awareness of how gender, class, and ethnicity influence how and what we learn. In my class, we discuss white privilege and the history and contemporary context of colonialism and racism, and we examine how this context affects our country's use and perception of violence, military force, and pacifism.

In a class studying war and violence, where I ask students to engage the wider community with a transformative project, the classroom itself needs to be a safe place for engagement, self-reflection, and transformation.[3] Learning involves taking risks, admitting that we don't know something, and then reaching for what we wish to learn. A sense of safety and connection invites students to take such risks. Lakey recommends beginning with introductions and icebreakers and setting up buddy pairs and support groups. Such activities foster connections and invite students to "share the job of building and strengthening the container."[4] The instructor can also build a safe learning environment by modeling and providing positive reinforcement of the attitudes, behaviors, and skills that are the goals of the class, including critical and creative thinking, curiosity, challenging questions, authentic conversation, admitting confusion, active listening, preparation, compassion, acts of courage, acknowledging and respecting differences, and sharing vulnerability.

Given the intensity of the subject matter that we study, I also encourage students to develop basic self-care skills, and I use Thich Nhat Hanh's meditation practice as the primary self-care skill for the course. Hanh connects meditation to a larger framework of peace building, and he proposes that work on inner peace is an essential foundation for outer peace in the community (Hanh, Peacemaking CD). Hanh argues that meditation helps us develop mindfulness, which leads to deeper patience and compassion, a better understanding of self and other, and a sense of co-responsibility for the problems and challenges around violence in the world (Hanh, Touching Peace). We practice this meditation in class a few times, and I encourage students to practice on their own. While meditation practice does not work for everyone, for many it offers an experience of serenity and grounding in their bodies and feelings while in the classroom, especially after a particularly intense classroom experience, such as viewing images of war and violence.

III. READINGS ON WAR AND PACIFISM

The first part of the semester examines the Just War Theory framework through the work of Michael Walzer and Brian Orend. Walzer's account of war is grounded within a framework of human rights. He uses many historical examples, especially from World War II and Vietnam. To provide students with some shared historical context, I show films like *Hearts and Minds*, a 1974 documentary about the Vietnam War, and *Why We Fight*, a 2006 documentary about the war in Iraq and U.S. militarism.[5] Walzer also discusses the responsibility of soldiers, officers, leaders, and citizens for war crimes. I show the 2007 film, *Taxi to the Dark Side*, a documentary about the U.S. military's abuse of prisoners in Afghanistan, Iraq, and Guantanamo. We then have a mock trial for war crimes committed by soldiers, officers, leaders, and citizens, where students take turns being prosecutors, defendants, and judges, and apply Walzer's arguments and international war crime standards like the Nuremberg Principles to questions of prisoner abuse by U.S. forces.

We then turn to Orend. Though much of his work follows and develops Walzer's ideas, Orend uses more recent historical examples, like the 2003 U.S. invasion of Iraq, and discusses emerging questions like humanitarian intervention and the use of drones. Throughout our rigorous theoretical discussions, I ask students to apply just war principles to their own experiences of force and violence. For example, we discuss the challenges of determining how much force is appropriate in personal self-defense when someone is under threat or attack. With a better awareness of complexities at the interpersonal level, we circle back to the international arena with a deeper understanding of the challenges of applying just war principles.

In our study of Just War Theory, students are often energized when we move from the conceptual generalization learning stage to discuss current violent conflicts. For the first iteration of the course, our class applied Just War Theory principles to drone strikes and the U.S. military presence in Afghanistan. That April, the bombing at the Boston Marathon took place. Students were greatly moved by that tragedy and wished to discuss it in light of what we had studied about violence, war, and pacifism. In the second iteration of the course, we discussed the U.S. bombing of the Islamic state in Iraq and Syria. In a role-playing activity, students represented the perspectives of the United States, the Islamic State, the Iraqi government, the Syrian government, and Syrian rebels, and offered arguments on the legitimacy of U.S. intervention from each point of view. We also had powerful discussions of cases of police killings of unarmed black men and children, including the morality of violent and nonviolent responses to incidents of police brutality.

It is critical to connect the study of the morality of war to current events that are relevant to students.

For this portion of the course, students work in small groups on class presentations. They develop a summary of the reading, evaluate the strengths and weaknesses of the argument, make connections to historical examples, engage the class with questions and activities, and discuss the author's or their own ideas for facilitating change at the personal, social, and/or institutional levels. Usually this last requirement is the most challenging aspect of the assignment. Students will often focus on the change that they want—for example, a more peaceful world or perhaps stricter standards for fighting a war—but miss the challenge of offering ideas of *how to facilitate that change* and make it a reality. This is a challenge I want them to wrestle with, since it brings them close to the heart of the course goals and prepares them for the final community engagement project.

We then examine Andrew Fiala's book *Practical Pacifism*. Fiala offers a philosophical and practical argument for pacifism, distinguished from "absolute pacifism." As a practical pacifist, Fiala believes that war is always tragic and almost always unjust but that there can be situations where the use of violence and war might be justified. Fiala's discussion identifies problems with militarism, the suffering and destruction that war causes, and the nation-state's tendency to seek empire, while arguing that the path to pacifism is built through personal freedom and education on the horrors of war. We close with Duane Cady's book *From Warism to Pacifism* and examine his argument for a moral continuum between warism and pacifism. I ask the students to locate the other authors we have read along this continuum and to evaluate whether Cady's framework is compelling and useful for understanding the range of different positions in pacifism and Just War Theory.

IV. CONFLICT AND GROUP DYNAMICS

While the students are reading about global issues of war and violence, they also study conflict resolution models which they are to use in their own lives (both in and out of the classroom.) Early in the semester, we study John Paul Lederach's framework for conflict transformation and his view that conflict episodes are opportunities to address deeper issues and promote constructive change. Conflict transformation seeks to create healthier and more just relationships that reduce violence in our communities. Lederach sees conflict as a natural part of human groups and calls us to develop creative and insightful responses to build a more peaceful and just world. Lederach's book offers not so much a conflict resolution tool but rather a framework for understanding conflict and a call to change our attitudes and expectations.

I also offer a practical model for working with conflict, developed by facilitator and community consultant Laird Schaub as a variant of nonviolent communication's four-step model of conflict resolution. Working in pairs, each participant takes turns sharing and listening to each other's experience and feelings resulting from the conflict; they then each articulate what's important/what's at stake; and finally, they each describe what they are willing to do to improve the relationship. This practical tool fits nicely with Lederach's vision of transformation because it asks those in conflict to identify what is important to them and make concrete commitments to create the type of relationships and communities they desire. I ask students to journal about their experiences of conflict and identify an especially challenging recent conflict they have faced. We use role playing to practice the conflict model and help students apply the model to their own lives and experiences.

Halfway through the course, we begin reading Peter Block's book *Community: The Structure of Belonging* to examine group dynamics and develop tools for working with groups. Block argues that we need to transform our communities in ways that better meet human needs and foster freedom, justice, and fulfillment. Block believes that we do this by looking at our stories about ourselves and our communities and shift from stories of problems, fear, and punishment to stories of gifts, gratitude, and possibilities. He argues that the unit of social transformation is the small group, where everyone shows up authentically and shares what is important to them, while also listening to and affirming what is important to others. Block proposes questions that are ambiguous, provocative, and open-ended, to allow people to meet one another genuinely and explore what they wish to create together. By taking responsibility for how we view the world and for what we wish to create, new possibilities emerge that can result in healthier, freer, and more just communities.[6]

Before students read this book, I break the class up into small groups and have them address a series of key questions from Block:[7] what is the price you and others pay for being here? What is the commitment that you brought into the room? How valuable do you plan for this experience to be? What have you said yes to that you no longer really mean? These questions invite awareness, authenticity, dissent, and deeper reflection. On another day, we go through a different sequence of questions: what is the current story you've been telling about problems with our society? What are your own contributions to the problems that you've been complaining about? What are some possibilities that inspire you and have the power to transform the community? In each sequence, I share one question at a time and give each student from one to three minutes to respond in a go-around format in small groups. I keep time and chime bells to cue them to switch to a new speaker. When everyone has spoken on a question, I write the next question on the board and we go around the circle again. By using the timer and the chimes, the group experiences a sense of discipline where no one person dominates the conversation and where everyone has the opportunity to practice speaking and listening. Small group formats, challenging questions, and discipline around speaking and listening are all tools that I encourage the students to use later as they create their final projects.

After reading half of Block's book, I ask the students to decide together how much the final project will weigh in their overall grade.[8] They must decide via consensus, and I give them a basic outline of consensus principles and a set of common values that are presented in the course syllabus. Based on these principles and values, they must reach a consensus decision. If another proposal is offered, students may block the proposal if their objections are based on common values and principles—they cannot block for personal reasons unrelated to group values. This activity allows them to make a group decision around something that matters to them and to gain experience of the gifts and challenges of deciding something significant together.

V. FINAL PROJECT: COMMUNITY ENGAGEMENT

The final project asks students to make a positive contribution to the community around issues of war, peace, and conflict. Students must clarify their own ethical positions on the justice of war and then design a community project that embodies their values. They must identify a target community, develop criteria for what counts as a positive contribution to that community, and develop a plan to measure the impact of their project on the target community. At the end of the semester, students submit a written summary of the project that includes a discussion of their ethical values; an explanation of why they chose this particular project; a description of the target community; a summary of work completed and course resources used; and an explanation of positive community impact and how it connected to their values. I grade their projects using criteria including clarity of values and goals; impact on community; creativity; effort; use of course resources; and quality of written work. Students may work alone or in groups.

During the final exam period, students discuss their projects in brief presentations. The first iteration of the course resulted in projects that included teaching conflict resolution skills at an afterschool program, creating a Facebook page to foster mutual understanding among Christians and Muslims, producing a radio public service announcement about military spending, showing films about war, creating art, photography, and billboard installations on campus to raise questions about violence and peace, and facilitating a youth group to discuss experiences of violence and trauma in the aftermath of the Boston bombing. The second iteration of the course produced projects that included maintaining a blog analyzing bias in the media and offering resources like video links, planning a daylong workshop on alternatives to violence, starting a "community police watch" to monitor the behavior of police in low-income and minority neighborhoods, creating a website to encourage peaceful methods of conflict intervention, leaving pocket watches around campus with messages of peace, preparing students for responding to threats during nonviolent protests, posting a discussion question about the causes of war on Reddit, making personal connections with homeless people, and collecting donations for the needy.

Many students reported waiting until late in the semester to get started and also struggled to develop realistic projects that they could both complete and that would make a meaningful difference in the community. Students who worked in groups seemed more successful and satisfied in creating and implementing plans that had a real impact on communities they cared about. Many students reported that Block's ideas on the small group as the unit of transformation were invaluable to their projects and helped them escape a paralyzing sense of not being able to do enough in a world with many overwhelming, large-scale problems.

One common pitfall occurred when students tried to rely on projects created through existing organizations. While established organizations can provide resources and opportunities, students drawn to such groups often end up struggling to connect their own values and ideas, find it challenging to take a leadership role, and have difficulties measuring the impact of their project in such organizations. In general, it was more fruitful for students to either create their own projects and implement them on their own or create their own projects and then partner with an existing organization (like a school or church or community group) to present them.

VI. CONCLUSIONS AND REFLECTIONS FOR IMPROVEMENT

Experiential learning brings vitality into the philosophy classroom while empowering students to create meaningful work and deeper understanding. This course simultaneously enables students to explore significant topics in the tradition of philosophy and address essential issues in the community around violence, war, ethics, and justice.

There are several ways the course could be improved. For example, I could bring in guests/visitors to teach self-care skills and also reserve time for students to teach each other. Second, the rhythm of the class requires balancing self-care and community/group facilitation skills along with theoretical studies and discussion of current events. Building tools and skills for community engagement throughout the course is essential, and it is tempting to spend much of our class time covering reading assignments. Furthermore, the students need additional structure for starting and completing the work for the final project, and I could include earlier timeline and due dates for project components that discourage procrastination. Finally, I would like to develop better standards of measure for a "positive impact" on the community.

My Just War Theory course highlights self-care and relationship building as essential aspects of an experiential learning environment where students develop critical thinking and philosophical skills and employ sophisticated concepts of Just War Theory and pacifism to analyze current international conflicts. By the end of the course, they have practiced self-care, group process, and conflict transformation skills, and they have worked at facilitating change in the community. Experiential learning in the philosophy classroom enables students to leave with deeper philosophical questions and a clearer personal vision of what it might mean to live a good life, seeking justice with and for others, in a conflict-ridden world.

NOTES

1. We alternate between rigorous theoretical exploration and experiential/practical activities. Rebecca Peters describes a "spiral of praxis" that "puts theory in conversation with action" by engaging students at both levels. "The theory informs their action and their action helps them to better understand the theory" (Peters 225).
2. "To learn requires facing and embracing differences" (Kolb and Kolb 207).
3. Kolb and Kolb also emphasize the importance of "creating a hospitable space for learning" (Kolb and Kolb 207). On the topic of personal transformation, Rebecca Peters points out that she cannot require transformation, only invite it.
4. Lakey 15. For example, I regularly pair students up at the beginning of class and give each of them three to five minutes to speak while the other practices active listening (paying attention, staying focused, being affirming, no commenting, interrupting, or questioning). After the allotted time for the first speaker, they switch roles. Though many teachers object that this is time-consuming, Lakey responds that students won't fully show up for learning until they feel connected and safe. Taking a few minutes at the start of class for connection-building activities saves time and creates a more productive and effective learning environment.
5. I also screen *Control Room, Dirty Wars, Battle of Algiers, Winter Soldier*, and *The Act of Killing*, as they are powerful sources of learning and discussion.
6. Block also recommends designing rooms and creating meetings that build more relatedness, accountability, and commitment (Block 152). "Every room we occupy serves as a metaphor for the larger community that we want to create."
7. It is critical for students to experience Block's questions and small group activities before reading and studying them in his book.
8. In the 2014 course, students decided to increase the weight of the final to 30 percent from 20 percent while decreasing the weight of quizzes and homework journals, where some students' grades were low.

WORKS CITED

Block, Peter. *Community: The Structure of Belonging*. San Francisco: Berrett-Koehler Publishers, 2009.

Cady, Duane. *From Warism to Pacifism: A Moral Continuum*. 2nd ed. Philadelphia: Temple University Press, 2010.

Fiala, Andrew. *Practical Pacifism*. New York: Algora Publishing, 2004.

Hanh, Thich Nhat. *Peacemaking*. Boulder, CO: Sounds True, 2002. Audio CD.

———. *Touching Peace: Practicing the Art of Mindful Living*. Berkeley, Calif.: Parallax Press, 1992.

Hearts and Minds. Dir. Peter Davis, 1974. Film.

Kolb, Alice Y. and David A. Kolb, "Learning Styles and Learning Spaces: Enhancing Experiential Learning in Higher in Higher Education." *Academy of Management Learning and Education* 4.2 (2005): 193–212.

Kolb, David A. *Experiential Learning: Experience as the Source of Learning and Development*. Englewood Cliffs, NJ: Prentice Hall, 1984.

Lakey, George. *Facilitating Group Learning*. San Francisco: John Wiley & Sons, 2010.

Lederach, John Paul. *The Little Book of Conflict Transformation*. Intercourse, PA: Good Books, 2003.

McDonald, Mark, Kirsty Spence, and Beth Sheehan. "Classroom-as-Organization: An Integral Approach." *Journal of Integral Theory and Practice* 6.2 (2011): 67–81.

Orend, Brian. *The Morality of War*. 2nd ed. Ontario, Canada: Broadview Press, 2013.

Peters, Rebecca Todd. "Teaching for Social Justice: Creating a Context for Transformation." *Journal of Cultural and Religious Theory* 12.2 (2012): 215–27.

Taxi to the Dark Side. Dir. Alex Gibney, 2007. Film.

Walzer, Michael. *Just and Unjust Wars*. New York: Basic Books, 1977.

Why We Fight. Dir. Eugene Jarecki, 2006. Film.

16 Minding Philosophy

Service Learning and Intellectual Disability

Donna S. Turney

I. EXPERIENTIAL LEARNING IN PHILOSOPHY

Philosophy is hardly known by the buzzwords of experiential pedagogies—internships, service learning, and active learning—the tradition of empiricism notwithstanding. While there are good reasons for the underwhelming presence of these pedagogies in philosophy, there are even better ones for working to reverse this. In this essay, I reflect on why philosophy has failed to be an impressive contributor at the forefront of experiential learning and how we might turn this around. If my argument succeeds, I am hopeful that the purported irony of service learning in philosophy will give way to a vision of a partnership between philosophy classrooms and communities in need.

At my institution, Randolph-Macon College, we use all three experiential pedagogies: service learning, internships, and active learning. Service learning is probably the least common of these. The presence of active learning in philosophy is probably the most common given the accepted, even canonical, use of the Socratic method in the philosophy classroom. We address active learning in a "write your own philosophy" capstone course in which our majors provide constructive criticism of others' ideas and develop their own in the production of a long essay. We require a philosophy internship to encourage the application of philosophy and exploration of careers. The philosophies of both internship and service learning provide students with practical engagement of social realities.

This chapter articulates the outcomes of a pilot yearlong service-learning course with first-year students, entitled The Minding Class, which was a course that pivoted around fostering relationships between students and members of our community with intellectual disabilities.[1] In the first section below, I discuss the practical matter of the structure and logistics of the course. I examine how my service-learning philosophy course involved students in service relationships with members of our community with intellectual disabilities. Next I address the effectiveness of service learning as pedagogy. I consider the student learning in terms of critical thinking, engagement in philosophy, including readings, and transformation of their lives. In the final section I ask how the discipline of philosophy can accommodate service by showing the impact of service learning on the methods and content of philosophy.

II. THE PRACTICAL MATTER: A CASE OF A SERVICE-LEARNING COURSE IN PHILOSOPHY

The Minding Class consisted in two linked four-credit general education courses, one in philosophy and one in psychology.[2] The students in the philosophy course in the fall term took the psychology course in the spring term and vice versa. The two courses shared a common theme for their content, in their respective disciplines, and met in adjacent rooms during the same class period. They also shared a service-learning component. With about eighteen students in each course, there were thirty-six students who participated in the service-learning component for the entire year. In what follows, I will first address the service component and then course theme and content.

The nonprofit organization we collaborated with is Hanover Arc, which serves people with intellectual disabilities and is a neighbor to the college.[3] Its clients came to campus for our class from different parts of the county as our "guest students" every other Friday for both the fall and spring terms. Each guest student was paired with two first-year students, one from philosophy and one from psychology. The two classes and the guest students convened at a local church affiliated with our campus on these service Fridays. The time the students and guest students met together was structured; half the time period was spent all together at the church in a common space, and the other half was spent in mixed groups of college and guest students in various places on campus. Both professors planned the activities for the groups, in consultation with the nonprofit. We scheduled cooking, crafts, and games for the common space. Field trips to different parts of the campus, such as the new student center, the athletic center, cafeteria, and bookstore, included activities appropriate to these destinations, such as playing basketball and eating ice cream. The idea here was for the guest students to experience college life. We had group lessons in Spanish, chemistry, and theatre in addition to exposing the guest students to the social side of campus life.[4]

In the fall term, the first-year students received training during the first two weeks of classes, prior to working with the population. They started meeting with the guest students in the third week. In the spring, we were able to begin the service learning during the first week since we did not have to repeat the training. In order to cultivate connection between the two courses, we had the class in philosophy and the class in psychology meet together for training. The students and guests exchanged biographies to get to know one another and facilitate relationship building. As the semester progressed, our students found that their relationships with their guest students grew more natural, developing to the point that they felt they did not need as much structure assigned for the time spent with their guest students. As a result, we amended the schedule for service to allow students and their guests to choose activities and also to allow for free time without activities.

The service-learning portion of The Minding Class created such momentum that we were encouraged to repeat it four times by the director of the nonprofit, its clients, our faculty and administration, and our students. The second time we taught it with the same content, but the two other times we offered new versions with different themes and respective areas of content. We kept the service-learning component with the same population each time we changed themes and content. We had the psychology and philosophy courses meet together about once every other week for interdisciplinary analysis of common readings in addition to meeting together for service on Fridays. While we had a different set of first-year students each time the course was offered, we had the same guest student population. (In fact, some of the guest students, who participated from the beginning, claimed they were back as graduate students.) Returning guest students were indeed the rudder of this ship. They were at crucial times more at ease in social interactions, quicker to participate in activities, and enthusiastic about coming to class. In many ways our guest students are better characterized as a population that served rather than a population that was served.

With service learning as the foundation, the different versions of The Minding Class were: (1) Minding Philosophy in 2004–2005 and again in 2009–2010, (2) Square Peg in a Round Hole in 2011–2012, and (3) Shoulda, Coulda, Woulda in 2013–2014. I will continue to refer to all three versions of the course as The Minding Class. The academic titles—Minding Philosophy, Square Peg in a Round Hole, and Shoulda, Coulda, Woulda—were on the books, but these were not generally used. The guest students who participated in the course are the ones who dubbed the three versions of the course The Minding Class. I have continued the guest students' linguistic convention because so doing highlights both the normative connotation of minding and the epistemic privilege of the guest students with intellectual disabilities.

In the first version of The Minding Class, Minding Philosophy, the theme for the philosophy was personal identity; philosophy topics included mind/body, memory, virtual reality, consciousness, and free will. Sample readings from this course are: Daniel Dennett (*Kinds of Minds)*, John Perry (*A Dialogue on Personal Identity and Immortality*), Sherry Turkle (*Life on the Screen*), and Clifford Williams (*Free Will and Determinism*). These readings offered approaches to personal identity, against which the experiences in the service-learning component could be examined. For example, John Perry's text offered concepts in the philosophy of mind such as memory and consciousness. I asked students to consider these in terms of their experiences with the Hanover Arc clients' memories and states of consciousness. I used

Clifford Williams's text to raise questions about free will and external influences, which they also considered in light of these service relationships. The final projects at the end of the year were joint projects for both philosophy and psychology. For this first offering the final project was an advocacy proposal for the Hanover Arc population. We asked students to incorporate concepts from their readings and their service in these proposals. We used additional readings, such as J. David Smith's *In Search of Better Angels: Stories of Disability in the Human Family*, to help students identify areas of advocacy. The college students worked in groups of five or six on these proposals. The proposals included a needs assessment, an initiative for programming, and an action plan.[5] In the needs assessment we asked them to reflect the needs of the guest students with whom they worked all year. In the initiative for programming, we asked them to suggest ways to address these needs, and in the action plan we asked them to outline steps to implement these suggestions at the college, state, and local government levels.

In the second version of The Minding Class, Square Peg in a Round Hole, the content for philosophy drew from theories of difference in feminist theory and disability studies. Sample readings from this course were: Sara Ruddick (*Maternal Thinking*), Carol Gilligan (*In a Different Voice*), and Susan Wendell (*The Rejected Body*). I used these readings to criticize canonical conceptions of normalcy and rationality. For example, I asked students to consider both Gilligan's and Ruddick's emphasis on women's experiences as points of departure for thinking about rationality. The project for this content area was for each group to produce a video documentary of their vision of a culture of difference. Students drew from what they learned from theories about feminism and disabilities and integrated this with their experiences from the service-learning component of the course.

In the third version of The Minding Class, Shoulda, Coulda, Woulda, the focus was on altruism; the topics for philosophy in this course included happiness, self-interest, duty, and self/other. Sample readings are: Aristotle (*Nicomachean Ethics*), Immanuel Kant, (*Foundations to the Metaphysics of Morals*), Peter Singer (*The Life You Can Save*), and Thomas Nagel (*The Possibility of Altruism)*. I used these readings to raise issues about altruism. For example, we considered Aristotle's concept of a weak will and Kant's insistence on thinking about persons as ends in themselves as they relate to altruism. The final project for this course was for each group of students to produce a documentary on "real life altruism." Students considered the problems the readings raised and reflected on what they themselves thought about problems with altruistic action on the basis of their service experiences.

III. THE IMPACT OF SERVICE ON STUDENT LEARNING

In all of its versions, The Minding Class inherited goals as part of the first-year curriculum requirement of which it was a part.[6] The goals of the first-year curriculum included critical and interdisciplinary thinking, active learning, speaking, and writing. As mentioned earlier, courses were four-credits each semester instead of three, eight over the course of the year. The fourth credit hour provided additional class time for the accommodation of these skills in innovative classroom settings. What we learned about the course from students' writing and speaking assignments, daily journals, essays, class discussion, and small group discussion was unanticipated and overwhelmingly positive; it pertained to the application of theory to practice.[7]

The learning outcome was for students to demonstrate that they could engage positions put forth in the readings using their experience from the service component as a basis. Our students went beyond connecting service learning with the concepts we studied. In their journal entries, we found that students did not just engage the readings; they were critical of the readings based on their service experience. I gave journal prompts for two or three entries a week for the entire year. The task changed as the term progressed. For the first month, I asked students to identify the main thesis or argument of the reading and discuss it. For the second month, I asked them to identify the thesis, provide an objection to it, and discuss the objection. For the last month, I had them identify the thesis, provide an objection, respond to it, and discuss the response.

In the objection part of their journals, most students used their service experiences to critique the readings. I had used this kind of journal assignment in traditional introductory classes without service learning and was struck by the difference between students' objections. Students in the traditional class did not draw from any particular source for their objections. Students in The Minding Class offered their criticism almost exclusively on the basis of their relationships from the service experience. This was a clear sign of the effectiveness of service learning in developing critical thinking. Moreover, what is especially surprising here is that this critical perspective emerged early in the academic year. Applying theory to practice was a goal for the final project at the end of the spring semester, but students were engaging, comparing, and criticizing theories on the basis of their service experiences before the midpoint of the fall semester. Students prioritized their service experiences over readings, reversing the epistemic privilege of the professional over the personal.

The college students had stories, included in their journal entries and final projects, about the friendship cultivated between themselves and their guests and the reversals of roles between them. An example of this was evident on a service day when the college students needed the guest students to help them with cooking. Having produced a batch of rice crispy treats that was very bland, the guest students corrected the college students' interpretation of the recipe. (Students had used the entire box of cereal in their cooking, a sorry state of affairs for the marshmallow-to-cereal ratio!)

Many of the college students shared the ways in which their relationships challenged them to examine how they think about themselves and the intellectually disabled. "Who is teaching who?" became the tagline of

The Minding Class and a reminder of the symmetry of real relationships. The designation of the service population as "guest students" was something of a misnomer given the kinds of interactions that occurred. On the first service-learning day the second year we offered the course, the guest students greeted us as we arrived, announcing who was or was not there yet. Each time we taught the course, we watched as the initial boundaries between the college students and their guests, between "us and them," gave way to reciprocal relationships between participants. One college student described the wisdom of advice received regarding a personal relationship with a significant other. Another canceled his participation in an important outing with his fraternity for one with his guest and family.

In addition to learning outcomes and personal growth, the service-learning component of The Minding Class has had the following effects: after two offerings of the course, the number of philosophy majors doubled from students who took the class; there is now an ongoing relationship between students and their guests outside the classroom, which continued after the course ended; students have chosen to work over the summer with the population; students chose career paths with the intellectually disabled; students have continued to work with faculty and students in other courses with service learning with the same population; and each year some of the students from The Minding Class have worked as volunteer mentors for service learning in disability studies.

IV. PHILOSOPHICAL IMPLICATIONS: METHODS AND CONTENT

A significant result of teaching this course is that it changed how I understood philosophy by reversing the way we generally understand epistemic privilege. Who is on the learning end of knowing? Who is on the teaching end? What about the comparative authorities of texts versus personal experience and theory versus practice? The adoption of a new yearlong, interdisciplinary, team-taught requirement for all first-year students at my college encouraged thinking outside the discipline, as we philosophers generally understand it. The synergy of working with a colleague in another discipline, support for development, and additional time for class meetings inspired me to challenge the ways in which privilege operates in organizing knowledge. Steeped in the privilege of a small residential private liberal arts college, it seemed sensible, if not long overdue, to think about how the production of knowledge in the academy could meet needs in our community.

What made this course unique was that its design was made possible by abandoning the assumption that course planning starts with what students should know. I began with how to meet the needs of people outside the academic community and then addressed the learning needs of students within the academic community. This violates the general practice of thinking about students as isolated from the community outside the academy.

Incorporation of service learning in the course meant starting with thinking about a community partner and target population as the point of departure for the course. Only then did I turn to considering the skill set of first-year students and identifying thematic content and readings. I exchanged the privilege of a student-focused mind-set from the perspective of working solely inside the academy for a community needs–based mind-set outside the academy. Philosophy curricula are primarily content-driven, but in this case, service determined content and not the other way around.

I noted earlier that in their written work, students granted more authority to their experiences than to the texts, another reversal of epistemic privilege. In thinking about philosophy in terms of their relationships with the guest students, the college students gave voice to perspectives otherwise absent in philosophical constructions of knowledge. They challenged the epistemic privilege of the intellectually able professional academic, first by the inclusion of intellectually disabled voices and second by empowering them as critical perspectives. The college students did not just include the points of view of their guest students; they took up their guest students' points of view in considering what philosophers said. In this way, students were minding philosophy, thinking about philosophical concepts such as personal identity, difference, happiness, and altruism on the basis of service learning. For example, in the essay exams in the 2009–2010 minding class on theories of difference, students argued for feminist constructions of gender, which reflected the intellectual disabilities of their guest students. In essays and class discussion for the 2013–2014 course on altruism, many argued that service to others contributes to happiness. Clearly, the individuals with intellectual disabilities from the community who participated in the service-learning component of the course were integral to minding philosophy.

Because The Minding Class was generated on the basis of an experiential pedagogy, service learning provided a way to approach disparate areas of content in philosophy for a common purpose, *viz.*, to sensitize students to essentialist generalizations and abstract discussions about human nature. In the altruism version of the course exclusively, students did not just direct their criticism against the readings. They also made their criticisms personal, directing them against themselves and against the structure of the course. Many asked how they could know if what they themselves were doing was really altruistic. Some questioned the wisdom of assigning service as a way of incentivizing altruism. Perhaps the fact that this occurred solely in the altruism course is due to the fact that the altruism content was closest to the service work. What is significant, however, is that the level of student engagement for this course was not different from the other versions of the course. What seemed important was not so much the more personal criticism produced by the altruism content but the high level of student engagement regardless of (different areas of) content. Furthermore, students in all versions of The Minding Class seemed more involved overall with the readings than students in other courses without service learning. I had used some of the materials on personal identity in another introductory general education philosophy course and did not see strong evidence in their journal entries of real engagement with the readings. This suggests that service learning made The Minding Class content effective, and not what we might expect—namely, that the course content made service learning effective.

My aim in this chapter has been to show that although philosophy may seem resistant to service learning, it can be greatly enhanced by integrating it into our courses. As a result of teaching this course, my colleague and I have made a continued effort to find a home for service learning in the changing landscape of higher education.[8]

NOTES

1. The service activities for this course and a summer stipend for course development were made possible by a grant Randolph-Macon College received from the Mellon Foundation and the Jesse Ball DuPont Foundation.
2. I am grateful for both the working relationship and friendship of my colleague Alva Hughes, professor of psychology, for teaching this course with me these past several years.
3. The circumstances of this partnership are serendipitous from start to finish. I knew the director of Hanover Arc, Lucy Cantrell, through our children. Lucy has been invaluable to the success of the course and to my learning about service.
4. Professors Mark Malin, Rebecca Michelson, and Joe Mattys were gracious in offering their time and talents as guest lecturers in the minding course.
5. On hindsight, the advocacy proposal in 2004–2005 was an overly ambitious project for the students with uneven results.
6. The first-year program ended in 2013. We are currently planning a fifth offering for the 2015 academic year as part of the honors program.
7. A faculty committee worked with the Office of Institutional Research in administering assessment of the first-year curriculum goals, but this assessment was not course specific. Assessment of students' writing and of interdisciplinary thinking was done in terms of essay scoring. While there were slightly higher results for the spring essays than for the fall essays, these were not statistically significant. Speeches were used for the assessment of the active learning goal, and these data did indicate improvement, which was statistically significant. There was additional evidence of success on active learning from NSSE, the National Survey of Student Engagement, for the first-year class, which went from below the fiftieth percentile for active learning before the first-year colloquia to the ninetieth percentile nationwide afterward. ETS, Educational Testing Service, results for the assessment of critical thinking increased, but these too were not statistically significant. NSSE and ETS results were measured by a voluntary online survey of students' perceptions of their first year at college. Thus, while NSSE and ETS results do not pertain to my course specifically, they do provide indirect confirmation of my positive impressions of the development of students' critical thinking skills in the minding course.
8. In light of the fact that both the grant and the first-year program ended, we are grateful for a donation from Carol Estes Williams, which will enable us

to continue to buy food and art supplies for the service activities and pay for the graduation party for the guest students who participate in The Minding Class. I also want to thank Julinna Oxley and Ramona Ilea for their careful and attentive editing of this essay.

WORKS CITED

Aristotle. *The Nicomachean Ethics*. Oxford (Oxfordshire): Oxford University Press, 1998.

Dennett, Daniel. *Kinds of Minds: Toward an Understanding of Consciousness*. New York, NY: Basic, 1996.

Gilligan, Carol. *In a Different Voice: Psychological Theory and Women's Development*. Cambridge, Mass.: Harvard University Press, 1982.

Kant, Immanuel. *Foundations of the Metaphysics of Morals, and What Is Enlightenment?* New York: Liberal Arts, 1959.

Nagel, Thomas. *The Possibility of Altruism*. Oxford: Clarendon Press, 1970.

Perry, John. *A Dialogue on Personal Identity and Immortality*. Indianapolis: Hackett Publishers, 1978.

Ruddick, Sara. *Maternal Thinking: Toward a Politics of Peace*. Boston: Beacon, 1989.

Turkle, Sherry. *Life on the Screen: Identity in the Age of the Internet*. New York: Simon & Schuster, 1995.

Singer, Peter. *The Life You Can Save: Acting Now to End World Poverty*. New York: Random House, 2009.

Smith, J. David. *In Search of Better Angels: Stories of Disability in the Human Family*. Thousand Oaks, Calif.: Corwin, 2003.

Wendell, Susan. *The Rejected Body: Feminist Philosophical Reflections on Disability*. New York: Routledge, 1996.

Williams, Clifford. *Free Will and Determinism*. Indianapolis: Hackett, 1980.

C. New Directions in Experiential Learning in Philosophy

17 Collaborative Research Groups in the Experimental Philosophy Seminar

Alexandra Bradner

Most people won't accept a claim until it is grounded by empirical data. For philosophers, however, that's not enough. Arguments grounded in data alone remain contingent upon that data. With new evidence, the ground could disappear. Philosophers ask that their claims pass a more extreme test: we hunt for alternative scenarios in which our principles fail to hold, and if we find one, we abandon the principle for its failure to universalize. We scroll through as many existing alternatives as we can find, but we imagine alternatives as well. These imagined alternative scenarios are called thought experiments. Perhaps, for example, we hold a principle that says we should not detach from a person if detaching from that person would kill him or her. Once we consider the imagined alternative scenario in which we've been forced to sustain the life of a famous violinist through a surgical connection to which we did not consent (Thomson), we lose confidence in the principle's ability to cover all cases—not just all existing cases, but *all* cases. At this point, we can abandon the principle or we can find a way to revise it, but we know, at least, on the basis of the intuition pumped by the thought experiment, that something is wrong.

Experimental philosophers are not completely hostile to this procedure. But they worry about the fact that the authors who present such important thought experiments to test claims simply guess at their readers' responses. So experimental philosophers run controlled experiments to study how people actually respond to philosophical thought experiments. In most x-phi studies, participants read a vignette in which a central character does something that raises a philosophically interesting question. Small changes are made to the vignette, and participants are tested to see how they react to the changes. Experimental philosophers identify the specific features of the vignette that trigger participants' responses and use this information: (1) to suggest new philosophical and psychological theories (the positive program) and (2) to criticize the arguments of philosophers who propose answers to thought experiments without testing for those answers (the negative program). The x-phi culture is distinctive. It's a young movement that has embraced teamwork and interdisciplinarity. X-phi studies are often coauthored, and research teams frequently consult with psychologists.

In a recent undergraduate seminar for advanced philosophy and psychology majors at Kenyon College, I brought x-phi's collaborative, interdisciplinary, empirical spirit to the classroom by asking students to work together in small groups on original, experimental research studies. This paper details the challenges and rewards of this on-campus form of experiential learning for both students and faculty, focusing, in particular, on the benefits of collaborative learning. By creating an environment of experimentation and support, in which undergraduates were able to float ideas without cost and access help from campus experts, we were able to run four original studies. Students left the course with valuable research experience and a sense of what it might be like to work as an experimental philosopher.

I. SETTING THE SCENE FOR STUDENT COLLABORATION

As a selective liberal arts college, Kenyon has high demands for student learning. Classes are small, and teachers are expected to think beyond the traditional lecture/discussion format. My seminar, PHIL 291, Experimental Philosophy, met for three hours on Thursday evenings and was almost fully enrolled at thirteen students. For the first day of class, I asked everyone to read Joshua Knobe and Shaun Nichols's "An Experimental Philosophy Manifesto," which argues that x-phi recalls a broader notion of philosophy that predates the onset of twentieth-century conceptual analysis (Knobe and Nichols 3–16), and Jesse Prinz's "Empirical Philosophy and Experimental Philosophy," which distinguishes empirical philosophers, who rely upon other scientists' empirical studies, from experimental philosophers, who conduct their own particular kind of studies (Knobe and Nichols 189–208). I closed the first day by presenting Judith Jarvis Thomson's (accessible) violinist thought experiment in class and conducting a Poll Everywhere survey to bring the two x-phi papers to life.[1] A lively discussion ensued, as we did not get the results Thomson predicts in her paper.[2]

For the second day of class, we studied the problem of the criterion, which raises worries about *a priori* conceptual analysis. We responded to that with David Lewis's "Elusive Knowledge" on epistemological contextualism, which allows for the proper ignorance of skepticism (i.e., the foundational use of empirical data, in some contexts) (Lewis). On the third day of class, I assigned three papers by Knobe on his side-effect effect—the asymmetry in the ascription of intentional action that is credited as the first phenomenon of the x-phi movement. I followed that with four papers critiquing Knobe, so the class could see how deep these discussions have become in such a short time. The students were hooked. For the rest of the class, we worked our way through x-phi studies on truetemp cases (Weinberg), descriptivist versus causal-historical theories of reference (Machery), compatibilism (Nahmias), moral relativism (Sarkissian), genes (Stotz), intelligent design (Keleman), norms (Uttich), gender (Buckwalter), and expertise

(Schweitzgebel), among several other topics. We also examined a series of more traditional philosophy papers on the justificatory role of intuitions (starting with Sosa).[3]

In order to write the three, four-page critical response papers (each worth 10 percent of the final grade) that were assigned in the first half of the term, students were forced to master topics in several different subfields of analytic philosophy, including metaphysics, language, epistemology and social epistemology, metaethics, biology, religion, and feminism. They were also asked to critique the studies from a scientific perspective: assess experimental methodologies by looking for sampling error and cognitive bias effects; critique graphical representations of data, such as bar charts, Gantt charts, treemaps, and networks; learn statistical methods, including chi square analysis, paired samples t-tests, and 2x2 ANOVAs, in order to check the data analysis; and consider the larger issues associated with experimentation on human subjects. None of the students came to the course with these skills at hand. The seminar required only one previous course in philosophy as a prerequisite. But through our in-depth discussions of the experimental studies, most students were able to develop the needed skills by the fifth week of class.

Midway through the term, I introduced our capstone experiential learning project: a staged assignment that was to develop out of one of the earlier response papers. Students were asked to organize into groups of three or four, according to interest, and design, run, analyze, and present four original x-phi studies. They wrote a two-page study proposal (5 percent of the final course grade), applied for clearance from Kenyon's Institutional Review Board (pass/fail), wrote a group lab report (15 percent), participated in a public PowerPoint presentation of their group's results (10 percent), completed a peer assessment of each member of their group (pass/fail), and wrote a more traditional, three- to-five-page, final critical response paper on an issue of their choice from the course readings (20 percent). We discussed topic suggestions in class and narrowed them down to four: Eddy Nahmias's experiments on compatibilist intuitions, Martha Nussbaum's objections to female genital mutilation, Bernard Williams's views on the Makropoulos case, and the identity problems raised by the ship of Theseus thought experiment. But how does one transform an objection to a philosophical argument into a scientific study?

II. COLLABORATIVE LEARNING FOR FACULTY AND STUDENTS

One of the widespread misconceptions about x-phi is that it aims to solve philosophical problems by "polling the folk." Experimental philosophers want to know whether or not free will is compatible with determinism, so they ask people on the street: "Does your intuition tell you that free will is compatible with determinism? Answer yes or no." I spent at least an hour in class explaining the difference between a poll and a controlled experiment. My students knew their experimental designs had to identify independent and dependent variables and that their analysis would have to compare survey responses to at least two vignettes, either two vignettes within one subject's test or two vignettes between two subjects' tests, in order to uncover some dependency relationship between the small change in the vignette's text and their participants' responses to the vignettes. The students were supposed to design simple, 2x2 studies. But those who had not taken a course in psychological research methods had a very hard time distilling their philosophical objections to the Nahmias, Nussbaum, Theseus, and Williams texts into the 2x2 format.

Respectable experimental design and compelling data analysis are won only by hard-earned, expert judgment—the kind of judgment that arises out of years of teaching and scholarship. Just as philosophers can look at a list of fifty sources and select five promising ones from the list, working scientists have a reliable sense about which experiments will work, which experiments are timely, and which experiments will build upon research programs that are already in progress. Most philosophers cannot claim these abilities. So before we ran our studies, I asked Kenyon cognitive psychologist Tabitha Payne to meet with the x-phi students over lunch and critique their experimental designs. Then, after we ran our studies, I asked nearby Denison University cognitive scientist and psychometrician Seth Chin-Parker to review the data and suggest appropriate statistical measures. This was an experiential learning course, so I wanted the students to conduct genuine x-phi studies, not classroom facsimiles. Students were to leave the seminar with publishable results and research they might pursue further over a summer or in graduate school. No college professor has time to teach someone else's course. But on rarified campuses like Kenyon's, where high-impact learning is supported by a high tuition rate, instructional collaboration with one's faculty colleagues is part of the culture. And this is to the good: faculty collaboration across the disciplines forestalls the common accusation from both psychologists and philosophers that experimental philosophers are dabbling in psychology, saves time, builds professional relationships, paves the way for future inter-departmental cooperation, creates institutional buzz surrounding innovative teaching, and most importantly, ensures that students receive the very best instruction.

Payne was central in helping students think about how to reorganize their theoretical interests into targeted, scientific studies. The Nussbaum group, for example, was curious as to whether peers would say FGM is wrong or whether they would hesitate to judge another culture's practice, regardless of how objectionable it might seem from their perspective. With a poll, the group would have been able to report the percentage of participants who expressed moral outrage and the percentage of those who did not. But that data would not have answered the why question: is female genital mutilation disturbing to Westerners because it eliminates the capacity for sexual pleasure, because the young women do not consent to the procedure, or both? Moreover, it's unclear how such data could serve as more than a footnote to Nussbaum's normative philosophical argument. Payne helped the group design a 2x2 within-subject study in which each participant encountered four randomized vignettes, evaluated the morality of the surgical procedure using a five-point Likert scale, and answered a series of demographic questions. The four eight-sentence vignettes were exactly the same, except for two possible points of change in each one: in the "con/no cap" vignette, the girl consents (con) and loses her capacity (no cap) for sexual pleasure; in the "no con/no cap" vignette, the girl does not consent (no con) and loses her capacity (no cap) for sexual pleasure; in the "con/cap" vignette, the girl consents (con) and retains her capacity (cap) for sexual pleasure; and in the "no con/cap" vignette, the girl does not consent (no con) and retains her capacity (cap) for sexual pleasure. The group hypothesized that on its politically liberal college campus, students would find, in opposition to Nussbaum, that the girl's lack of consent was more objectionable than the loss of sexual capacity. No longer conducting a mere poll of the folk, the group was now empowered to support a claim about *which* contextual factors routinely motor judgments of wrongness—the girl's lack of consent, the girl's loss of sexual capacity, both, or neither—and to what quantitative extent these factors mattered. After our luncheon, Payne offered us access, through Sona Systems, to the psychology department's participant pool. Without this access, we would never have been able to run our studies within the context of the semester.

Once the experimental designs and initial proposals were complete, each group had to secure IRB approval, in order to conduct human subjects research on campus. Our projects were the very first faculty or student x-phi studies to seek such approval. I expected the process to require some attention to detail, as passing the IRB can be challenging even for experienced faculty members. But my expectations were exceeded: this turned out to be the most time-consuming stage of the assignment. Fast-track approval took more than thirty days. Students had to program their studies into Qualtrics and submit the link as part of their application, so the IRB prompted yet another round of institutional collaboration with the director of institutional research, who gave the students access to Qualtrics and remained available to answer programming questions. By this point in the term, on the heels of our several collaborations, the students were arriving to class with provocative observations about the social epistemology of science and the sociology of philosophy—that is, about the ways in which the social organizations and cultures of the disciplines can affect and limit the kinds of knowledge they can generate.

Once the data were in, I asked the students to write a lab report based upon an eleven-page assignment sheet, a three-page statistics primer for x-phi, an in-class statistics boot camp (completed with the help of several YouTube videos), and what they had learned in their science courses. This is where the collaboration with a nearby psychometrician became helpful. Professor Chin-Parker graciously reviewed our data and based upon the number of participants and factors in each study, suggested an appropriate statistical measure for each group's analysis. The data supporting the Nussbaum group's hypothesis was highly significant: the p-value for consent was 0.00, which is less than 0.05 and the most significant value that could have been generated. The p-values for capacity and the interaction between consent and capacity were 0.543 and 0.840 respectively. Both of those values are higher than 0.05 and thus, statistically insignificant. In other words, when the girl did not consent to the procedure, participants' responses shifted dramatically toward the "immoral" end of the scale. But when capacity for sexual pleasure was eliminated, participants' responses hung to the "slightly immoral" option. The presence or absence of consent more significantly affected participants' responses than the presence or absence of capacity. This original research passes along a fact: it reports that Nussbaum's approach is not intuitive (for some populations). But the study also contributes to a more normative philosophical debate by showing that consent is a far more important factor than capacity (for some populations) in determining the morality or immorality of an action. The data shift the burden of proof back on to Nussbaum.

The three other studies were equally provocative. The Ship of Theseus group designed vignettes to address the questions: how do intuitions about identity/persistence change when the vessel named in the thought experiment is a ship versus a body? Do responses about identity/persistence depend upon which vessel is encountered first? The compatibilism group designed vignettes that asked: will people retain their compatibilist intuitions about free will and moral responsibility in progressively deterministic contexts? And finally, the Makropoulos group designed vignettes to get at the question: what weakens the desire for immortality more—accomplishing a primary goal or working forever toward a continuing series of smaller goals?

With our collaborations, we were able to generate focused experimental designs, gain IRB approval, test enough participants to achieve statistically significant results, and employ sophisticated, *au courant* statistical measures. This illustrates Prinz's view that "when researchers trained at each pole convene at the middle, that can be highly fruitful" (Knobe and Nichols 207).

III. FOSTERING SMALL GROUP COLLABORATION

The class worked with external faculty and staff, but students also had to collaborate within their groups. Philosophers have been slow to embrace group work, for good reason. The problems with unmonitored think-pair-share activities are myriad and pronounced to anyone who has tried them: most groups end up with members who have not completed the homework readings and can't participate; students work on task for a short period of time and then chitchat; good students take over the task so their grades won't suffer at the hands of weaker members; and valuable class time that might have been spent mastering another reading is lost to an unsatisfying discussion. But many, if not all, of these issues can be preempted with a little preparation and attention. Experiential learning requires especially tight monitoring of student groups because the groups operate primarily outside of class—beyond the instructor's purview—and in the presence of course collaborators, study participants, and the general public. Because experiential learning courses are often on a very tight schedule, problems with free riders, overbearing leaders, conflicting personalities, missing/overlapping talents, and floundering have to be identified quickly and resolved.

Before we began the experimental studies, I spent an hour of class time running through a handout on group work: why we were doing it, how to work in a group without frustration, and what an effective group looks like. Temple University's handout "Creating Effective Collaborative Learning" (Fiore) and Harvard University's "Working in Groups: A Note to Faculty and a Quick Guide for Students" (Sarkisian) served as models. Some of the more useful group work guidelines culled and revised from the Temple and Harvard handouts, with a few additions, include:

- Limit groups to no more than four to five members.
- Plan the group assignment for the middle or end of the course, after students have had time to learn the new skills required by the course and the new themes introduced by the course.
- Make sure the task assigned is relevant, fits your students' abilities (i.e., is not too hard or too easy), and does not repeat anything your students already have completed.
- Make sure the task *requires* collaboration/interdependence (i.e., that your assignment cannot be completed without collaboration).
- Plan for group work by producing clear assignment sheets for each stage of the project, with templates, whenever possible. Explain in class how the groups will operate and how students will be evaluated. Consider developing a RAP (readiness assurance process)—perhaps a diagnostic, multiple-choice test—to gauge whether the students are ready for teamwork (Michaelsen, "Readiness").
- Give the groups ten minutes in class right after the initial constitution to work out a weekly meeting time. Give the groups thirty minutes in class each week to work so you can observe dynamics and answer questions.
- Check in with each group weekly by meeting face-to-face with one member. Ask about group functionality on a brief midterm course evaluation.
- Provide "official" mechanisms the groups might use to deal with free riding, dominating, floundering, digressing, and minimizing/pessimistic

behavior. Tell students to confront problems early, and remind them that they can work with people they do not like (Bowen and Jackson).
- Finally, give students an opportunity to evaluate the effectiveness of their groups and their group's members with a confidential, end-of-project peer assessment. Have each student assess the other group members in four distinct areas: leadership/initiative, cooperation/communication, work ethic/engagement, and quality of work.[4]

With these practices in place, the practical benefits of group work will start to shine through: students are never bored; the group work keeps everyone—even under-performers—on task, because everyone becomes answerable to one another's mutual expectations; and students receive more feedback and more immediate feedback on their ideas because they must float them past the group.

In our seminar, a rare class synergy developed. The atmosphere was demanding and spirited but informal and collegial at the same time. In the early stages of the final project, for example, I asked each group to present their nascent designs impromptu to the rest of the class for feedback. These discussions, in which the audience anticipated objections to the designs, were some of the best discussions we had all semester. Relying on criticisms raised earlier in their critical response papers, some students worried that their peers' results would be skewed by the collegiate demographic; some pointed out the ways in which a proposed design was not going to target the phenomenon in which the group was interested; some uncovered confounds; some raised concerns about misleading scales of measurement; some gave advice about how to avoid ordering effects; and all of them noted how the freedom scientists have in establishing operational definitions seems to support contextualist or constructivist theories of knowledge: scientists make their own choices about how to operationalize key terms, and these choices affect what data is received and what data is not received. The students had found a routine way to proceed within the plurality of topics we had studied. One by one, my cautious, skeptical philosophers became rowdy, try-anything experimentalists with fixed opinions about how to trace worldly regularities—a memorable transformation.

IV. MEANINGFUL PEDAGOGICAL INNOVATION AND THE TRANSFORMATIVE POWER OF HIGH-IMPACT LEARNING

It can be distracting and disorienting to add pedagogical innovations to a course just for the sake of trying a technique that's presently *en vogue*. When adding bells and whistles to a course, form should fit function. There should be a reason available to the students on reflection as to why a group assignment appears. In philosophy, group work can be especially appropriate when the readings interrogate, for instance, the concept of the individual: are you studying the moral luck associated with praise and blame, dependents' "unfair" demands on their caregivers in the ethics of care, the rights objection to utilitarianism, the rise of modern liberalism in the wake of medieval serfdom, Frege's problem of cognitive significance for proper names, the referents of context-sensitive expressions, participation in Plato's Forms, or Darwin's species concept? Pedagogical innovations are transformative when they can reinforce the course content at the metalevel. In this case, the messy experience of designing and running an experimental study during the second half of the term served as a contrast to the tidy lecture-and-discussion format of the first half. At the start, students' thoughts were constrained only by the resistance of their interlocutors, while, later on, the narrowness of the studies prevented students from drawing sweeping conclusions. This communicated the x-phi lesson that *a priori* analysis aimed at certainty can be wildly unconstrained in comparison to philosophy practiced within the constraints of existing empirical data, even when that data is treated as a fallible starting point.

The director of the National Institute for Learning Outcomes Assessment and NSSE founding director, George D. Kuh, places both collaborative assignments and undergraduate research among the ten "high impact educational practices": "Collaborative learning combines two key goals: learning to work and solve problems in the company of others, and sharpening one's own understanding by listening seriously to the insights of others, especially those with different backgrounds and life experiences" ("Overview"). Undergraduate research connects

> . . . key concepts and questions with students' early and active involvement in systematic investigation and research. The goal is to involve students with actively contested questions, empirical observation, cutting-edge technologies, and the sense of excitement that comes from working to answer important questions. ("Access")

Instructors who have combined these two high-impact practices have found that the small group deliberations assist retention by reinforcing content, creating a personal connection to the material, increasing the motivation to learn, providing a series of local leadership opportunities, and building classroom community. We humanists often complain that, unlike our counterparts in the sciences, we cannot conduct research with undergraduates. Research in the humanities is all about having an original idea, and only one person can have an idea—or so the story goes. We can take on independent and summer research students, but the advising relationship remains a completely altruistic one. X-phi, in contrast, offers philosophers the opportunity to genuinely collaborate with students, who are able to assist by contributing to experiment and materials design—enlisting and monitoring participants, running statistical analyses, and creating conference posters, among other things.

My end-of-term course evaluations suggest strongly that the experiential portion of the seminar had a positive impact. Though three students expressed concerns about the demanding workload and the ever-developing syllabus, all thirteen reported that they enjoyed the course. One student wrote: "It is hard to pin-point [just one memorable reading] because we engaged so much in all the material, and it was such an open learning environment where we challenged each other and still respected each other afterwards." Another wrote: "I am very glad with what I took away from the course. I was able to participate in a new field of academia and help design a thought experiment and actually run an empirical study. It was definitely exciting to be a part of." Another wrote: "It's been a lot of hard work, but it has forced me to examine what I want/need out of philosophy in a way that I'd never been allowed to do in an academic setting. It was very, very interesting." And, importantly: "This course was stimulating the whole way through."[5]

NOTES

1. In one of the only other papers on teaching x-phi, Thomas Nadelhoffer and Eddy Nahmias detail some of the virtues of taking time out in an x-phi class to poll students. They find that polling increases comprehension of the study at hand and generates both student investment and high-quality class discussion (Nadelhoffer 2008).
2. For similar data, see Alexandra Bradner's "When the Violinist Is Your Half-Sibling: An Experimental Study of Thomson's Classic Thought Experiment," with Jeanine Weekes Schroer and Seth Chin-Parker, Poster Session, Eastern Meeting of the American Philosophical Association, Washington, DC, December 27–30, 2011.
3. All of these papers, except the Kelemen and Stotz, appear in the Knobe and Nichols's anthologies *Experimental Philosophy* and *Experimental Philosophy, Volume 2*, which we used as our course texts.
4. For additional resources on best practices in collaborative learning, see the University of Michigan's Center for Research on Learning and Teaching webpage "Cooperative Learning: Best Practices" ("Cooperative Learning").
5. Thanks to Tabitha Payne, Seth Chin-Parker, Jami Peelle, Erika Farfan, and the students of the Spring 2014, Kenyon College seminar PHIL 291: Experimental Philosophy—Brian Andrews, Adam Brill, Timmy Broderick, Michael Burten, Will Friedlander, Max Kalifut, Alexa McElroy, Kristina Miklavic, Rhodes Sabangan, Mara Vulgamore, Carter Walker, Justin Weidner, and Lauren Zoppo—for joining me in this semester-long experiment.

WORKS CITED

Bowen, Donald D., and Conrad N. Jackson. "Curing Those Ol' 'Omigod-Not-Another-Group-Class' Blues." *Journal of Management Education* 10 (1986): 21–31. Accessed February 22, 2015. doi:10.1177/105256298601000402.

"Cooperative Learning Best Practices." University of Michigan Center for Research on Learning and Teaching. Accessed February 22, 2015. http://www.crlt.umich.edu/publinks/clgt_bestpractices.

Fiore, Stephanie. "Creating Effective Collaborative Learning." Temple University Teaching and Learning Center. Accessed February 22, 2015. http://www.temple.edu/tlc/resources/workshop_handouts/Collaborative_handout_fiore_FALL10.pdf.

Kelemen, Deborah. "Are Children Intuitive Theists? Reasoning about Purpose and Design in Nature." *Psychological Science* 15.5 (May 2004): 295–301.

Knobe, Joshua and Shaun Nichols, eds. *Experimental Philosophy*. New York: Oxford University Press, 2008.

———. *Experimental Philosophy*. Vol 2. New York: Oxford University Press, 2014.

Kuh, George. High-impact Educational Practices: A Brief Overview. Washington, DC: Association of American Colleges and Universities, 2008. Accessed February 20, 2015. http://www.aacu.org/leap/hips.

———. High-impact Educational Practices: What They Are, Who Has Access to Them, and Why They Matter. Washington, DC: Association of American Colleges and Universities, 2008.

Lewis, David. "Elusive Knowledge." *Australasian Journal of Philosophy* 74.4 (1996): 549–67.

Michaelsen, Larry. "Readiness Assurance Process." 2013. Accessed February 22, 2015. http://www.teambasedlearning.org/page-1032387.

Michaelsen, Larry, Michael Sweet, and Dean X. Parmalee, eds. "The Essential Elements of Team-based Learning." Adapted from chapter 1 of *Team-Based Learning: Small Group Learning's Next Big Step: New Directions in Teaching and Learning*. San Francisco, CA: Jossey-Bass. Accessed February 22, 2015. http://cit.duke.edu/wp-content/uploads/2012/09/Essential_Elements_of_TBL.pdf.

Nadelhoffer, Thomas and Eddy Nahmias. "Polling as Pedagogy: Experimental Philosophy as a Valuable for Teaching Philosophy." *Teaching Philosophy* 31.1 (2008): 39–58.

Nussbaum, Martha. "Judging Other Cultures: The Case of Genital Mutilation." Sex and Social Justice. Ed. M. Nussbaum. New York, NY: Oxford University Press, 1999. 118–29.

Sarkisian, Ellen. "Working in Groups: A Note to Faculty and a Quick Guide for Students." Derek Bok Center for Teaching and Learning, Harvard University. Accessed February 22, 2015. http://isites.harvard.edu/fs/html/icb.topic58474/wigintro.html.

Stotz, Karola and Paul Griffiths. "Genes: Philosophical Analyses Put to the Test." *History and Philosophy of the Life Sciences* 26 (2004): 5–28.

Stotz, Karola, Paul Griffiths, and Rob Knight. "How Biologists Conceptualize Genes: An Empirical Study." *Studies in History and Philosophy of Biological & Biomedical Sciences* 35 (2004): 647–73.

Thomson, Judith. "A Defense of Abortion." *Philosophy & Public Affairs* 1.1 (Fall 1971): 47–66.

18 Philosophy as Practice

Zen and Archery

Gregory A. Clark

Zen and Archery teaches philosophy to students by training them to shoot a bow. The goal of the course is to examine the notion of practice philosophically and practically by engaging in various practices, including archery, reflective writing, and philosophical reflection. It is experiential in a broad sense: it engages the student in an experience, models and calls for reflection on that experience, and thereby draws its subject matter, namely, philosophical reflection, out of the experience. In principle, a philosophy course such as this could accomplish the same goals by paying close attention to other practices: painting, sewing, or baking, and even eating. The course provides concepts, categories, readings, and writing assignments to help students reflect on what is happening in their specific activity and in other analogous practices. For the purpose of this course, I adopt Alasdair MacIntyre's definition of practice as "any coherent and complex form of socially established cooperative human activity through which goods internal to that form of activity are realized in the course of trying to achieve those standards of excellence which are appropriate to, and partially definitive of, that form of activity with the result that human powers to achieve excellence, and human conceptions of the ends and goods involved are systematically extended" (MacIntyre 187).[1]

In this chapter, I will explain how naming specific activities as practices opens students to a dialogue with philosophical reflection. That is, when an archer can name archery, for example, *as* a practice, then her eyes may be opened to aspects of archery she never noticed before. Likewise, when a philosopher names archery as a practice, then he may find that archery can fit that description only in unique ways. My hope is to ignite the imaginations of the readers to develop courses that draw on their own areas of expertise.

I. THE COURSE

The namesake for Zen and Archery is Eugen Herrigel's book *Zen in the Art of Archery*. Herrigel (1884–1955) visited Japan as a lecturer from 1924 until 1929. He wanted to experience Zen Buddhism, but he could not find a way in. Friends advised him to take up a practice as a "preparatory school" through which to approach Zen. Any one of a number of practices—ink painting, flower arranging, tea ceremonies, swordsmanship, cooking, etc.—may function as a gateway to Zen by disengaging from the "utilitarian" function and instead engaging the practice for its own sake, as a rite or a ceremony (Herrigel chapters 1 and 5). These practices then play a role analogous to sitting in Zen meditation. Herrigel decided to take up archery, *kyudo*, the way of the bow. Herrigel thus learned Zen by learning archery, and he learned archery as a form of Zen.

Zen reordered Herrigel's experience of archery through two of Awa Kenzo's teachings. These teachings, which Herrigel calls "The Great Doctrine," exhibit the puzzling character that Westerners have come to expect from Zen pronouncements, and Herrigel insists that they cannot be understood apart from the practice of Zen. First, according to Kenzo, archery is not a matter of following steps; it is an "artless art," and one must put one's entire life into each shot (see Kushner). That is, archery becomes a meditative ceremony once we no longer need to concentrate on the successive steps of shooting. Only then will we be able to attend entirely and exclusively to the current shot. Second, when one does this, it is not the individual self that shoots, but rather "it shoots." That is, we no longer experience ourselves as active agents, with the bow, arrow, and target as passive objects on which we act. Rather, we experience ourselves differently, as part of an interconnected whole. "Shooting happens."[2] If the practice of archery has the aim of consistently hitting the bulls-eye, the aim of Zen is to consistently hit the archer. As Herrigel says, "fundamentally the marksman aims at himself and may even succeed in hitting himself" (Herrigel 5).

Herrigel's work provides the initial exemplar and the inspiration for the course, which I supplement in three ways. First, reading about archery is not the practice of archery; it is not a preparatory school for Zen. Thus, reading is supplemented with real world training with a bow. The students travel each week to Archery Bow Range Chicago (ABRC) for an hour of archery instruction and practice in Western archery (not kyudo), where they have the opportunity to progress from novice to varying levels of competence. Second, Herrigel does not provide a clear or authoritative account of Zen. Thus, I have the students read an introduction to Zen, such as *How to Cook Your Life: From the Zen Kitchen to Enlightenment*, by Roshi Kosho Uchiyama, a Japanese Zen priest. Uchiyama provides more robust definitions of Zen that Herrigel neglects, such as "big mind," "parental mind," and "joyful mind." He also corrects some common misunderstandings (e.g., that being present in the moment is incompatible with careful and calculative thinking or reasoning).

Third, though Herrigel was a German philosopher, he does not make a clear or strong connection to Western philosophy. Thus, I assign Alasdair MacIntyre's *After Virtue*, which provides the real philosophical source for practice-based education. MacIntyre's concept of a practice is grounded in an Aristotelian account of practical reason (*phronesis*) and a Marxist accounts of praxis, both of which attend to how our practices shape our character (or in Herrigel's language, how the marksman hits himself) (MacIntyre 187–94). MacIntyre provides a formal definition of a practice that makes the concept analytically useful. A practice is any human activity: A) that is coherent and complex, B) that is socially established and cooperative, C) through which goods internal to that activity are realized by trying to achieve the standards of excellence appropriate to and definitive of that activity, and D) that results in systematically extending both (i) human powers to achieve excellence and (ii) human conceptions of the ends and goods of the activity (MacIntyre 187).

II. COURSE STRUCTURE AND "PRACTICE"

MacIntyre's definition provides the vocabulary for thinking about practices as practices, and it offers an organizational framework for the course. Every student in the course assumes some responsibility for four practices: archery, reflective writing, a third practice chosen by the student, and philosophizing.

Archery is the paradigm case of a practice in this course in that we spend the most time on it and we make sense of MacIntyre's categories by reference to it. I don't actually grade the archery component of the course. I keep attendance and observe to make sure everyone participates. There is a tournament at the end, and I give extra credit for the two highest scores. But students don't need the external good of a grade to motivate them to loose arrows. They signed up for the course so they could go to the archery range.

Students have been writing since early elementary school, so they think they know about writing, and yet they are still novices. They generally don't enjoy it, and they look on it as a necessary evil. But students have not understood writing as a practice in MacIntyre's sense of a "practice." I assign Annie Dillard's *The Writing Life* and Anne Lamott's *Bird by Bird* for the students to see excellent models of reflective writing, as well as to encourage writing as a practice in ways that are consistent with MacIntyre's account of practice. Both texts can be read as belonging (albeit problematically) to the "Zen and Writing" genre. We take the time to provide a similar analysis for reflective writing as we did for archery in the section above.

Experiential learning is tailor-made for reflective writing. The instructor structures an experience with certain outcomes in mind, but the experience is always less than, more than, and other than what was intended. Responses to reflective writing assignments can indicate progress toward intended outcomes. Just as important, they can name those unintended outcomes that the instructor could not anticipate and that the student too may have missed if the writing assignment had not provided the opportunity to capture it.

Reflection paper prompts may be as simple as, "Describe the difference in your experience between shooting at a blank bale and shooting at a target face." A prompt that asks them to reflect on the reading (Tom Kelly's *The Tenth Legion*) with an eye to their own paper looks like this:

> Who are the "deer hunters" of your practice? Describe them in unflattering ways. Who are the "old people" who fake it for external rewards in your practice (Ch. 2)? Describe them in unflattering ways. Who is the 10th Legion of your practice? Why should your readers respect and admire them? Describe them and praise them.
>
> Who or what is the "turkey" in your practice? Describe the turkey and the demands it makes on its pursuers.

Perhaps the most important experience for students in the practice of writing is rewriting in the context of a writing community. Their final paper must progress through four distinct drafts. In the process, students conference together and help each other with their papers by forming a type of writing community. Most of the grade for the class is based on a combination of following the writing process and on the quality of the final paper. The external reward of grading remains necessary.[3] The prompt for the final paper with rubrics and grading criteria may be found at the course website. (For the syllabus, schedule, writing prompts, etc., see: http://philosophiablog.net/practical-philosophy/zen-and-archery/.)

Students learn more when they can be the experts and teach others. So for a third practice, students choose a practice in which they already have some expertise and then teach the class some aspect of that practice in a fifteen-minute presentation. They present on longboarding, coffee making, running, jewelry making, piano playing, ballet, cooking, singing, mustard making, home brewing beer, martial arts, wood-working, pie making, and so on. The final paper is, at the simplest level, a how-to paper on their chosen practice. At a deeper level, the paper analyzes the practice *as* a practice, specifying its communal dimensions, its internal and external goods, and the virtues it is likely to require of its practitioners. At another level, the paper shows what it would mean for the practice to be a preparatory school for Zen, to be a means of Zen meditation. Indeed, the working title for their paper is "Zen and [my practice]." But at the most rarified level the paper is also to be a meditation on how the practice teaches us to live. Or put differently, each paper must answer the question, "If a practice is training in a vision of the good life for humans, what is the good life for human implied by your practice?"

The fourth practice of "Zen and Archery" is philosophy. I begin the course by trying (and failing) to understand archery on the model of mechanistic or genetic accounts of action. I then try (and fail) to understand archery on an intellectualist, or purely rule-based, account of action. My goal, of course, is to lead the students into a series of *aporiai,* dead ends. I hope to give them a sense of being puzzled and not just frustrated.

My long-range goal is to articulate the concept of "practice" as a response to those inadequate accounts. However, I cannot hand the students an answer. The answer would already be fairly abstract, and they haven't yet felt the need for it. They need to try working it out in their own experience and through reading thick, non-philosophical accounts of practices. I want them to see that philosophical problems are found not primarily in philosophical journals but the things they love to do. Experiential education provides the ideal way to make this connection.

That said, part of the practice of philosophy is reading. We aren't the first to confront these philosophical challenges, and we must consult "the many and the wise." Tom Kelly's *The Tenth Legion* offers an outstanding, thick description of a practice. Aristotle would have classified him with "the many" (*hoi polloi*) that we should consult, but his philosophical instincts are gold. Most of the readings try to bridge the gap between everyday practices and the philosophical reflection on those practices: Herrigel, Mipham or Uchiyama, Crawford, and even MacIntyre. Students find these readings more than challenging. Canonical philosophical readings—Aristotle, Marx, MacIntyre—require time and care. I prefer to conduct classes as dialogically as possible, and I can usually do this with my best students participating. However, I often get wider class participation if I lecture on a few principal concepts at the beginning of each class so that we all start from the same place.

III. THE PRACTICE OF ARCHERY

What exactly do students learn in the course? How will our students philosophize about archery? How will archery inform their philosophizing? In this section, I will show how "Zen and Archery" examines the notion of practice-based philosophy of education in three ways: as the concept of practice is experienced as (1) coherent and complex, (2) a socially based and cooperative venture, and (3) achieving goods internal to the practice. I will use both MacIntyre's and Herrigel's concepts to illustrate this as I explain how the course works.

Archery clearly exhibits coherence and complexity. During the first session at ABRC, the instructors, Bill Munson and Eva Yam, introduce the students to some three basic safety rules: 1) don't get shot; 2) don't shoot anyone; and 3) don't dry-fire your bow. (There is a fourth rule: "Have fun." But this is a rule that challenges certain ways of applying rules.) The instructors also introduce the students to the basic steps of how to shoot a bow and arrow. The steps are similar to the steps found in Herrigel's book: a) grasp the bow; b) nock the arrow; c) raise the bow; d) draw and hold; and e) loose the arrow. Later they will learn the rules for scoring and for line etiquette in a tournament. Further, in the classroom, they will learn how a bow works and about how the materials and design of the bow and arrow have developed across time and cultures.

These rules, steps, settings, and equipment introduce the students to the coherence and complexity of archery and by analogy, all practices. We can find these features in how-to books, in instruction manuals, on YouTube videos, etc. They offer an entryway into the practice for the novice, a beginning point for a teacher, and a first approximation for a philosopher thinking about a practice. But the rules and the steps are not adequate to coherence and complexity of archery or of any practice. Following the steps of shooting an arrow is not enough to make you a good archer. The execution of each step may need modification to account for the unique structure of an archer's body. Further, the archer must perform each step automatically rather than with conscious effort. The movements must be fluid. Unless this happens, the steps and rules will actually distort the practice. They will have the practitioner attending to this, when she ought to attend to that. To move beyond the novice stage of a practice requires that the practitioner master steps and rules so that they function as intuited or tacit knowledge. This allows the practitioner both to determine where attention is needed and to have the freedom to attend there.

Herrigel's way of explaining this is to say that we must move beyond simply following steps in three ways. First, he practiced only the form of shooting for almost one year before he ever shot at a target. Further, each step in kyudo begins with breathing in, sustaining the breath, and exhaling. Breathing weaves each step into a larger whole; it was the breathing that led Herrigel from practicing a series of steps to practicing kyudo. Finally, his Zen training continually reminded him that kyudo is not *about* executing the steps, nor is it *about* even hitting the target. That is, part of his training was learning the difference between the steps of the practice and the practice itself.

But now let us take a step back and ask if archery might teach us something about the character of coherence and complexity. Someone might claim that archery is not actually a practice but a mere skill. MacIntyre is vague here. He never specifies how much complexity and coherence is required to move an action from a mere skill to a practice, and he is content to list examples of what seem right to him: playing the game of football is a practice, but throwing a football is a skill.

Further, we know that a machine can shoot a bow more consistently and accurately than can any human. Perhaps archery's complexity can be reduced to rule-following, in much the same way that we can now program machines to play chess better than we do. And this might threaten archery's status as a practice. On the other hand, those who maintain that chess is a practice (indeed, judging by how often it is cited, it is the paradigm of a practice) insist that machines and humans play chess differently and that chess remains a practice for humans. What, then, is the nature of the coherence and complexity of archery that makes it a practice?

Students meet other employees and associates of ABRC. Bill and Eva are joined by a rotating but stable cast of helpers: Sue, Ryan, James, Mischa, and Sergey. We are generally the first group of the evening to arrive, but by the time we are leaving, other groups are filing in. One group comes in to prepare for the World Cup at Vegas, and then later in the semester they begin preparing for indoor nationals at Louisville. Another group comes in from the Rehab Institute of Chicago. The students come to realize that they are at a hub of the archery community in Chicago. The pictures on the wall, the trophies on the shelf, and the announcements on the bulletin board show that ABRC is connected to other ranges and clubs and to organizations at the local, state, national, and international levels. Archery was not handed to humanity by Apollo or Artemis. The rules, the styles, and every aspect of the practice is an expression of the communities that keep it alive.

IV. PRACTICE AND THE COMMUNITY

Students learn that there are two parts to the idea that practices are socially established and cooperative. First, though a practice like archery may seem like it could be solitary, it is not. Practices are not invented or reinvented by each person who takes it up anew, and neither are they stored in the genetic memory of each individual. Communities of practitioners promote, sustain, and develop the practice. But on the other hand, different communities will almost certainly do some things differently. No one community carries out a practice the "natural" way, while all others deviate. Practices are both constituted by and help to constitute culture. In this regard, communities form around practices, and practices express the life of a community. Practitioners establish societies, associations, or institutions to nurture, promote, and strengthen the practices, and those societies produce new, and hopefully better, practitioners. Novices join the community by learning from those whom the community recognizes as having more expertise. One does not simply learn a practice; one must be shaped by the community of practitioners.

When Herrigel set out to learn Zen through learning archery, he relied on this dimension of practices. The community dimension of practices is also the aspect that could have prevented him from learning archery. The kyudo community in Japan, and Awa Kenzo, who eventually became his teacher, was not open to a Westerner joining the ranks. When he was finally allowed in, Herrigel needed to learn not only archery but also the proper way to behave within that community. He could learn the practice only by respecting the community formed by and around the practice. Only because they allowed him into their community could *Zen in the Art of Archery* become the face of the kyudo community to the Western world when he returned to Germany.

ABRC does not practice kyudo; they teach indoor target archery. So while there are similarities between the students' experience of archery and Herrigel's descriptions, the differences are just as striking. I noted above that Herrigel identifies the same steps of shooting a bow that I and my students use. However, the actual execution of each step is so utterly different that the skills are not transferable. The archers grip the bow differently, place the arrow on opposite sides of the bow, draw differently, anchor (or not) differently, release differently, and follow through differently. Awa Kenzo even claims that one need not aim. Likewise, the methods of instruction in Japan in the 1920s and in the United States in 2010s are incommensurable. Japanese instruction relied on deference to and imitation of the teacher in ways unimaginable for Westerners, then or now. To fully grasp these differences, the class experiments with some of the techniques that Herrigel discusses: the students have two sessions of blank-bale shooting; I sometimes teach through imitation rather than explanation; we give more attention to breathing and rhythm than we otherwise would. We ask students to allow their minds to rest on only one thing: the arrow that they are about to loose.

Because practices are socially established and cooperative, we can articulate how they are always relative, but not viciously so. This dimension of practices presents the challenge, the possibility, and the reward for cross-historical and cross-cultural dialogue. Archery provides an ideal basis for cross-cultural engagement because nearly every people group from prehistory to the present has an archery culture. Archery, then, provides a bridge between Eastern and Western philosophical traditions.

Registration for Zen and Archery always hits the enrollment cap quickly. The range fees cost extra and are passed on to the students. It requires an entire evening once a week. Yet I've never had a student ask me, "But what can I do with that?" or "How will this help me get a job?" Students don't cut class if they can help it. They know why they are there; they say it is "fun." It is a highlight of their week, and of mine. Nonetheless, it is difficult to keep students in the course focused on the mere experience of learning about and reflecting on philosophy and archery. When the targets go up, students see how their friends shoot. They compare scores. That young woman who otherwise appears clumsy shoots the high score, and people see her differently. Some archers hold their heads high, while other heads are wagging. I would not be surprised to find that students sometimes wager on how people will perform each evening. What initially seemed enjoyable for its own sake can become an exercise in frustration and disappointment when the focus subtly shifts from fun to competition.

Herrigel and MacIntyre both offer analyses of what is going on here. The archers are initially attracted by the act of archery for its own sake. But when they start shooting at targets, external elements enter, and it changes their experience of the act. And yet this summary remains superficial. It covers over the differences in the ways Herrigel and MacIntyre parse the act of archery (and so also difference in their philosophies). What does it mean to practice archery "for its own sake"? Neither author means "for fun." Herrigel means that it can be separated from its utilitarian function and made into a ceremony. But is hitting the bulls-eye a utilitarian function, external to the practice of archery? Is using archery as a form of meditation to train the mind doing archery for its own sake? Likewise, MacIntyre would name and distinguish the internal and external goods of archery. The external goods (e.g., fame, money) are necessary to promote the practice, but they open the possibility for its corruption. Internal goods—those elements of the act that we enjoy when the act is well-executed—are integral to the activity and are available only through that activity. In order to achieve excellence in the practice, competition is necessary but also dangerous. Herrigel and MacIntyre, then, disagree on what is integral to archery. Students can unpack these differences for themselves by reflecting on whether and in what ways the practice of archery is advanced or hindered by competition.

IV. CONCLUSION

In addition to teaching this experiential learning course, I teach traditional philosophy courses. At the introductory level (Logic, Modern and Contemporary Philosophy) I tend to focus on elementary cognitive outcomes. I introduce theses, illustrate how they apply in paradigm cases, and ask students to apply those theses in similar cases. My advanced courses (Hermeneutics, Directed Research) tend to aim at more challenging cognitive outcomes. Students conduct research, derive theses from primary source readings, summarize the conversations around what those theses are and how they do or do not apply, and make an argument for how they think we should understand or apply the theses.

My experiential-learning courses, of which "Zen and Archery" is one, differ from the traditional courses. Affective and behavioral outcomes play a central role without pushing the cognitive outcomes to the side. That is, I can count on students bringing some enthusiasm to the course. Students will be physically engaged in the subject matter. As a result, the students' knowledge of the material is not secondary, derived from reading only. Their experience gives them a direct authority from which to think and speak.

In a traditional class, I can give a brilliant, insightful lecture, and it will generate an introductory discussion. In an experiential-learning class, I can give an introductory lecture, and the students won't allow me to finish. They will launch into an advanced-level discussion of the nuances of a thesis. Non-majors will ask questions I'd expect from majors; majors make arguments I'd expect of graduate students.

Zen and Archery teaches philosophy to students by training them to shoot a bow. If my theses on practice are correct, students will be able to practice archery and engage in sustained philosophical reflection on the other practices they engage in long after the course is over. The course will come to mind and be instrumental in their philosophical reflection. When it does, the bow will become their teacher.

NOTES

1. For an approach to the philosophy of education congruent with this approach, see Higgs.
2. I believe, "It shoots" should be read as we would read, "It is raining." We are not attributing agency to an "It" that rains, nor to an "It" that shoots. We are just saying, "Shooting happens." Awa Kenzo used the phrase to identify when the shooting was going well, so a paraphrase might be, "Now shooting is really happening."

WORKS CITED

Dillard, Annie. *The Writing Life*. New York: Harper & Row, 1989.

Dōgen and Kōshō Uchiyama. *How to Cook Your Life: From the Zen Kitchen to Enlightenment*. Trans. Thomas Wright. New York: Shambhala, 2005.

Herrigel, Eugen. *Zen in the Art of Archery*. Trans. R. F. C. Hull. New York, NY: Pantheon, 1953.

Higgs, Joy. *Practice-based Education: Perspectives and Strategies*. Rotterdam: SensePublishers, 2012.

Kelly, Tom. *Tenth Legion: Tips, Tactics, and Insights on Turkey Hunting*. Guilford, CT: Lyons, 2005.

Lamott, Anne. *Bird by Bird: Some Instructions on Writing and Life*. New York: Anchor, 1995.

MacIntyre, Alasdair C. *After Virtue: A Study in Moral Theory*. Notre Dame, IN: University of Notre Dame, 1984.

Mipham, Sakyong. *Turning the Mind into an Ally*. New York: Riverhead, 2003.

19 Teaching Philosophy by Designing a Wikipedia Page

Graham Hubbs

I. INTRODUCTION

Many technological advancements do not readily lend themselves to incorporation into a philosophy curriculum, but Wikipedia is an exception.[1] Courses can be designed around implementing or improving Wikipedia pages, which will help students both learn technological skills and engage with the world beyond the classroom walls. This essay recounts my experience leading such a class; my hope is that it may serve as a guide for developing similar courses in the future.

II. COURSE DESIGN: LEADING UP TO THE PROJECT

In the fall of 2012, I led an upper-division undergraduate class on collective intentionality. At the time, there was no Wikipedia entry on the topic. I decided that the class's final project would be to design and to implement that entry ("Collective Intentionality"). The fit between topic and project was excellent: we would study collective intentionality by engaging in the collectively intentional act of creating the Wikipedia page on collective intentionality. The match between topic and method does not need to be this tight, however, for the project of designing a Wikipedia page to be pedagogically useful. There are scores, if not hundreds, of specialized philosophical topics that do not yet have Wikipedia entries; any instructor who wants to teach one of these topics could make the design and implementation of a Wikipedia page a group project for her/his class.

Over the course of the semester, we read and discussed the literature on collective intentionality. Students wrote blog posts in response to the readings, which provided the base material for composing the first drafts of the page's content. We used the blog feature on BlackBoard Learn, the University of Idaho's online course service; other services could have been used instead.[2] The recent literature on collective intentionality is not voluminous, so the students were able during the semester to master all they needed to know to develop the page. Some students suggested that the course would have been better if we had spent the first few weeks discussing intentionality more generally, which would have provided a broader framework within which to understand the debates on collective intentionality. This suggestion, I think, was a good one. If I organize a course around producing a Wikipedia page again, I will not jump in to the specialized literature without first presenting more general, framework-setting material.

This is probably good advice for anyone who wants to incorporate a page-design project into her/his course, but achieving the right balance of framework setting and specialized focus is no easy matter. It is only made more challenging if the specialized topic is one with a large literature. Take, for example, semantic externalism. There is a very brief Wikipedia page on the topic, which has just two citations ("Semantic Externalism"). By contrast, on the Stanford Encyclopedia of Philosophy's entry on content externalism, the subsection on semantic externalism has five citations and is nearly twice as long ("Externalism about Mental Content"). Now, one can only hope to scratch the surface of the literature on semantic externalism in an undergraduate course; indeed, one could easily spend half of the course reading Frege, Carnap, Quine, etc., to set up the discussion of the topic. It should be obvious, however, that the current Wikipedia page on semantic externalism could be improved, even by a class that only manages to cover the topic's seminal papers. Again, this is sure to be true of scores, if not hundreds, of specialized philosophical subjects.

III. COURSE DESIGN: THE PROJECT

Returning to the class on collective intentionality, two-thirds of the way through the semester, with six weeks to go before its end, we began composing the page. We spent one class session reviewing the how-to materials available through Wikipedia's "Article Wizard," which includes information about their editing standards and instructions for first-time page developers ("Wikipedia: Article Wizard"). The focus at this point was strictly on the page's content, so we did not spend time learning Wikipedia's various editing commands. We then turned to settling on the page's organization. The students decided the clearest way to present the contemporary philosophical debates on collective intentionality was by author. Other topics might be subdivided in different ways: sticking with the example of semantic externalism, one might subdivide that page into the different debates (e.g., those concerning self-knowledge, those concerning the relation between mental and semantic content) that emerged after the presentation of the original position.

Once our method of sub-dividing was settled, the class split into various teams to work on different parts of the page. Many of the teams focused on individual authors and, drawing on the material from their blog posts, began composing the author sections. One team worked on the page's introduction. Another team researched Wikipedia for all entries related to collective intentionality; these entries would then be hyperlinked with our page. Another team researched non-Wikipedia websites on collective intentionality, to which external links would be made. The last team did little at this point but was to be responsible for final grammar checking and editing once a full draft of the page was established. The teams posted their work to a private Wikispace, which then served as a rough draft for the page's content and links.[3]

A word is in order here on the amount of guidance I offered as the course instructor throughout this process. When experiential learning involves not merely perceiving the world but altering it in some way, part of its pedagogical value comes from the responsibility students take when they believe their work has an impact beyond the classroom. That sense of responsibility is enhanced if the students are not merely carrying out orders or following instructions but are making impactful decisions. It is nevertheless the role of the instructor to offer guidance, giving helpful suggestions when needed, overruling bad ideas, and resolving disputes. So when I say that the students decided to organize the material around the authors on collective intentionality, that is not to say that I did not participate in the decision-making process; I facilitated it from an arm's length, as is appropriate for experiential learning. The same is true of my facilitation of the content production. I advised the students along the way to improve the content, but the final decisions were ultimately up to them. One's own pedagogical preferences will determine the extent to which one is hands-on or hands-off at this point in the process. It is best to encourage student responsibility, which I think speaks in favor of being as hands-off as possible, but I doubt there is anything like a firm rule on the issue.

While the students were developing the page's first draft, we continued working through the literature. We concluded our review of each of these later articles with a discussion of what place, if any, it should have in the Wikipedia page. We did not end up incorporating much of this later material, but it would not have been problematic had we decided to do so. After the literature review was complete, the students spent two weeks composing their page on the private Wikispace. We might have instead used a personal Wikipedia Sandbox for page development, but to keep attention focused strictly on the content and its organization, we held off on adding anything to Wikipedia itself until near the end of the project.[4] In-class time was devoted to allowing students to break into their small groups to work on their specialized projects. The students appreciated this, but the time allotment was not necessary; the small groups could have conducted their work outside of class. At this point, we also spent in-class time reviewing Wikipedia's editing commands and content policies.[5]

One of the more pedagogically useful aspects of this project was the way it reinforced the importance of clean prose, straightforward and accurate presentation of others' ideas, and adequate citation of sources. These are features of good writing that any teacher should want to convey to her or his students, but students can fail to recognize the importance of these features. It is easy for students to complain that a teacher is being too strict or simply mean when high standards of writing are enforced. Wikipedia's policy to maintain such standards creates a space in which to discuss the importance of clear, accurate, and well-sourced writing, and it also can help students to be more accepting of these standards rather than seeing them as the imposition of a tyrannical teacher.

There are several ways one might go about assessing whether the standards are met, which can help ensure, in turn, that the page will survive once it is taken live. One would be to tell students that the page will not go live until the project is of B or perhaps A quality. Another is simply to take the page live in whatever shape it is in while there are still a few weeks left in the semester and let the students learn from the edits that ensue (more on this below). I did neither of these. Instead, I hoped that the team of final editors would do their job well enough to produce a page that conformed to the standards. I got a bit lucky here; one of the editors was one of the best students I have ever had and is currently pursuing a PhD in philosophy. One cannot always expect to be so lucky, however, so this issue is worth thinking through when organizing a page-design project.

When the content was ready to go, we copied it from the class's Wikispace to a Sandbox we opened for developing the page. Several tasks remained before activating the page. First, the team that had worked on internal Wikipedia links needed to link our page out to the relevant pages and link those pages in to ours. This included inserting links into the body text as well as developing and implementing a "See Also" section. The team that had worked on the external links had to create these links; these were divided into the page's "Further Reading" section and its "External Links" section. The team that had worked on the page's citations had to produce these, which included generating links to the footnotes in the page's body text. The editing team was responsible for checking the page's internal organization, making sure that the headings and subheadings linked to the table of contents as we had planned, and proofreading the prose. Finally, one last team found some appropriate images and added them, with captions, to the page.

IV. ASSESSMENT

Standard survey methods were used to assess the effectiveness of the project. The following response is representative of most students' reactions: "The course was like nothing I have taken before. It was nice to work towards a common goal, and to thoroughly flesh-out a single idea rather than to temporarily cram a dozen different concepts into a semester. It forced me to think about things in way I never have—or have had time to, think about them before. . . . It will also be really neat to have a finished project that exists in the real world and to know I worked to create it."[6] Note that this student claims to have had a unique learning experience, not only because of the in-depth focus on a single topic over the course of the semester but also because his/her work resulted in something that now "exists in the real world." This is exactly the sort of response for which an instructor hopes when s/he engages in experiential learning.

Wikipedia itself also offers several ways to assess the project's success and impact. First, one can review the page's revision history.[7] If the project has been executed well, then there should be minimal revisions to the prose, the content, or the links. Saying "should" is important here, of course, as revisions can themselves be erroneously made. One thing I did not do but would likely do in the future is organize the syllabus so the page can go live while there are still a few weeks left in the semester. Doing so would allow the class to review revisions to the page and to discuss whether the revisions are corrections or are errors that need to be undone. Wikipedia also allows one to know the page's view history.[8] These data can help students appreciate the impact of their work beyond the walls of the classroom.

V. CONCLUSION

As stated at the outset, this project, I believe, can serve as a model for other upper-division philosophy courses. Again, to improve upon the course I led, I would recommend contextualizing the specialized topic within the broader philosophical landscape and, as just mentioned, time the project so that the Wikipedia page is activated a few weeks before the course's end. For topics that already have Wikipedia entries, one could make improving the existing page the class's collective assignment. The philosophical implications of such projects are potentially quite rich: students not only reap the rewards of contributing to public knowledge, but they also learn how public knowledge is produced. This, in turn, helps them to be more aware—and when appropriate, critical—of the sources of knowledge on which we all rely in our daily lives.

NOTES

1. For background on Wikipedia, see their self-description at "Wikipedia."
2. Blackboard's blog tool is described at "Course Blog Tools: Blogs."
3. For more on Wikispaces, see "Wikispaces."
4. For more on these Sandboxes, see "Wikipedia: About the Sandbox."
5. Information on both editing commands and content policies can be found at "Wikipedia: Contributing to Wikipedia."
6. This anonymous quote was posted to the University of Idaho's Online Course Evaluation for the class. No public URL exists for this evaluation.
7. For the Collective Intentionality page, this revision history can be seen at "Collective Intentionality: Revision History."
8. For the Collective Intentionality page, this view history can be seen at "Wikipedia Article Traffic Statistics: Collective Intentionality."

WORKS CITED

"Course Tools: Blogs." *Blackboard Help*. Blackboard Inc., 26 March 2013. Web. 26 March 2015.
"Collective Intentionality." *Wikipedia*. Wikimedia Foundation, 7 October 2014. Web. 26 March 2015.
"Collective Intentionality: Revision History." *Wikipedia*. Wikimedia Foundation, 7 October 2014. Web. 26 March 2015.
"Externalism about Mental Content." *Stanford Encyclopedia of Philosophy*, Metaphysics Research Lab, CSLI, Stanford University, 22 January 2014. Web. 26 March 2015.
"Semantic Externalism." *Wikipedia*. Wikimedia Foundation, 21 January 2014. Web. 26 March 2015.
"Wikipedia." *Wikipedia*. Wikimedia Foundation, 24 March 2015. Web. 26 March 2015.
"Wikipedia: About the Sandbox." *Wikipedia*. Wikimedia Foundation, 17 November 2014. Web. 26 March 2015.
"Wikipedia Article Traffic Statistics: Collective Intentionality." *Wikipedia*. Wikimedia Foundation, 26 March 2015. Web. 26 March 2015.
"Wikipedia: Article Wizard." *Wikipedia*. Wikimedia Foundation, 18 February 2015. Web. 26 March 2015.
"Wikipedia: Contributing to Wikipedia." *Wikipedia*. Wikimedia Foundation, 20 March 2015. Web. 26 March 2015.
"Wikispaces." *Wikispaces*. Tangient LLC, 2015. Web. 26 March 2015.

20 Museums as the Philosophy Lab

Technology and Cognition Beyond the Brain

Robin L. Zebrowski

1. INTRODUCTION

Philosophy classes often seem to be resistant to experiential learning opportunities. There are no easy lab activities for most traditional readings, and even in the cases where we do have common experimental references, they tend to be thought experiments. Yet clearly experiential learning is a powerful pedagogical technique, and as philosophers, we really must start talking about how we can bring these experiences into our classrooms. In this chapter, I discuss my use of campus museums for experiential learning (EL) activities relevant to philosophy courses, in the hopes that this discussion will encourage other philosophy instructors to buck the traditional lecture-and-discussion model that so many of us were raised on for the purpose of increasing student engagement and learning. I will also discuss some other uses of the museums across disciplines to show more ways we can adopt these uses in philosophy courses.

While I will not speak in detail about the pedagogical theories of experiential learning, I will mention that my use of the phrase draws heavily on Kolb's explorations into the topic (Kolb 1983). Kolb offers a working definition of learning as "the process whereby knowledge is created through the transformation of experience" (Kolb 38). He goes on to emphasize the process itself:

> First is the emphasis on the process of adaptation and learning as opposed to content or outcomes. Second is that knowledge is a transformation process, being continuously created and recreated, not an independent entity to be acquired or transmitted. Third, learning transforms experience in both its objective and subjective forms. (38)

Importantly, my takeaway of Kolb's summary reminds us that learning is not a case of mere knowledge transmission and that learning takes place in an environment of active inquiry. As philosophers, we ought to be an excellent group to emphasize process over outcomes, but it can be quite difficult to sell this model to administrations, which are increasingly worried about outcomes assessments and testing. When I speak of my own students engaged in experiential learning, I mean simply that they are creating knowledge themselves through activities that reach beyond just reading and discussing and that this active step of the learning process is necessary before reflection on that knowledge can occur. In this way, at least, I think many philosophers are often engaged in a kind of experiential learning in the classroom because I've rarely seen a philosophy class where the goal was strictly the transmission of knowledge rather than creating an environment where students generate their own knowledge. Here I discuss a use of museum collections that I think brings that attitude one step further.

II. OBJECTS

There are several reasons to believe that the examination of objects can help teach the philosophy of mind (which is my area) or philosophy more generally, in a way that is more effective than the traditional use of thought experiments or lecture and discussion. First, as Bartlett, Meister, and Green note in their paper on "Employing Museum Objects in Undergraduate Liberal Arts Education" (2014):

> Objects make excellent foci for inquiry-based and active learning methods. The use of these techniques fosters increased skill in higher-level critical thinking, greater acceptance of conceptual change, increased student investment (through ownership of the process. . .), knowledge retention and transfer through application in different contexts, and better understanding of complex material. (3)

There are data to back up each of these points (Bartlett, Meister, and Green), and each point is itself something we strive toward in the teaching of philosophy. Thus using objects makes our students better able to do the work of philosophy itself.

Second, and perhaps more mundanely, being out of a traditional classroom and engaging in activities beyond listening and speaking makes it more difficult for students to fail to engage with the material. While this is true of EL generally, as this volume demonstrates, object-based engagement in particular make it quite difficult for students to be checking social media or their phones because their hands are otherwise occupied with a new object they are unfamiliar with and that they must come to understand using the course concepts.

III. CAMPUS MUSEUMS AND COURSE STRUCTURE

Let me offer a bit of context. I have the good fortune of being employed by a liberal arts college, where the staff of our campus museums has historically encouraged faculty members to make use of the museum collections in our teaching. This use of museums in teaching stretches back at least to 1911 at our institution, Beloit College, but a Mellon Foundation grant in the 1990s reignited this approach (Bartlett and Meister). We are a school fairly famous for our experiential learning across the curriculum, but philosophy tends to lag behind other disciplines when it comes to this sort of teaching and learning, generally as a result of the historical methods of teaching philosophy.

At Beloit College, we have two primary museums that have been used as teaching resources: the Logan Museum of Anthropology and the Wright Museum of Art. The Logan, founded in 1893, has long been used as a teaching resource. Philosophers at larger institutions are likely to have access to a similar museum, probably already used by their anthropology departments, although many liberal arts and community colleges may not. Luckily, the Logan, like many museums of this sort, has a digital collection available now with online access, so activities using museum collections are not prohibitive at any sort of institution. My discussion of experiential learning will focus on my use of the Logan, but I will also highlight ways that colleagues in other disciplines have engaged in with our art museum, too. Many of these activities that were used in other disciplines can be adapted to philosophical concerns or may at least encourage creative thinking about other uses of your own museums, so it seems worthwhile to include them in this discussion.

I teach a course called Cyborg Brains and Hybrid Minds, which is a semester-long, interdisciplinary examination of the Extended Mind Hypothesis put forth by Andy Clark and David Chalmers in their 1999 essay. This reading has become standard in many philosophy of mind courses, as well as courses on metaphysics and in discussions of personal identity. In this course, we examine both the idea of minds as embodied, embedded, and ultimately, extended, and also the broader idea of the cyborg as a human inextricably wedded to her technologies. This notion of the cyborg is widely discussed in the literatures of various disciplines in ways relevant to philosophy, including neuroscience, art, psychology, literary studies, disability studies, and cultural studies. Understanding a bit of the Extended Mind theory will help make sense of how I chose to engage with EL, but I make no argument as to the correctness of the theory here.

The basic idea of the Extended Mind Hypothesis (EM) is that cognition is not confined to "skin and skull" but rather that certain operations of our minds literally take place outside of our bodies, in the environment and in interaction with tools in that environment. In his book on the theory, *Natural Born Cyborgs*, Andy Clark takes up the Heideggerian notion of ready to/present at hand in making the argument for EM, claiming that the tools become invisible in use and thus emphasizing our bodily phenomenology over the traditional inner/outer split between body and world. As Merleau-Ponty demonstrated, if the stick of a blind individual feels like a bodily sense organ rather than something being held, the experience of our own bodies is malleable. The neuroscience of tool use backs up this experience, and tools or other external objects or activities appear to be allotted representational space in our brains as body parts (Cardinalli et al.; Nicolelis and Chapin; Shokur et al.). What this means is that our bodies and minds are much more problematic than the straightforward understanding of each we tend to have.

Andy Clark has referred extensively to humans as "natural born cyborgs," going so far as to dedicate an entire book to this idea. By this, he means that it is in our nature (or it is our nature) to be bound to our objects, as they are genuinely a part of our mental apparatus. We are creatures who cannot be separated from our tools and technologies, and the environment is the location of some of our cognition. Take Scrabble, to use Clark and Chalmers's example. They note that, rather than mentally shuffling the tiles to attempt to find a word, there is evidence that physically shuffling them prompts word recall. As they point out, "the rearrangement of tiles on the tray is not a part of action; it's a part of *thought*" (Clark and Chalmers 10). This all contrasts with the traditional representational theory of mind, wherein cognition is an internal process confined (traditionally, if somewhat mysteriously) to the brain.

Overall, this course is focused on a close examination of the nature of our minds, but we do this through a constant revision of what it means to have a human body. We discuss classic cyborgs, real stories of prosthetics and disability, and broad ways in which our tools expand various human cognitive capabilities (including some discussion about what features do or do not mark a capability as cognitive to begin with). While on the face of it, we are talking about minds, what we really do is talk about bodies.

IV. BODIES AS OBJECTS

While I will describe my museum engagements as discrete activities, I do so only because they were a pilot case for this sort of EL project in my classroom, and they can be enhanced to structure a greater portion of the course. Each visit was followed by a full debriefing discussion among the entire class, so that I could get a sense of what they took away from the exercise and also get them to begin the process of reflection and knowledge creation. They then wrote reflective papers where they discussed the theory we'd been studying in terms of their experiences at the museum. The first time I brought my class to the museum, the activity was designed to further problematize our bodies in interaction with the world. Designed specifically for my class by the Logan's Curator of Collections and the Curator of Exhibits and Education in conversation with me and the course's literature, a number of unfamiliar tools were made available to my students to actually experience up close. (This is something that I would expect many teaching museums could arrange, having a special collection of touchable artifacts, or at least artifacts that can be pulled from the collection to be examined closely without touching.) The tools selected for the exercise were at least unknown in contemporary American culture and often obsolete entirely. A close examination of them and the ability to touch and manipulate some without explanation was coupled with a prompt for the students to try to determine what physical activities these tools would've enabled their users to engage in that would otherwise have been impossible.

Imagine a small, bent piece of metal. It doesn't lend itself to any immediate analogy with any tool you've ever used. The students' first encounter required that they figure out what it could be used for, given the material and shape and attributes of the object, and then determine what this enabled a given culture to do with their bodies that wouldn't have been available otherwise. This led to a discussion of examining all the accompanying insights about the culture and lived experiences such a tool might bring. As the students realized they did not know how to interface with some of these tools, their own bodies became the object of study. This is the very point: you don't even know how to hold this foreign object or which way it faces. You don't even know for sure it is something you use with your hands! Perhaps it rests on your lap.

When given these unfamiliar tools, the students couldn't help but notice that their own bodies were suddenly awkwardly in the way of the interaction. And as they had learned from Clark all semester, our tools, those we are comfortable with, those that are invisible in use, make us cyborgs through our being intertwined with them. And yet here they saw what their bodies could be with very visible tools. With a new insight into Clark's "natural born cyborg" hypothesis, these students returned to the classroom with a new way of seeing the tools they use every day: their laptops, their phones, their notebooks—things that have long since become more or less invisible in use—and a new way of understanding cognition in the world and the challenges to traditional theories of mind. It is impossible for us to step outside of ourselves to study how our tools impact our cognitive experiences. But when shown tools that were foreign, the students were much better able to view the bodies and experiences of the users with a (variety of) objectivity, bringing the metaphysical claims about these things into much sharper relief.

While I am lucky to have our highly engaged museum curators, it is possible to engage in this activity even without the ability of students to touch the objects (since not every museum is a teaching museum). Indeed, even a good digital collection will enable students to examine these objects in some detail and imagine how their bodies might engage with them. It's true, however, that the actual hands-on activity brings with it numerous additional benefits in the case of this particular experience. As my colleagues Dan Bartlett and Nicolette Meister point out, "these kinds of connections (and for our purposes they don't need to be profound) can create a greater curiosity about, or sense of ownership of, an object. These can be useful in engaging students in the classroom both with the content and with each other . . ."

(Bartlett and Meister). There is a Deweyan lesson here with hands-on experience, but the application to EM in particular is profound, if a bit beyond the scope of this paper. (It is, after all, a theory about tool use.)

V. REPRESENTATION

The second experiential learning activity I engaged my students in occurred later in the semester, at a time when the students were more familiar and comfortable with the idea that the mind might do some of its work in the environment. This activity was designed to facilitate more examination of the notions of representation and information as they are used in the philosophy of mind and in particular EM. By this point in the course, the students were finding the usual examples mundane. For example, the notion that the notebook or hard drive might literally be part of our minds began to seem cliché (though the students certainly fail to agree on the fact of the matter). The students, in general, had a hard time understanding the very idea of mental representations (and who could blame them?). It shortly became clear that the very notion of representation was unclear. So back to the Logan Museum we went, this time to examine a group of about ten Wayang Kulit, which are Indonesian shadow puppets. These puppets have the status of the person they represent encoded in various visual ways (through the clothing they wear, the size of the doll, the details, the body shape, etc.). The students were led in a close examination (but no touching!) by the museum director. They were asked guided questions about what they might guess about what kind of person was being represented by the dolls and why.

Examining the Wayang Kulit employs a fairly straightforward literary technique, by examining cultural and social concepts of representation and what it requires on the part of the observer/interpreter. However, using objects that are culturally *unfamiliar* (and they were, as none of the students knew about Wayang Kulit in advance) required the students to be much more deliberate and look much more carefully at the objects to decode how and what they represent. It was made clear to them that we can expect that these dolls encode for a different kind of social structure than we are used to, and they were primed with ideas about how representation itself works. Viewing the dolls raised the students' awareness of the role cultures play in their understanding of representation and information, insofar as it is implicit. As most of us working in the philosophy of mind can attest, this is largely absent in the canonical literature, which has historically imagined our mental representations as objective facts, a special case of representation in general.

The goal of this activity was to get the students to think about what it means to represent information, broadly speaking, so we could start to make inroads on the notion of mental representation. In their post-museum debriefing sessions and discussions, as well as their reflective written work, the students admitted this activity was not as successful overall as the first had been in challenging or clarifying their thinking. In part, I believe this is because the nature of mental representation remains somewhat elusive to them even after a thorough exploration of the nature of representation more generally. We can understand representation (and they did), but to then apply it to mental representations is a leap that continues to challenge even many professional philosophers. This activity could rather serve as an excellent model for anyone daring to embark on the philosophy of information, however. I would imagine anyone teaching, for example, Luciano Floridi's work would find clear value in this exercise. Space limits a discussion of this here, but I hope it provides a valuable starting point for anyone working on these topics.

VI. CREATIVE ENGAGEMENTS WITH MUSEUMS

I mentioned earlier that the Logan Museum, as well as many other university anthropology museums, has an online digital collection available. Particularly as the exhibits in any museum make up only a small part of their overall collections, access to a digital collection opens up wider EL opportunities for philosophers who may want to structure an entire course around thinking with objects in this way. In a Philosophy of Mind course, for example, one could have each student choose an object early in the semester and use that object as a focal point for thinking about how tools challenge our traditional ways of doing the philosophy of mind throughout the entire course. All sorts of activities might follow from this sort of structure. For example, a student might be asked to write or present on how that object changes the capacities of the person who has access to it (once they know what it is), or as my first activity, simply to bring the student's own body into focus as the object of study (if they do not know what it is). This is especially valuable for a class like mine, where we talk about bodies throughout the semester, questioning what "normal" bodies are and examining the very idea of "disabled" bodies. The student ought to read the literature with this object in mind, after some time exploring it in person (if available) and time reflecting afterward on how that piece offered something new to the literature itself. How would Andy Clark's hypothesis that we are natural born cyborgs intersect with a culture that had this object? If possible, students ought to go out into their community (or a community) and talk to people with different-than-average bodies. They could talk to people with prosthetics, or cochlear implants, and learn how those bodies are lived and how those tools are both invisible and indispensable. Are these tools doing cognitive work? In so many ways, using objects like this must necessarily change the conversation and the way students read this literature (and therefore, the knowledge they create throughout the course). With the focus on new and emerging technologies like neural implants or easily accessible pocket computers, it is too easy to see Clark's cyborg as some sort of future being, the stuff of science fiction. But the claim is that we have always been this being; our technologies have always moved some of our cognition out of our heads and into the world. Students who visited the museum reported that the very plausibility of the claim shifted merely by reframing the conversation from emerging technologies to antiquated technologies.

At Beloit College, a number of my colleagues in other departments—departments not traditionally engaged in work with museums or artifacts—have used our museums in creative ways. To encourage philosophers to see museum collections in a new way, as a resource for all kinds of new approaches to our teaching and learning, I'll briefly offer one example. My favorite example of creative use of our collections involves a music course and the Wright Museum of Art. My colleague, Dr. Susan Rice, taught a course titled Hidden Harmonies, in which she paired a piece of art from the Wright with a piece of music for her choral students to learn. The artwork had no immediate or obvious connection to the piece of music. She then asked various professors from other disciplines to engage with that piece of artwork through their disciplinary lenses, without hearing the musical piece she chose to go along with it, and give a lecture to her class. I was asked to engage with a self-portrait of an artist (Robert Arneson) who I knew nothing about and give a talk on how a philosopher might encounter such a work. This is a terrifying challenge, even for someone who is used to working across disciplines. But of course, what could be more philosophical than the question of selfhood? Prompted only with a self-portrait, I was able to teach the students about theories of personal identity, intersubjectivity, and intercorporeality. Other professors were able to offer their own discipline-specific lectures from similarly unfamiliar art objects. Flip this so the student is charged with this task, and this is an activity that would engage any Introduction to Philosophy student in a much deeper way than only reading the text. Any introductory course could follow this model with great success, assigning students a piece of artwork and asking them to talk about a philosophical problem encountered through it (without making the problem explicit). My own experience of having been placed in the role of student for the sake of this course was that it is terrifying to be asked to do something with so little structure, and then so incredibly fulfilling when you find a way to approach the work. It is what we call an ill-defined or ill-structured problem in cognitive science.

Finally, let me emphasize that any philosophy course or topic could use museums as a lens through which to encounter that topic. For example, when I teach the topic of personal identity in my courses, there are a handful of canonical readings and approaches I generally take. We might talk about persistence of soul, of consciousness, or of body. Students generally understand these ideas. But what do we make of the objects in our museum that have been believed by their cultures to hold (or be) the souls of people who once possessed them? Or think of how much richer a discussion of cultural relativism might be if we bring our students to see the tools of a culture that practices infanticide rather than just telling them such groups exist.

I'm not suggesting we simply bring students to the museum to look at these objects. We can give them questions to guide their experiences or ask them to explore other objects in use by the same culture, filling out a larger and more immediate picture of why that culture practices what they do. And when I do bring my students to explore these objects in the future, I expect that we will have the same sort of discussion we always have about the persistence of souls or bodies or minds but that the students will have a much richer and more memorable experience of that conversation than they do merely by reading the texts. They will (hopefully) be motivated to explore more, see more, do more, and learn more about the situations we ask them to evaluate. And this is what is so valuable about experiential learning techniques and opportunities: we have empirical data that shows the many ways that object-based instruction enhances and deepens student learning and retention (Bartlett and Meister). Using objects to enrich our experiences of philosophical questions, and to help us determine which questions to ask (and of course, drawing on the rich resources of our museums) seems like an amazing way to increase the effectiveness of the sorts of philosophical instruction we already do.

WORKS CITED

Bartlett, Dan and Nicolette Meister. "Objects and Instruction: Materiality at Beloit." Beloit, WI: Beloti College. 30 April 2014 Faculty Forum Presentation.

Bartlett, Dan, Nicollete Meister, and William Green. "Employing Museum Objects in Undergraduate Liberal Arts Education." *Informal Learning Review* 124 (2014): 3–6.

Cardinalli, Lucilla, Francesca Frassinetti, Claudio Brozzoli, Christian Urquizar, Alice C. Roy, and Alessandro Farnè. "Tool Use Induces Morphological Updating of the Body Schema." *Current Biology* 19.12 (2009): 478–79.

Clark, Andy. *Natural Born Cyborgs: Minds, Technologies, and the Future of Human Intelligence.* Oxford: Oxford University Press, 2003.

Clark, Andy and David Chalmers. "The Extended Mind." *Analysis* 58.1 (1999): 7–19.

Kolb, David A. *Experiential Learning: Experience as the Source of Learning and Development.* New Jersey: Prentice Hall, 1983.

Merleau-Ponty, Maurice. *The Phenomenology of Perception.* Trans. Colin Smith. London: Routledge Classics, 2002.

Nicolelis, Miguel A. L. and John K. Chapin. "Controlling Robots with the Mind." *Scientific American Reports* 18 (2008): 72–79.

Shokur, Salaiman, Joseph E. O'Doherty, Jesse A. Winans, Hannes Bleuler, Mikhail A. Lebedev, and Miguel A. L. Nicolelis. "Expanding the Primate Body Schema in Sensorimotor Cortex by Virtual Touches of an Avatar." *Proceedings of the National Academy of Sciences* 110.37 (2013): 15121–26.

Contributors

Minerva Ahumada is an associate professor at LaGuardia Community College. She teaches philosophy courses such as Ethics and Moral Issues, Latin American Philosophy, and Social and Political Philosophy. Her research focuses on the intersections between philosophy and literature, especially the way in which different literary genres address epistemological issues related to moral philosophy. Her teaching aims to create a democratic and reflective learning environment for herself and her students. She earned her PhD in philosophy from Loyola University Chicago.

Alexandra Bradner is a philosopher of science and biology who has taught at Northwestern University, University of Michigan, Marshall University, Denison University, University of Kentucky, and Kenyon College. She presently chairs the American Philosophical Association's Committee on the Teaching of Philosophy and teaches at Eastern Kentucky University. Her scholarship investigates the pragmatics of explanation and understanding.

Michael D. Burroughs is senior lecturer of philosophy and assistant director of the Rock Ethics Institute at Pennsylvania State University. Dr. Burroughs's research interests include philosophy of education, ethics, social ontology, and publicly engaged philosophy. Dr. Burroughs developed and taught undergraduate courses on philosophy and experiential education at the University of North Carolina at Chapel Hill and has founded and/or led philosophy outreach programs at the University of Memphis, UNC-Chapel Hill, and Pennsylvania State University. Through these programs and relevant publications, Dr. Burroughs specializes in introducing philosophy to children and teachers in K–12 schools.

Gregory A. Clark, PhD., is professor of philosophy at North Park University. He initially learned about experiential education in the early '80s through his training to lead wilderness trips in the boreal forests of northern Minnesota, Wisconsin, and Michigan. He has been experimenting with teaching philosophy on that model ever since. He teaches

Zen and Archery and several other experientially based courses, including The Zombie Apocalypse, Philosophy of Nature, and Intentional Christian Community.

Joe Cole earned his PhD in philosophy from Duke University and is currently a visiting assistant professor of philosophy at Guilford College, where he teaches courses on Ethics, Pacifism, and Just War Theory. He also works as a facilitator, consultant, and trainer with nonprofit organizations, consensus-based groups, and intentional communities.

Brian Glenney received his PhD in philosophy at the University of Southern California in 2007. He is assistant professor of philosophy at Gordon College, where he received the 2013 Junior Distinguished Faculty Award. He has published articles on art (especially social design), the history of early modern philosophy (especially Adam Smith), and the philosophy of cognitive science. Brian began collaborating with Sara Hendren (Harvard) in 2009 on reimagining the "handicap" symbol, which presents a more active and embodied figure, and is thrilled that their collaboration has coalesced into a community movement featured in the *Boston Globe, The Chronicle of Higher Education,* and *Good Morning America.*

Maurice Hamington is director of university studies and professor of philosophy at Portland State University. He is the author of nineteen articles in refereed journals and fourteen book chapters and the author or editor of eleven books, including the digital textbook, *Revealing Philosophy* (Thinking Strings), *Contemporary Feminist Pragmatism* (Routledge 2012) edited with Celia Bardwell-Jones, and the forthcoming, *Care Ethics and Political Theory* (Oxford 2015) edited with Daniel Engster. His works focus on care theory from a feminist and pragmatist perspective.

Susan C. C. Hawthorne is an assistant professor in the Philosophy Department at St. Catherine University. She has assigned civic engagement projects classes on environmental ethics and socially engaged philosophy. She and Ramona Ilea coauthored the article "Beyond Service Learning: Civic Engagement in Ethics Classes." Her core research, which investigates how epistemic, practical, and ethical features of clinical science and medical practice affect individuals and society, crosses the boundaries between philosophy of science and medical ethics. Her book *Accidental Intolerance: How We Stigmatize ADHD and How We Can Stop*, was published in 2013 with Oxford University Press.

Karen Hornsby is an associate professor of philosophy at North Carolina A&T State University. She was selected as a 2005–2006 Carnegie Scholar to conduct research on the development of undergraduate students' moral reasoning skills. Currently, she serves as a Teagle Assessment Scholar and codirects the Wabash/Provost Scholars—a group of undergraduate researchers who gather and analyze qualitative data about the student learning environment. In 2012 Karen was conferred the Outstanding Faculty Advisor Award for Region 3 by the National Academic Advising Association. She regularly conducts workshops on scholarly teaching and has published articles on student learning nationally and internationally.

Graham Hubbs is assistant professor at the University of Idaho. He is the author of several articles on practical rationality and is coeditor of *Pragmatism, Law, and Language* (Routledge, 2014).

Ramona Ilea is associate professor and chair of the Philosophy Department at Pacific University Oregon. Her research focuses on demonstrating that philosophical work can contribute to public debates and social issues. She writes about civic engagement, empathy and sympathy, animal ethics, environmental ethics, and normative ethics. She coedited (with Avram Hiller and Leonard Kahn) *Consequentialism and Environmental Ethics* (Routledge Press, 2013). She has implemented civic engagement projects in eleven classes, published "Beyond Service Learning: Civic Engagement in Ethics Classes" with Susan Hawthorne, and has presented on civic engagement at over fifteen conferences.

Monica Janzen is an adjunct professor at Hennepin Technical College in the Philosophy Department. Her research interests focus on how individuals and communities work to create more just societies. She utilizes civic engagement projects as a method of community-based learning in her ethics classes as well as her critical thinking classes—even when these classes are exclusively taught online. She has presented about civic engagement at numerous conferences. In addition to her extensive work with civic engagement in the classroom, she is interested in concepts of hospitality, civic responsibility, and social guardianship.

Kathie Jenni, PhD, is professor of philosophy and director of human-animal studies at the University of Redlands. Her teaching and research focus on animal ethics, environmental ethics, and moral psychology. She is coauthor, with Mylan Engel Jr., of *The Philosophy of Animal Rights: a Brief Guide for Students and Teachers*; her published essays include "Vices of Inattention," "The Power of the Visual," and "The Moral Responsibilities of Intellectuals." Her community service learning course *Taking Animals Seriously* won the University of Redlands' Outstanding Faculty award for Innovative Teaching. Kathie lives in Southern California with six adopted animal companions.

Katherine E. Kirby is associate professor of philosophy and director of the global studies program at St. Michael's College and is the recipient of the 2011 Vermont Campus Compact Award for Excellence in Community-Based Teaching. She offers courses integrating philosophical theories of "otherness," interdisciplinary examination of marginalization, and community-engaged learning with senior citizens and others, including a course that takes students to Guyana to work with vulnerable communities. Recent publications include an article on service-learning in *Teaching Philosophy* and a variety of articles on theoretical and applied ethics. Recent presentations focus on integrating philosophical ethics with politics, media, and economics.

Wade Maki is a senior lecturer in the Philosophy Department at the University of North Carolina Greensboro. He is currently codirector of the university's Faculty Teaching and Learning Commons and director of BB&T Program on Capitalism, Markets, and Morality. Wade serves on the faculty senate, chairs the Senate Online Learning Committee, and was nominated for the UNCG Excellence Award in Online Education.

Sharon M. Meagher is dean of the College of Arts & Sciences and professor of humanities at Widener University. A cofounder and codirector of the Public Philosophy Network, Meagher is the editor of two books and the author of many articles on feminist philosophy, social and political theory, and ethics. Meagher is former chair of the Department of Latin American Studies and Women's Studies and professor of philosophy at the University of Scranton.

Julinna Oxley is associate professor of philosophy and director of the Women's and Gender Studies Program at Coastal Carolina University. Her research focuses on issues in feminist philosophy, the emotions, applied ethics, and political theory. Her book *The Moral Dimensions of Empathy: Limits and Applications in Ethical Theory and Practice* was published by Palgrave Macmillan in 2012. She regularly teaches courses in feminist philosophy, biomedical ethics, and contemporary moral issues and has implemented experiential learning in several upper-division courses.

Ericka Tucker is an assistant professor in the Department of Philosophy at Marquette University. She received an AB in philosophy from Brown University (1999) and a PhD in philosophy from Emory University (2009). Her research areas are early modern philosophy (Spinoza, Hobbes, history of moral and political philosophy), social, moral, and political philosophy (democracy theory, global justice, theories of normativity, social ontology), and feminist philosophy. She recently served as a postdoctoral researcher at the University of Helsinki in the Philosophical Psychology, Morality, and Politics Research Unit.

Donna S. Turney teaches philosophy at Randolph-Macon College, a small liberal arts college in Ashland, Virginia, where she serves as department chair. She is currently a service-fellow and part of an initiative to explore service-learning opportunities in the general education curriculum. She has a PhD in philosophy from the University of Pennsylvania. Her interest in experiential service-learning is a result of an experiment teaching freshmen, though on a trajectory from her study of the failure of logical positivism to feminist epistemology.

Chad Wiener is currently a visiting assistant professor of philosophy at Pacific University, where he teaches various ethics courses, including a course that combines ethics and civic engagement. He also works and publishes on ancient Greek philosophy, especially Plato and Aristotle.

J. Jeremy Wisnewski is an associate professor of philosophy at Hartwick College, and the editor of the *Review Journal of Political Philosophy*. He has published widely in moral philosophy and phenomenology.

Dan Yim is an associate professor of philosophy at Bethel University in Saint Paul, Minnesota. He has a PhD in philosophy from the University of Southern California. He is interested in the cross sections between moral psychology, racialization, and contact theory. He created the school's first philosophy course dedicated to concepts of race and gender and has been teaching it yearly since 2007.

Robin L. Zebrowski has a joint appointment in philosophy and cognitive science at Beloit College, a liberal arts college known nationally for its commitment to experiential learning. She has received grants to pursue these opportunities with her classes. Dr. Zebrowski has published and presented widely on topics related to artificial intelligence, cyborg theories, and embodiment theories more broadly, with a focus on conceptual metaphor and the ethics of emerging technologies.

Megan Halteman Zwart received her PhD in philosophy from the University of Notre Dame in 2010; she currently is assistant professor of philosophy at Saint Mary's College, Notre Dame, Indiana. Megan teaches classes in twentieth-century philosophy, ethical theory, and applied ethics, including experiential learning classes in Medical Ethics and Social Justice. Her research interests include contemporary European philosophy, Hellenistic philosophy, food ethics, and pedagogy.

Name Index

Adams, Carol J. 141
Ahumada, Minerva 6, 12, 65, 237
American Association of Colleges and Universities 18, 44, 156, 157
American Association of Philosophy Teachers 10, 17
American Friends Service Committee 163
American Philosophical Association xiv, 10, 13, 17, 33, 115, 210, 237
Andresen, Lee 22–3, 35
Animal Welfare Act 134
Arendt, Hannah 153
Aristotle 12, 23–5, 34–5, 66, 71, 81, 87, 192, 197, 216, 241
Armstrong, Susan J. 132,139

Bamber, Philip M. and Mark A. Pike 175, 178
Banaji, Mahzarin 91–3, 97, 98–9
Beard, Colin 22–3, 35
Best Friends Animal Sanctuary/Society 132, 136, 138
Block, Peter 184, 187
Boal, Augusto 56, 61, 63
Boss, Judith 102, 115
Boston Globe 238
Botzler, Richard G. 132, 139
Boud, David 22–3, 35
Bradner, Alexandra 6, 15, 201–11, 237
Burroughs, Michael D. 5, 12, 21–36, 237
Butler, Judith 58, 63
Butler, Samuel 119, 129–30

Cady, Duane 183, 187
Callicott, Baird 134
Campus Compact 10, 17, 239
Carlson, J.A., 119, 130
Carter Center 163
Chalmers, David 230, 231, 236
Clark, Andy 230, 231, 232, 234, 235, 236
Clark, Gregory 6, 15, 212–21, 237–8
Cohen, Ruth 22–3, 35
Cole, Joe 6, 9, 179–88, 238
Crabtree, Robbin D. 175, 178

Damasio, Antonio 133, 139
DeGrazia, David 139
Dennett, Daniel 191, 197
Descartes, Rene 133, 139
Dewey, John 3, 6–7, 12–13, 21–2, 25–6, 28, 31–2, 34–5, 37–9, 49, 66–9, 74–6, 79–80, 88, 153, 233
Dillard, Annie 214, 221
Donovan, Sarah K. 35, 99
Duley, John 41, 49

Emory University 165, 240
EngagedPhilosophy.com, xiv 10, 17, 33, 35, 87, 115

Fiala, Andrew 183, 187
Finley, Ashley 156
Fitzgerald, Patrick 17, 35, 103, 115, 148
Foos, Cathy Ludlum 4, 17
Francione, Gary 134
Freire, Paulo 13, 39, 49, 61, 63, 75, 79–80
Frye, Marilyn 153, 156

Georgia Coalition for the People's Agenda 163
Gibbs, Graham 39–40, 43, 50
Giebel, H.M. 4, 18, 102, 115, 148

Gilligan, Carol 192, 197
Giving Game xii
Glenney, Brian 6, 13–14, 119–30, 238
Greene, Maxine 52, 63
Greenwald, Anthony 91–3, 99
Greenwood, Dennis 173–4, 178

Hadot, Pierre 142–3, 147–8
Hamington, Maurice 6, 12, 52–64, 238
Hanh, Thich Nhat 181, 187
Harrison-Pepper, Sally 54, 63
Haste, Helen and Hogan, Amy 4, 17, 18
Hawthorne, Susan C.C. xiv, 5, 9, 13, 101–16, 147, 148, 238
Hayek, Friedrich 141
Heidegger, Martin 230
Herrigel, Eugen 212–14, 216–21
Higgs, Joy 221
hooks, bell 150, 156
Hornsby, Karen 5, 9, 12, 37–51, |238–9
Hubbs, Graham 6, 11, 15, 222–7

Ilea, Ramona i, v, xiii, xiv, 1–18, 101–16, 139, 147, 148, 197, 238, 239
International Rescue Center 163
Itin, Christian M. 22, 35, 79, 88

James, William 38, 50
Jamieson, Dale 134
Janzen, Monica xiv, 5, 9, 13, 17, 101–16, 239
Japan 130, 212–13, 218–19
Jenni, Kathie 5, 8, 14, 15, 131–39, 239
Johnson, Allan G., 153, 156, 157
Johnson, David W. 69, 76
Johnston, D. Kay 59, 63

Kahneman, Daniel 90, 98–9
Kant, Immanuel 31, 66, 72–3, 172, 192, 197
Kelly, Tom 215–16, 221
Kenzo, Awa 213, 218–19, 221
Kirby, Katherine E. 4, 6, 9, 14, 16, 18, 169–78, 239–40
Knobe, Joshua 202, 210–11
Kolb, Alice 41, 50, 53, 55, 63, 65, 68, 76, 180, 187–8
Kolb, David 2, 18, 22, 35, 39–41, 42–3, 48, 50, 53, 54, 55, 63, 65, 68, 69–70, 74, 76, 180, 187–8, 228, 236

Kuh, George 8, 18, 156–7, 209, 211
Kuhn, Thomas S. 14, 119–20, 129–30
Kyudo 213, 217–19

Lakey, George 181, 187–8
Lamott, Anne 214, 221
Latin American and Caribbean Community Center 163
Learn and Serve: America's National Service Learning Clearninghouse 2, 10, 18
Lederach, John Paul 183–4, 188
Lerne, Linda 151, 157
Levinas, Emmanuel 16, 169, 173–4, 176–8
Lewin, Kurt 22, 38–9, 50
Lewis, David 202, 211
Likert Scale 155, 205
Lipman, Matthew 28–9, 33–5

McDonald, Mark, Kirsty Spence, and Beth Sheehan 180, 188
MacIntyre, Alasdair C. 212–14, 216–17, 219–21
McNair, Tia 156
Maki, Wade 5, 9, 12, 37–51, 240
Manen, Max van 42, 48, 51
Marton, Ference 44, 50
Matthews, Gareth B. 30–1, 36
Meagher, Sharon M. 5, 14, 149–57, 240
Mentkowki, Marcia 44, 50
Mill, John Stuart 66, 141, 147
Mipham, Sakyong 216, 221
Monopoly 153, 156
Moon, Jennifer 65, 68, 76
Moore, David Thornton 44, 49–50

Nadelhoffer, Thomas 210–11
Nagel, Thomas 192, 197
Nahmias, Eddy 202–4, 210–11
National Association of Colleges and Employers, The 44, 50
National Research Council 43
Noddings, Nel 60, 63–4
Nozick, Robert 141
Nussbaum, Martha 112 203–6, 211

Orend, Brian 182, 188
Oxley, Julinna i, v, xiii, xiv, 1–18, 139, 197, 240

Palmer, Clare 134
Perry, John 191, 197
Peters, Rebecca Todd 187, 188

Philosophical Horizons 10, 18, 27, 34, 36
Piaget, Jean 22, 38–9, 50, 129
Plato 12, 21, 23–5, 34, 66, 81–3, 209, 241
PLATO: Philosophy Learning and Teaching Organization 10, 18, 33, 36
Prinz, Jesse 202, 206
Project Implicit 98, 100
Public Philosophy Network 10, 18, 240

Rachels, James 134
Radio Diaspora 163
Rawls, John 141, 147, 161, 168
Refugee Women's Network 163
Regan, Tom 132, 135, 139, 141
Rollins, Bernard 134
Rousseau, Jean-Jacques 3, 12, 21, 24–5, 34, 36
Ruddick, Sara 192, 197

Säljöl, Roger 44, 50
Sandel, Michael 147–8
Schön, Donald 40, 48, 51
Seider, Scott 103, 114, 116, 147–8
Sen, Amartya 161, 168
Shor, Ira 79–81, 87–8
Singer, Peter xi–xii, 8, 75, 132, 134–5, 139, 141, 169, 178, 192, 197
Socrates xi, 7, 13, 18, 77, 82–5, 87, 89–90, 153
Spurlock, Morgan 57, 64
Stanovich, Keith 90, 100
St. Catherine University 103, 109, 115, 238
System 1 and System 2 90–4, 96–8

TeachingChildrenPhilosophy.org 10, 18, 35, 36
TeachPhilosophy101.org 10, 18
Thayer-Bacon, Barbara J. 55, 64
Thomson, Judith Jarvis 201–2, 210–11
Truth and Reconciliation Commission of Liberia 163
Tucker, Ericka 5, 8, 9, 14, 15, 161–8, 240
Turkle, Sherry 191, 197
Turney, Donna S. 5, 15, 189–97, 240–1

Uchiyama, Kōshō 213, 216, 221

Verducci, Susan 56, 64
Volgistics 10, 18

Walzer, Michael 182, 188
Wartenberg, Thomas E. 34–6
Watts, Margit 44, 51
Wendell, Susan 192, 197
West, Richard 90, 100
Wiener, Chad xiv, 5, 9, 13, 101–16, 241
Wikipedia 6, 15, 222–7
Williams, Clifford 191–2, 197
Wilson, John P. 22–3, 35
Wisnewski, Jeremy J. 5–6, 11, 13, 77–88, 241
Wurdinger, S.D. 119, 130

Yim, Dan 6, 13, 89–100, 241
Youth Convergence Project 163

Zebrowski, Robin L. 15–16, 228–36, 241
Zen 6, 212–15, 217–21
Zull, James E. 43, 51
Zwart, Megan Halteman 5, 14, 140–8, 241

Subject Index

ableist 126
accessible icon project 6, 119–20, 127–8, 129
activism xiii, 3, 5, 9, 78, 104, 107, 113, 137, 167
adaptation 22–3, 38, 41, 120–1, 228
agency xii, 13, 32, 69, 74–5, 89–92, 101, 103, 113–14, 171, 221
altruism 99, 192, 195, 197
animal rights 132, 135, 139, 239
animals xii, 2, 5, 8, 14, 49, 131–9, 141, 143, 146, 239
animal welfare 134–5, 138–9, 146
anthropocentrism 134, 138
archery 6, 9, 15, 212–14, 216–20
art 10, 14, 43, 51, 63, 64, 123, 126–8, 130, 185, 188, 197, 212, 215, 218, 221, 230, 235, 238
assessment xiv, 43, 47, 58, 90, 93, 95, 97, 101, 103–4, 107, 113, 115, 149, 154–5, 192, 196, 203, 208–9, 225, 228, 238; *see also* course evaluations
assessment, post-course survey 13, 101, 103–4, 106–8, 113
assessment, pre-course survey 13, 101, 103–5, 106–8, 113
assimilation 38

banking model of education 39, 61, 75, 79
blogs i, 46–8, 102, 126, 164, 167, 185, 215, 222–3, 226–7
business ethics 5, 12, 37, 45–6

care ethics 6, 12, 52, 54–5, 58, 60, 63, 238
care-giver 53, 56, 58, 170, 173, 209
Catholic social teaching 141
change-maker 101
citizenship 4, 6, 9, 13, 17–18, 81, 86–7, 101, 103–6, 108, 112–14, 168–9
citizenship, global 6, 169
civic engagement xiv, 2–3, 5, 7, 9–11, 13–14, 17, 101, 103–6, 108, 110, 113–14, 149 238–9, 241
civic engagement project xiv, 9, 101, 104–6, 108, 115, 147, 238–9
cognitive dissonance 12, 37, 41–2, 46, 48, 94, 98–9
collaborative learning 46, 53, 65, 72, 74, 180, 202–3, 207, 209–11; *see also* group work
collaborative projects i, 1, 3, 6–7, 9, 68–9, 74, 119, 153, 156, 174, 201
collaborative writing 11, 17, 222–7; *see also* writing
collective intentionality 15, 222–4, 226–7
community xiii, 2, 4, 6, 8–12, 14–18, 28–9, 31, 33, 44, 46–7, 49, 60, 65–6, 74, 76, 95, 97, 100, 102, 104–12, 114, 115 120, 132, 136, 141–6, 148–52, 155–6, 159, 161–7, 170–2, 176–7, 179–81, 183–7, 189, 194–5, 209, 215, 218, 230, 234, 237–40
community college 11–12, 65, 230
community engagement 15, 33, 95, 143–5, 159, 162, 179, 183, 185–6
community radio 163, 165–6
community service i, xiv, 1–11, 17–18, 21, 33, 95, 99, 104, 107, 114, 116, 144, 146, 149, 151, 156,

159, 166, 169–70, 172, 175, 177–8, 180, 189–96, 239; *see also* service learning and volunteering
compassion 14, 78, 131, 138, 176–7, 181
consumption 134, 141
cooperative learning 50, 69–75
course evaluations 13, 101, 103, 107, 109, 112, 143, 176, 207, 210
crisis 120–2
critical reflection 7, 39, 41–2, 44, 58, 97, 103, 154 172
critical theory 78–9, 86–7
critical thinking 1, 4–5, 8, 10, 13, 18, 44, 64, 78, 80–3, 85–6, 90, 93, 101, 103–6, 108, 112–13, 181, 186, 189, 193, 196, 229, 239
cross-cultural 5, 99, 219
cyborgs 230–2, 234–6, 241

deep learning 2, 16, 44, 47, 49, 54
direct education 180–1
direct instructional guidance 45
disability 5, 14–15, 120, 123, 126–8, 189, 192, 194, 197, 230–1
dissociation 94, 98
distributive justice 141
dramaturgical exercises 12, 55–6, 58, 59, 61–2
dualism 133
dual-process model of mind 6, 89–90, 92, 98–9

educational fair 5, 14, 149, 152–3, 155–6
embodiment 57–9, 62, 241
emergent learning 6, 14, 119–21, 129
emotions 7, 22, 50, 57, 61, 62, 91, 96–7, 133, 134, 137, 139, 161, 168, 172 180, 240
empathy i, 6, 52, 58, 62–4, 101, 239–40
engaged learning 48, 50, 54, 161–2, 164–8, 240
epistemology 31, 41, 51, 54–5, 58, 60, 67, 87, 202–3, 205, 237, 241
ethics i, xii, 5–6, 8, 12, 14–15, 17, 21, 25, 31–2, 35, 37, 42, 45–50, 52–5, 58, 59, 60–6, 69, 72–5, 77, 99, 102–3, 107, 112, 115,127, 131–2, 134, 137, 139, 141, 147–8, 152, 165–6, 169, 174, 178–9, 186, 192, 197, 203, 209, 238–41
evolution i, 38, 83, 120, 127, 129
experiential learning, i, xi, xii, xiii xiv 1–18, 19, 22–3, 25–9, 31–5, 37–48, 50, 52–6, 58–63, 65–6, 68–75, 76–8, 82–3, 85–9, 92–5, 99–100, 114, 119–20, 128–9, 133, 140–2, 144–7, 149, 151, 161, 166, 168, 179–81, 186–9, 204, 207, 214, 220, 224, 226, 228–30, 233, 236, 240–1
experimental philosophy 6, 15, 201–2, 210–11
extended mind 230, 236

female genital mutilation (FGM) 203–4
feminism i, 5, 7, 12, 14, 54–5, 58, 61, 63, 72, 116, 137, 149, 150–7, 165, 192, 195, 203, 238, 240–1
field trips 65, 75, 81, 95, 131, 142, 144, 170–1, 177–8, 190, 237
food desert 96, 141
food ethics 141, 241

games 12, 24, 34, 55, 63, 149, 153, 156, 190, 217
gender i, 2, 7, 13, 57–8, 63, 89, 92, 94, 96, 98–9, 141, 151, 153, 157, 162, 167, 181, 195, 202, 241
global justice 2, 8, 14, 161–5, 167–8, 240
group dynamics 38, 151, 155, 183–4
group work 6, 119, 151, 155, 206–8; *see also* collaborative learning

habits 12, 24, 34, 54–6, 58, 59–60, 67, 79, 89–90, 141, 143
high impact educational practices 8, 11, 16–17, 156, 157, 209, 211
high-impact learning 204, 208
high-risk class environment 119
hospitality 170–1, 239
human rights 162–3, 182

identity 53–5, 58–9, 93, 115–16, 191, 195–7, 203, 206, 230, 235
immigration 162–3, 167
implicit association test 92–3, 94, 97; *see also* implicit biases
implicit biases 13, 89, 92–3, 96–8, 126; *see also* implicit association test

independent study courses 6, 13–14, 119, 121, 127 129
injustice 14, 61, 106, 138, 141, 144–6, 161, 174
institutional review board (IRB) 15, 205–6
integrative learning 121, 128, 133
intellectual disabilities 15, 189–90, 195
interdisciplinary 11, 35, 63, 87, 191, 193–4, 196, 202 230, 240
internet 154, 197
internships 5, 8–9, 14, 21, 47, 65, 78–9, 138, 151, 162–8, 189

journaling 2, 95, 142–3, 147
justice 2, 8, 14, 32, 109, 137, 141–4, 147–9, 152, 155–6, 161–5, 167–8, 172, 174, 179, 181, 185–7, 211, 240
just war theory 6, 15, 179, 182, 183, 186, 187, 188, 238

libertarianism 141

metacognition 38, 47
metaphysics 7, 31, 55, 58–60, 63, 66, 192, 197, 203, 230, 232, 237, 240
militarism 182–3
modeling 37, 60, 181
moral education 18, 23, 34, 59–61, 64, 115
moral reasoning 4, 14, 102, 131, 133, 238
museums 5, 9, 16, 65, 81, 126, 228–36

non-profit organizations 15, 105, 108, 132, 138, 154, 163, 166–7, 190–1, 238
normalcy 192

oppression 61, 62, 141, 150, 151, 153, 156, 181

pacifism/peace building 15, 163, 179, 181–3, 187, 238
patriarchy 153, 157
pedagogy 1, 3, 5, 12–14, 31–3, 35, 37–9, 48–9, 54, 63, 77, 79–80, 88–90, 98, 119–20, 149–50, 152–7, 167, 179, 189, 195, 211, 241
pedagogy, feminist 149–50, 153–5, 157
performativity 54–5, 58, 61–3
philosophy with children 12, 21, 25, 27–36
philosophy as a way of life 14, 140, 142, 146, 148
political philosophy *see* social and political philosophy
poverty xii, 14, 137, 141, 163, 170, 197
practical rationality 42, 239
practice i, 1–3, 5–8, 11–12, 14–18, 21, 27–8, 30–5, 37–40, 42–6, 48–51, 55–6, 60, 65–6, 68, 74, 76, 78–9, 85, 87, 90–1, 101–2, 120, 131–2, 134–5, 137, 142, 144, 149–50, 153, 156–7, 161, 164–5, 171, 179–81, 184, 187–8, 193–4, 204, 208–21, 236, 238, 240
presentations, student 13–14, 46–8, 58, 59, 70–3, 76, 84, 101, 102, 120, 122, 126, 128, 152, 154–6, 164–6, 182–3, 185, 203, 208, 215; *see also* teach in
privilege 6, 10, 21, 79, 141, 153, 181, 191, 193–5
progressive education 66–7

rationality 42, 90, 99–100, 192, 239
reflection 186
reflective equilibrium 41
repeated reflection 12, 37, 42, 46–8
representation 58, 89, 120, 130, 152–3, 203, 233–4
respect 28–9, 80, 92, 101, 132, 134–5, 180, 215
rights 53, 55, 132, 135, 139, 162–3, 172–3, 182, 209, 239
role playing 61–2, 98, 182, 184

same-sex marriage 52–3
savior complex 175
self-care skills 181, 186
self-deception 133, 138; *see also* implicit biases
self-interest 169, 172–3, 175, 192
semantic externalism 223, 227
semiotics 127
sensory substitution device 119, 121–3, 125, 130
service learning i, xiv, 1–5, 7–11, 14, 17–18, 21, 33, 35, 95, 99, 102, 114–16 140, 142, 144–8,

151, 166, 170, 172, 175, 177, 189–91, 193–6, 238–9; *see also* community service and volunteering
sexism 150–1, 153, 156
social change 61, 63, 102, 114, 117, 138, 179
social justice 5, 14, 32, 109, 137, 140–1, 144, 149, 152, 156, 161, 179, 188, 211, 241
social and political philosophy i, xii, 8, 14, 77 165, 178, 237, 240
spect-actor 56
stereotypes 13, 89–92, 94, 96–9, 138, 151
street art 14, 126–8
structured scaffolding 12, 37, 42, 46, 48
student research 2, 13, 121–7, 129, 135, 142, 152, 154–6, 163–7, 180, 196, 202, 204–6, 209–10, 220, 224
study-abroad i, 1, 3, 5, 7, 8, 9, 11, 13, 14, 18, 77, 81–3, 170–3, 175–7
symbol 14, 120, 123, 126–30, 238

teach-in *see* education fair
theatre of the oppressed 56, 61, 63
theatrical acting 6, 14, 52, 56–8, 61, 64
thought experiments 1, 18, 66, 201–3, 206, 210, 228–9
tool use 230, 233, 236
transactive education 23, 80, 82, 87

urban gardening 142, 143
utilitarianism 54, 66, 72, 73, 76, 112, 141, 172, 209, 213, 220

violence 62, 162, 167, 181–3, 185–6
volunteering 9, 14, 28, 78, 102–4, 110, 112–14, 122–3, 125–6, 131, 136–8, 145–6, 163, 166–7, 170, 172, 174–6, 178, 194; *see also* community service

war 6, 15, 162, 179–83, 185–8 238
wildlife rehabilitation 132, 134, 135
women's studies i, 54, 150, 155, 157, 240
writing 2, 7, 11, 15, 17, 48, 65, 68, 77, 82–3, 97, 102, 104, 106–7, 109, 113, 129, 151, 172, 174, 193, 196, 212, 214–15, 221, 224–25